Introduction to prepress

Hugh M Speirs MA BA FBIM FIIM FIOP LCGI

pira BPIF
PUBLISHING

Acknowledgements

The British Printing Industries Federation and Pira wish to thank all who have provided assistance in any way with the production of this book, including equipment suppliers, manufacturers and PR companies who have supplied invaluable information, technical literature, digital data, photographs, transparencies or film for reproduction, without whose help this publication would not have been possible.

ISBN 1 85802 309 2

Typeset and created by Hugh Speirs using Adobe PageMaker 6.0 including some imported data; main typefaces used are Palatino, Industria Solid, Stone Sans and Stone Sans Bold. Cover and page design by Aleksander Marinkovic.

Printed in England by Biddles Ltd., Guildford, Surrey

British Printing Industries Federation
11 Bedford Row, London WC1 R 4DX
Telephone (+44) (0) 0171 915 8300, Facsimile (+44) (0) 071 405 7784

Pira International
Randalls Road, Leatherhead, Surrey KT22 7RU
Telephone (+44) (0) 0372 802080, Facsimile (+44) (0) 0372 802079

Contents

• •

Introduction

● ●

This book follows on from the previous publication *Introduction to Printing Technology* which had appeared previously in four separate editions over a period of 30 years covering the wide range of prepress, printing, finishing and associated areas.

When a new edition/replacement publication was considered it was decided that due to the massive changes which had occurred, especially to prepress, since the last publication date in 1992, two companion publications - *Introduction to prepress* and *Introduction to printing and finishing* have been prepared. By splitting the subject matter into two distinct areas it allows the opportunity of producing updates for the two sectors at different time intervals to reflect the changes that have taken place over an intervening period of time.

As stated in the book printing has now the potential of utilising and working with a wide range of equipment and operations in one digital workflow, to the extent that digital systems are the central driving force behind all major current developments in the printing industry. When reflecting on the actual position in printing and print-related areas in general however, the situation is very different in that the many and varied players and contributors to printed work - publishers/print-buying customers, designers and printers, etc - are all preparing, or handling mixed media in the form of traditional/conventional artwork and analogue film as well as digital data. This book intentionally covers both traditional and digital reproduction, in recognition that both systems are very much in evidence in day-to-day working practices but also from the perspective that at least a basic background to traditional methods of working will enhance an understanding of the many facets of prepress.

The format has been carefully chosen to stand as both a general reference book for the industry, and as a technical handbook for students. It is intended primarily for new entrants to the printing industry, and provides an overview of all technical aspects of the industry. Modern printing is complex and constantly influenced by technological developments. An individual can no longer rely solely on a knowledge and understanding of the equipment and processes in his or her own company. This book will also prove useful to individuals whose job functions or interests are linked to the printing industry, through areas such as desktop publishing or print buying.

As with previous *Introduction to technology* books this book underpins the British Printing Industries Federation's technical, as well as commercial qualifications, and should be of particular value to students studying through the British Printing Industries Federation open learning courses or colleges in technical and print-related subjects.

The *Glossary, Bibliography* and *Index* provide additional details about particular areas. The reader can build on the foundation provided in this publication by reading technical articles, journals and books on the various subjects covered and, where possible, by direct observation or involvement with particular processes or operations.

Dedicated to my brother John who died last year after over 40 years service to the printing industry and to my father, George Speirs, who worked in the family printing business for over 50 years.

one

THE STRUCTURE AND ORGANISATION OF THE PRINTING INDUSTRY, PRINT-RELATED PRODUCTS AND SERVICES

The printing industry is a strange paradox in the sense that there have probably been more radical changes to it in the last 15 years than the previous 500, yet we still retain generally the same basic means of applying printing images, discovered and developed over centuries.

Printing companies, where once they were in charge and control of the complete print chain from design to typesetting, graphic repro, printing and print finishing, mainly on an 'in-house' basis, now find themselves dealing with customers and suppliers across a wide range of print-related services and products.

New technology, or more correctly, the application of new technology to the printing industry, continues to have a marked effect on printers and print-buying customers alike. Printing is a bespoke industry producing products and supplying services in a tremendously wide range from business cards to large posters, from leaflets to case-bound books, from plain packaging to complex multi-coloured cartons. The range of printed products and services is endless and it is increasing rather than decreasing with the passage of time. There is not one aspect of the world economy which is not touched by the printing industry and its wider role in the developing communication and media industries.

There are around 15 000 companies trading as printing firms in some form or other in the UK, although with the spread of desktop publishing *(DTP)*, laser printers and photocopiers/printers it would be difficult to find a company without some contact or other with printing. Although there have been tremendous changes in industrial and business organisation in the 1990s throughout all business sectors, the printing industry is still predominantly a relatively small-scale bespoke industry in economic and structural terms - *see Figure 1.1* for confirmation of this.

Printing companies, through increased and intense competition, are more and more reviewing their position in the market place and trying to establish a niche or sector within which they can concentrate to achieve expertise with the aim of gaining higher margins and improved added value products and services.

The majority of printers still operate in the *jobbing/general centre ground*, although specialism in this area is still a major consideration with companies differentiating in terms of price, service, quality combination; sheet size, number of colours; partial or complete print service, print processes, etc.

Company size by number of full-time employees	Total number of companies	% of full-time labour force	% change of full-time labour force from 1990*
1 - 9	968	7.7	+ 2.7
10 - 24	878	17.1	- 1.1
25 - 49	381	17.1	+ 1.2
50 - 99	194	17.2	+ 8.2
100 - 149	69	10.7	- 7.0
150 - 249	46	10.6	- 22.0
250 - 499	36	16.5	+ 54.2
500 +	4	3.1	- 53.0

Figure 1.1: BPIF Manpower Survey 1996

Historically, printing companies set up close to a business community which would require their products and services. This is still true today of a great number of companies, although with digital links such as modem and Integrated Services Digital Network *(ISDN)*, geographical position matters considerably less than in the past. Some printers are indeed 'local' printers serving a very narrow catchment area of customers, whereas others could, in fact, cover the whole of the UK and parts of Europe or are truly global in outlook.

The table above reveals that just under 20% (19.6%) of the full-time labour force is employed in companies of 250 employees or more; 41.9% in companies of 49 employees and less and nearly 60% (59.1%) in companies of 99 employees and less - it should be noted that the figures relate to BPIF members only and the fourth column (*) is computated from the BPIF Labour Force Inquiry 1990.

The figures show that, of the BPIF firms in the survey, 72% employ less than 25 people: the situation in the EU of printing companies being 'small-scale' in size and structure is even more pronounced, with over 80% of the printing companies employing fewer than 20 people.

Specialist printers have taken a conscious decision to concentrate in a specific narrow band of products in which they have set up to gain maximum expertise and sector knowledge, offering a clearly defined range, aimed at achieving 'economies of scale' and market advantage by their clearly defined activity - examples include cartons, business forms, self adhesive labels, books, magazines, financial security printing, etc. *Figure 1.2* shows a breakdown of printing, composition and platemaking, graphic services, stationery and packaging covering the UK for 1996.

UK manufacturer sales (PRODCOM) - 1996	(£ million)
Printing	
Newspaper printing	232.5
Other printing, of which major areas are:	8622.1
Books, brochures, leaflets, etc	1990.4
Advertising literature	2003.4
Periodicals	1048.3
Security printing (stamps, cheque books and bank notes)	316.1
Printing of programmes, tickets, etc	1478.5
Registers, account books, receipt books	76.2
Notebooks, letter pads, etc	184.9
Diaries	69.9
Engagement books, address books, etc	8.8
Exercise books	14.7
Binders, folders and file covers	167.5
Continuous business forms	247.4
Other business forms	180.1
Albums for samples or for collections	11.0
Playing cards	n/a
Blotting pads and book covers	20.6
Maps, charts and globes	22.9
Postcards and greetings cards	173.2
Printing of transfers (decalcomanias)	57.4
Calendars	48.9
Pictures, designs and photographs	99.6
Printing onto plastic, glass, metal, wood and ceramics	335.7
Bookbinding and finishing	
Books	99.3
Brochures and magazines	170.5
Other	140.8
Composition and platemaking	
Composition, platemaking services, typesetting, etc	716.3
Printing components	199.9
Other printing activities	
Graphic services	557.3
Stationery	
Continuous stationery	138.1
Other stationery	208.4
Labels	456.0
Packaging	
Folding cartons, boxes and cases	1210.5
Box files, letter trays and storage boxes	33.0
Source: Office for National Statistics	

Figure 1.2: Printing and print-related UK manufacturer sales

Other significant areas in the generation of print and related services are inplants, facilities management and print shops, Print-on-Demand *(PoD)* and Small Office Home Office *(SOHO)*.

Inplants

These units are generally sited in the host organisation's premises, or within close proximity, with the main objective of supplying at least the majority of day-to-day print requirements in the short-run single and spot colour areas. Multi-colour and long-run work are often placed with a commercial printer possessing larger multi-colour presses, gaining 'economies of scale' and lower unit costs: some inplants, can of course, be large in their own right, with comprehensive production facilities including large sheet and web presses.

Facilities management

The central thrust of this arrangement is for the printing/supply company to undertake the management, production and/or sourcing of all, or a high proportion of, a customer's day-to-day requirements covering stock management of printed matter - eg - stationery, forms, order processing and distribution documentation, promotional and technical literature, etc, maintaining stock levels, including replenishment and disposal, as well as database management linked to a wide range of on-line electronic- based services. Facilities management is also now being offered on a short-term project by project basis, or longer-term basis: the facility and organisation can be very portable in that it can be set up and go live in a very short time span, depending on the circumstances.

Print shops

These were initially set up to some extent to compete with the traditional local 'High Street' jobbing printer and although starting from humble beginnings have grown tremendously, introducing a highly professional 'quick print' service and response. The growth of electronic printing has helped print shops respond in a positive way, resulting in a much higher profile, higher added value, and a quick response personal print service. In an attempt to gain 'economies of scale', group support, established profile and increased publicity, franchises have become popular with print shops, leading to service and product identification in particular market sectors.

Print shop services can cover from design, copying, printing - conventional and digital - to print finishing, data processing and management across a wide range of communication-related services and products - ie - a 'one-stop print shop concept' - with DTP driving the prepress links to the copiers and digital printers/presses.

Print-on-Demand

An emerging market born out of the application of new technology is distributed PoD where printers, through a digital network such as the World Wide Web *(WWW)*/Internet can print and deliver to 'local' customers within a very short period of time. Distributed printing is based round a hub of high speed printing systems accessed through a dial-up central database arrangement.

A further extension of this concept is *dial up digital artwork/picture/graphics libraries* where companies can seek and search through indexed lists and 'pictorial thumbnails' of pictures and graphics.

Small Office Home Office

New working practices are springing up as telecommunications become quicker and cheaper, allowing companies and individuals to work effectively in very small and often remote units: this arrangement is increasingly identified under the umbrella of SOHO, the structure and organisation of which is well suited to providing print, publishing and electronic-centred products and services.

The paperless office

We are somewhat removed from a 'paperless office' at the present time but it cannot be denied that electronic database management is a trend which will be adopted by an increasing number of companies, large and small. The impact of this trend will mean a reduction of printed paper documentation in the office. Also when hard copies of the electronic data are required they will generally be printed 'in-house' for small quantities, or through an electronic print service such as PoD or digital print centre for higher volume and distributed requirements.

The digital revolution

Predictions abound as to the impact of the digital revolution on long-established communication technologies, such as print, as well as new, evolving ones. Printing is currently adapting and adjusting to be a major player in the converging telecommunications and information-centred industries.

Far from digital 'non-print' means of reproduction and communications replacing print almost entirely within a relatively short period of time, as has been suggested in some quarters, it has so far proved to be complementary, as the overall business expands exponentially in terms of speed and impact.

Printing is still expected to be a major player in multi-media/communications well into the next millennium - possibly commanding at least 50% share by the year 2010.

It is now accepted that we live in an increasingly information-led world - where information in the form of data, text and images is created, manipulated and repurposed to produce an endless array of goods and services which often can be competitively and efficiently satisfied by print-related companies.

A further, new, digitally-led service taken up by some printers is *on-line publishing* which can be seen in electronic versions of magazines and newspapers available through the WWW.

An area where electronic-accessed data is replacing printed media is in software and other data-related manuals which are increasingly being offered on CD, disk and electronic manuals, often in the form of tutorials: use of the Internet to download software is another increasing non-print option. Many other traditional printed jobs such as catalogues, financial research papers, parts lists, etc, are still being printed, albeit in some instances with much lower print runs than previously, but increasingly electronic versions, such as in the form of a Portable Document Format *(PDF)* file are produced to allow access and use of the data through PCs, using on-screen services, etc. However, in most cases the printed product retains a major and central role in publishing with electronic formats or copies being produced as an additional service to the printed version, not as a replacement; print still remaining the most accessible and simplified means of accessing information for most people.

Printing companies, through their need to develop and utilise an efficient digital workflow, essentially in prepress but also increasingly in the pressroom and in print finishing, are building up a digital expertise which goes well beyond just the production of printed products, so extending the value-added business opportunities open to them.

The changing roles of the designer, customer and printer in preparing printed material

Traditionally, especially with printed products which require a certain level of design input, it has been the normal practice for a graphic designer or design agency to produce the initial sketches, visuals, dummies, layout and possibly made-up finished flat artwork from paper paste-up and airbrush techniques which were then passed on to the printing company for printing. This long-established labour-intensive, multi-operational approach has now been revolutionised by DTP-driven facilities.

It is interesting to note that the whole area of prepress can now be manipulated and prepared on DTP digital data, even up to the final stages of making printing plates.

New technology is relatively accessible to anyone, so that the design agency, customer and the printer can produce directly or through a second party - ie - a bureau - the amount of work required, therefore controlling and managing the whole prepress area. It is, however, more common for each of the 'players' involved in the *design-and-print cycle* to prepare only part of the prepress requirements - eg - *customers* producing 'copy' on word processors, IBM compatibles or Macs, with the electronic data being sent on to the *graphic designer* to produce visuals for approval, followed by preparation of the finished design, again in digital form. Finally, the *printer* generates the required film on scanners, imagesetters and workstations for subsequent platemaking, or, if applicable, goes direct-to-plate or cylinder.

There are certainly an increasing number of customers handling multi-page publications such as weekly and monthly magazines, journals and reports who are controlling the whole prepress operation up to the stage of supplying fully formatted PostScript disks or similar data through digital links to a bureau, repro house or printer for outputting on their imagesetter or scanner. Some print buying customers have even installed their own imagesetting and colour scanner/make-up facilities in-house so that final digital data or composite film is supplied to the printer.

Printers in recent years have moved towards seeking to form *partnerships* with customers, adopting a far more *active order-creating role* rather than the more traditional passive order-taking role. The objective of this approach is to deliver as high an added-value product or service to the customer as can be achieved with, if possible, some unique features which will help to cement a long-term profitable relationship.

In time, closer and closer *printer - customer links* are likely to develop in all areas of print-related services and products; customers will increasingly decide how involved they wish to become in generating, manipulating and producing the finished printed result. Previously discrete and separately defined areas are merging more and more into each other with a wide array of options open to the creator and user of print alike.

7

two

CHANGING ROLE OF PREPRESS

Printing as highlighted in *Chapter 1* has now developed into far more than an 'ink on paper/board or other substrate' process, positioning itself in an increasingly multi-media communications arena.

Data is increasingly being generated by, or on behalf of, the customer and sent to the printer to be manipulated, planned and repurposed into a wide range of printed products, as well as additional related services such as final electronic document generation, low- and high-resolution scanning, data management, on-line business, etc.

To encompass these changes and respond to an increasingly digital world, prepress has had to take on board a much more important role than was the case in the past when prepress operated within a printing company as a 'closed/ black art' activity. Previously the only production-type contacts with customers were confined to the receipt of hard copy manuscript, originals for reproduction such as photographs, transparencies, drawings, etc; plus hard copy proofs, passing between printer and customer in a mainly staggered, irregular form which, depending on the type of work involved, could take weeks or even months to conclude.

In response to the massive changes in the way that print and other modes of communication are organised, prepress has become the central and pivotal point of printing and print-related operations - ie - *the communications centre*: directly interfacing and interacting with customers across an increasingly wide spectrum, from the one person business scenario operating simply and basically from a word processor/hard copy base to global requirements across complex print, Internet and other multi-media options.

Today, anyone in prepress, from the self-employed graphic designer or photographer, to the largest printing company or multi-national corporation, is increasingly involved in the convergence of different technologies, such as telecommunications, computing, animation, digital photography, colour processing, image format, databasing of images and printing standards. These areas will be dealt with in more detail in later chapters.

There is even an increasing trend towards pre-communications, rather than prepress, where digital workflows and networks replace print as well as support it. As can be seen from *Figure 2.1* the end result of a print-orientated fully digital workflow is computer-to-plate, though increasingly this will be computer-to-print - *see Chapter 10, 'Computer-to-print and beyond'*.

Printers are increasingly aligning themselves as multi-media organisations with printed products as only one of their options, albeit a very important and major one. The ability to do this is based around their well-tried creative and digital manipulative skills which are still paramount in ensuring the work generated can run across different platforms, systems and media.

Printers' customers and printers alike are therefore increasingly involved in digital workflows and many of the decisions made, especially investments in software and hardware, are customer generated, directly or indirectly.

Prepress workflows

Workflows are systems, consisting of inputs and outputs which, increasingly in the case of prepress, are digital in nature. The measured control and management of workflows has become a major consideration and requirement in prepress as in some ways digital working processes are 'invisible', but unfortunately they cannot be said to be truly 'seamless'. The complexity of the digital reproduction route outlined in *Figure 2.1,* reveals that the *management of digital data from creation to output* provides plenty of opportunity for minefields of incompatibility. The proliferation of systems available demands that where fast and speedy exchange and transfer of data digital is required, it is important to ensure that all parties are working with compatible processes, procedures and systems.

Preflight checking is a type of troubleshooting procedure which has been developed to help highlight any problems, bottlenecks or hold-ups in input or output stages, which could, or are likely to, occur in the workflow process. The objective is to rectify these in 'advance', so alleviating, or at least minimising, workflow hitches. An example of a preflighting software utility is Barco 'PS Fix' which, for example, will identify and fix PostScript data problems in the digital workflow.

Figures 2.2 and *2.3* illustrate typical digital/electronic workflows used by medium- to large-sized printing companies, and by large repro companies/ bureaux showing the range of services offered to printers and print-related organisations respectively.

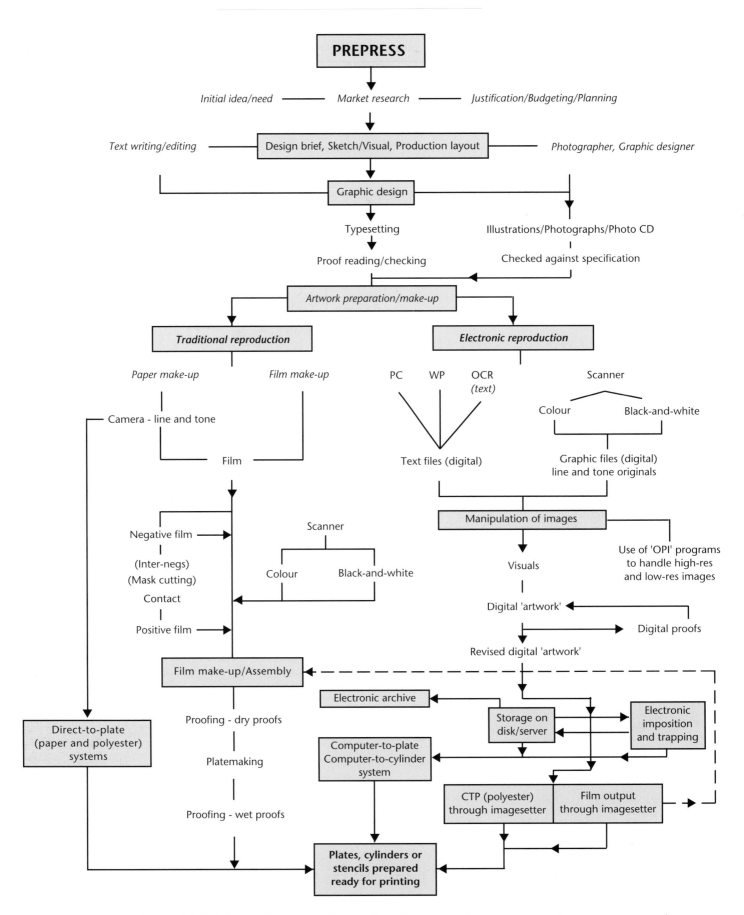

Figure 2.1: Workflow diagram illustrating the wide range of prepress operations, processes and routes which are commonly used in traditional and electronic reproduction

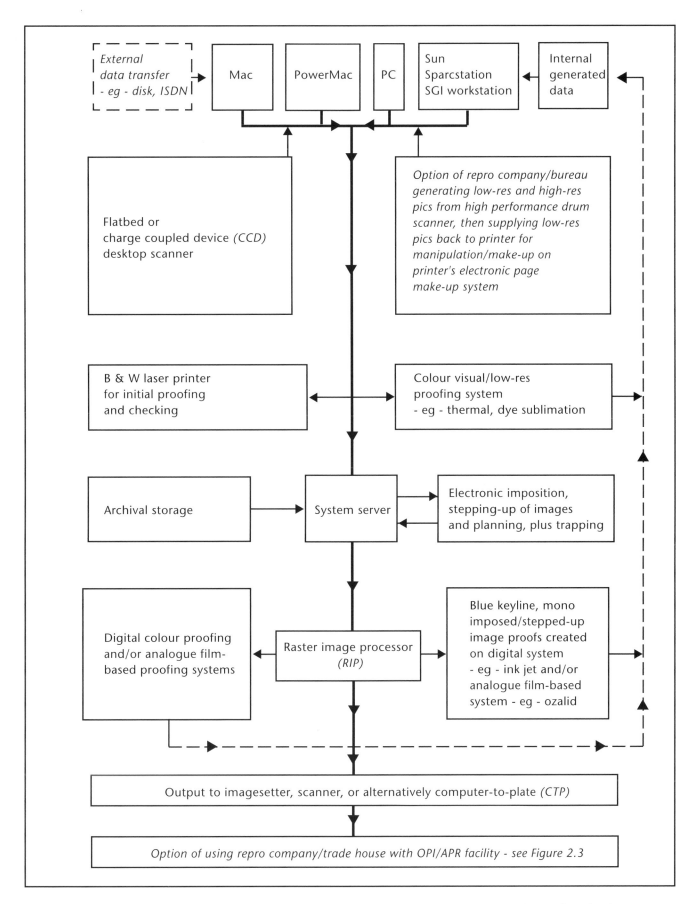

Figure 2.2: Workflow diagram of typical digital/electronic networks used by medium- to large-sized printing companies

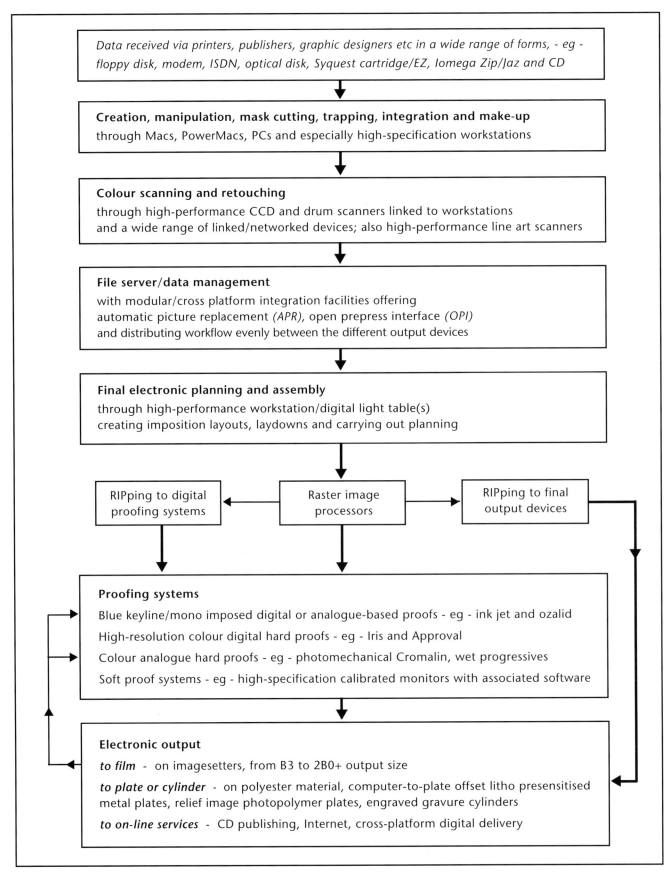

Data received via printers, publishers, graphic designers etc in a wide range of forms, - eg - floppy disk, modem, ISDN, optical disk, Syquest cartridge/EZ, Iomega Zip/Jaz and CD

Creation, manipulation, mask cutting, trapping, integration and make-up
through Macs, PowerMacs, PCs and especially high-specification workstations

Colour scanning and retouching
through high-performance CCD and drum scanners linked to workstations
and a wide range of linked/networked devices; also high-performance line art scanners

File server/data management
with modular/cross platform integration facilities offering
automatic picture replacement *(APR)*, open prepress interface *(OPI)*
and distributing workflow evenly between the different output devices

Final electronic planning and assembly
through high-performance workstation/digital light table(s)
creating imposition layouts, laydowns and carrying out planning

RIPping to digital proofing systems

Raster image processors

RIPping to final output devices

Proofing systems
Blue keyline/mono imposed digital or analogue-based proofs - eg - ink jet and ozalid
High-resolution colour digital hard proofs - eg - Iris and Approval
Colour analogue hard proofs - eg - photomechanical Cromalin, wet progressives
Soft proof systems - eg - high-specification calibrated monitors with associated software

Electronic output
to film - on imagesetters, from B3 to 2B0+ output size
to plate or cylinder - on polyester material, computer-to-plate offset litho presensitised metal plates, relief image photopolymer plates, engraved gravure cylinders
to on-line services - CD publishing, Internet, cross-platform digital delivery

Figure 2.3: Workflow diagram of typical digital/electronic networks used by large repro companies/ bureaux showing the growing range of services offered to printers and other print-related organisations

Outline of prepress workflow - traditional and electronic

The following precis links to *Figure 2.1*, with greater detail in the areas covered appearing in the appropriate places, later in the book.

As printing is largely a bespoke industry, the earliest stages of a job such as *initial idea/need; market research; justification to proceed, budgeting and planning* up to the *design brief stage* will rest largely with the customer. Once the decision has been reached to produce a printed or print-related product, various options are then available.

Design brief - sketch/visual

This stage will normally commence with the customer or customer's representative briefing the person responsible for preparing the initial sketches and visuals. The type of product, its use, house style, corporate image, illustrations, photographs and materials to be used will be discussed at this stage, as well as the proposed budget and schedule. A great many problems and misunderstandings can be eliminated at the outset if preliminary discussions take place between the person responsible for co-ordinating the work for the customer and printing company's staff. This is to ensure the artwork, film or digital data is prepared in the most effective manner and to the correct specification. The drive towards electronic/digital generation of printed images was reflected as far back as 1992 when the findings of a survey stated that over 70% of the participating design houses and advertising agencies used computers - 85% for page layout and 67% for 'drawing and 'painting'.

Text writing and editing

These are processes which would either be carried out by a member of the customer's staff or handled by a professional copywriter. The text can be generated on a word processor or other digital media form, also in certain cases clean hard copy suitable for optical character reading is supplied.

Photography

Photography undertaken by lay persons will vary considerably in quality depending on the skills of the individual, the equipment used, plus the lighting and subject matter conditions at the time. Professional photographers are often commissioned to take a series of shots to a specific brief of subject matter, composition and balance, etc, but the results may still require retouching to ensure the required printed result can be achieved. The conventional photographic products used for printing reproduction fall into the main categories of monochrome or colour photographs, colour negatives or positive transparencies.

The application of new technology has impacted on photography to the extent that higher quality digital imaging is now available through the use of *digital cameras* and *Kodak Photo CD*. The quality of digital photography is increasing all the time and the method avoids a number of intermediary processes and associated problems found in traditional photographic properties, such as a tendency for emulsion fading and colour casts. A further development is the use of digital picture libraries.

Production layout

Unless the graphic designer prepares the combined design and image elements on a DTP/Computer Aided Design *(CAD)* system up to the stage of outputting to an imagesetter or other means of output, a *production layout* must be prepared for each job to ensure that the desired printed result is expressed in the elements or components necessary to create the printed images required. The designer will, whatever system is adopted in preparing the work, still need to produce sketches and visuals at the required stages to ensure the customer's approval to proceed, and to discuss reproduction aspects with the printer. Production layouts are simply the equivalent of what in engineering would be drawings or blueprints. Coloured pencils, felt tip pens and markers can be used to good effect, or a digital equivalent produced on a computer, indicating the use and split for colour. Professionally prepared, they can result in high quality production visuals allowing the customer an ideal, inexpensive preview of the finished job.

Graphic design

Graphic design for print has changed dramatically in the last decade through the application and adoption of CAD in the form of relatively standard and popular software programs run on Macs and PCs, as well as dedicated high-end design systems, which are aimed mainly at specialist areas of printing such as packaging, labels, direct mail and business forms. These systems are capable of generating digital files of text and graphics in colour, separated for the individual colours, retouched and redrawn to suit particular requirements. The designs are stored in digital form and are therefore easily accessible for amendment, once the basic design parameters are prepared.

Typesetting

Nowadays word processors mostly capture the keystrokes in a transferable form - for example, formatted disks, as well as producing a hard typewritten copy for checking. This eliminates, or at worst reduces, the need for a printer's typesetter to key again after the customer has created the approved manuscript.

14

Technology has advanced so rapidly with the advent of DTP and the use of terminals allowing sight of 'What You See Is What You Get' *(WYSIWYG)* working procedures that the customer can prepare or interface with the printing company's equipment to produce digital data in finished form. *Proof reading* and *checking* is increasingly being undertaken by the person/department generating the key strokes, which today tends not to be the printer: for further details - *see Chapter 3, 'Typography'*.

> *The pace of change and development in printing and print-related industries in the last decade has been nothing short of extraordinary, none more so than in the area of prepress.*
>
> *Processes which traditionally utilised a wide range of equipment and different operations can now be carried out in one integrated digital workflow.*
>
> *Although it cannot be disputed that printing, as part of the wider communication industries, is moving more and more towards a fully digital prepress scenario, the reality is that printing companies and print buyers are at widely varying points along the digital prepress journey/solution.*
>
> *This publication, as an introduction to prepress, acknowledges that digital systems are the central driving force behind all major current developments in the printing industry.*
>
> *There is a further factor, however, in that although traditional methods of working are by-and-large dated, they nevertheless show the principles and activities of prepress much simpler and clearer than digital: in addition it should be noted that the length allocated to a specific topic in the book does not necessarily equate with its importance as again it generally takes much longer to explain and outline the main prepress functions which have mainly been looked at from a traditional perspective. The aim is to provide a better learning perspective in a balanced approach.*

Traditional reproduction *- see Figure 2.1*

Up to the stage of platemaking, traditional (often previously referred to as *conventional*) reproduction involves a wide range of operations, all producing a 'physical-type' product which is passed on to the next stage for processing, converting and positioning into the required format:

• **Typesetting**, although declining rapidly to be replaced by DTP-based systems, is still carried out, albeit in a very limited form, on imagesetters producing bromide paper or film for at least partial manual make-up.

• **Photographs, transparencies, artwork** reproduced traditionally on *graphics arts cameras* again producing paper bromide or film output.

• **Film make-up** using negative or positive film, along with *inter-negs, mask cutting* and *planning* onto plate flats or foils - for further details, *see Chapter 6, 'Make-up, planning and assembly'.*

• **Proofing** produced using film-based/analogue processes as dry photo-mechanical proofs or wet proofs using plates.

• **Platemaking** from punch-pin register film, negative or positive, in the form of flats or foils contacted onto presensitised plates in a printing-down frame. Polyester/Silvermaster-type plates can also be produced from special camera systems: for further details - *see Chapter 9, 'Output systems and the preparation of printing surfaces'.*

Electronic reproduction

The principle of electronic reproduction is radically different from conventional reproduction in that the system creates and manipulates digital/ electronic data. It only produces 'physical' or 'mechanical' data when required as part of the process - such as completed hard copy proofs from a laser printer, or finished film from a scanner or imagesetter, also polyester plates from an imagesetter when required, retaining its digital form in the host storage system:

• **Text input** ranges from *word processors, PC/Mac disks* or input from *Optical Character Recognition (OCR) systems* into *electronic text files.*

• **Photographs, transparencies, artwork** are scanned into the system, using a scanner either for colour or black-and-white reproduction.

• **Digital cameras,** as previously commented upon, can supply digital images direct to the receiving DTP system. Graphics generation can also be produced using specialist software manipulation programs. Desktop colour systems have now developed to such an extent that they have overtaken the previously dominant proprietary Electronic Page Composition *(EPC)* systems, apart from some highly specialised areas.

• **Final image/page make-up -** during this process all the subjects needed for a job - type, photographs, graphics and tints, etc - are scanned or input into the system by other means. Also, as far as possible, the colour balance and other reproduction parameters are set up at the input stage.

• **Digital proofing** takes place at various stages including black-and-white page/ one-up laser proofs, up to high-end inkjet colour proofs - *see Chapter 8, 'Proofing'.*

• **Outputting** can be in the form of *computer-to-film* or *computer-to-plate*; whatever method is used, electronic software will allow imposed page images or multiple images to be produced on imagesetters or platesetters.

Receipt, distribution and storage of digital data

As can be seen from *Figures 2.1, 2.2* and *2.3,* digital data can be received from many different sources. The means of receipt and distribution of digital data is again wide and varied - from physical media such as floppy disk, cartridge and CD, etc, to data transfer such as ISDN, modem and Internet - *see Glossary,* for further details of these items.

All forms of digital data rely on storage to hold the digital data and to provide the means of distributing and receiving it. Storage is measured in bytes and multiples of bytes: one byte can store one character, while one kilobyte *(kb)* can store in excess of 1000 characters, one megabyte *(Mb)* in excess of one million characters and one gigabyte *(Gb)* in excess of one billion characters. Storage media store data as 'ones' and 'zeros', presence/absence of a charge, formed by a read/write head. AppleMacs have a peripheral connection/data bus connection protocol called Small Computer Systems Interface *(SCSI),* whereas on a similar basis, Integrated Drive Electronics *(IDE)* is a common connection drive on PCs allowing external drives such as storage systems to be connected to the computer for receipt, distribution and storage purposes of digital data. SCSI 1 and 2 support up to seven devices, such as external storage systems, as well as scanners, printers, communication links, etc, plus the host computer: SCSI CD-ROM drives are also now available on most recent models of PCs and AppleMacs. Re-writable CDs are also available.

Memory and storage

There are two types of memory for storage - Random Access Memory *(RAM)* used to retain a computer's operating system and applications: data produced in RAM is lost when the computer is switched off. Data which is to be retained and stored, uses Read Only Memory *(ROM),* with the digital data being put onto suitable storage media. Digital graphics files are in most cases very large and even using compression software a considerable amount of RAM is required, including fast access storage systems. A medium-sized bureau's ongoing network server requirement can be 5Gb or more.

On a computer the most common type of storage is the internal hard drive which is a 'fixed' form of storage. Due to the requirement to send and receive digital data, plus back-up files, create archives and 'top up' the available fixed data, a wide range of removable storage media have been developed.

Removable media

These have the advantage of portability and the facility to store and distribute data with potentially no limit to the amount of data that can be stored and retained.

The options available in this area have expanded considerably in recent years from the ubiquitous 3.5" *floppy disk* capable of holding 1.44Mb, fitted to all modern PCs and AppleMacs, to systems capable of storing multiple Gb of data.

Magneto optical *(MO)* disks are another form of large removable storage media: the drives have the added advantage of being practically an indestructible form of media. A further option of high volume storage are Write-Once-Read-Many *(WORM)*, or multiple optical type disks which can hold up to 15Gb of data single sided.

Compact Disk Read-Only-Memory *(CD-ROM)* is a form of volume, highly portable low cost data storage with 650Mb capacity on a disk where the data is burnt onto the plastic carrier disk by laser.

Hard drives

All modern computers are fitted with an *internal hard drive* with the main objective of retaining and storing digital data. 40Mb internal hard drives were common in the mid 1980s, so highlighting the massive explosion in use and complexity of computer requirements which can be gauged by the multiple Gb hard drives which are now available on computers.

Due to computer requirements such as the size of operating systems and applications appearing to increase daily and become almost insatiable in terms of storage requirements, *external hard disks* are becoming a part of everyday prepress operations. To assist in coping with these massive storage and retrieval requirements, 'juke box' and other systems are now available.

A Redundant Array of Independent Disks *(RAID)* system works on the principle of several combined disks culminating in fast access, working on the basis that if one disk fails (becomes redundant) a 'spare' hard disk is brought into operation. A further option on similar lines is *data mirroring* where data is written simultaneously to two hard disks so that if one crashes the other will retain a copy. The purpose of RAID is mainly to provide system redundancy in the event of failure in mission-critical systems.

Data juke boxes or *towers* are a system of combining a number of drives with the object of forming one large storage facility. They are capable of holding multiple storage disks or WORMs and CDs with data capacity in excess of 2 terabytes (2000Gb) but they lack the functionality of RAID systems.

Data back-up procedures

Back-up of data in the prepress area can be undertaken on 4mm or 8mm tape, normally DAT *(digital audio tape)*, cassettes or CD. Tape systems are relatively cheap, which make them ideal for back-up purposes, but are slow in comparison to other systems.

> ***Note:*** *As time passes, all forms of computer-related software and hardware will improve in terms of speed, performance and cost: in addition, some systems will become redundant, as well as new ones introduced.*

Desktop computers

There are three main types of desktop computers - AppleMacs and PCs, both of which fall into the category of micro-computers, and the more powerful mini-computers, such as those produced by Sun Microsystems, Silicon Graphics and Windows NT servers made by most of the major computer companies. The term desktop is often not strictly accurate as most systems are now mainly developing into tower-based systems which, instead of sitting on a desktop, reside under it.

Computers are made up of their *computing platforms* which consists of hardware and operating system, plus *software,* which is designed to run on a particular computer platform or range of platforms.

AppleMacs

An AppleMac comes as a complete configured system with its own operating system. The features that have made the Mac particularly popular with the graphics-centred industries is the user-friendly working environment, with the use of a simple Graphical User Interface *(GUI)*; icons, in the form of graphical representations; easy mouse control - a hand-controlled device, which, when operated, moves the cursor on the computer screen to the point required - and consistent working practices, which remain consistent from program to program, so allowing the user to confidently move around the system. The range of machines now cover from smaller home-use to powerful units which are capable of competing with UNIX-based workstations in certain classes of work: there are also systems developed which allow UNIX implementation on PowerMacs.

PCs

PCs differ from AppleMacs in that they are built by a wide range of companies, using different but compatible components, and up until recent years, were generally accepted to be less user-friendly than Macs.

PCs were originally developed by International Business Machines *(IBM)*, although the great majority of machines are now IBM-compatibles. The initial operating system, Microsoft Disk Operating System *(MSDOS),* which is based on a command line interface - eg - the typed instruction *'c:>cd dir'* instructs the computer to the change directory on drive c, which is much less user-friendly than the Apple system. In order to overcome this fact, Windows 3.1 was developed which still required DOS to be installed. Windows 95 and 98, further developments, gave advantages over 3.1 of built-in greater functionality and user-friendliness, more powerful environment, along with multi-tasking, plug-and-play and Internet access facilities. Windows NT *(New Technology)* has also been developed, resulting in a very powerful network management operating system.

Sun Microsystems and Silicon Graphics

Sun Sparcstation and Silicon Graphics machines are based on the UNIX operating system. Both machines come with built-in networking, multi-tasking and ISDN facilities, high quality colour monitor and are very fast and powerful in operation.

Sun Sparcstation machines are mostly used in the graphics-related industries for high-end colour and image manipulation: Silicon Graphics Indigo *(SGI)*, has also developed workstations.

Software programs such as Adobe Photoshop and Illustrator have been developed for the UNIX-based machines, but the range of available software programs is much more limited than for the AppleMac and PC. A further use for the machines is in RIPing and as a host file server for high-end graphics creation/retouching systems such as Quantel 'Paintbox/Printbox'.

It is claimed by major users of UNIX-based machines that they are much more productive than even the top-end Macs by up to tenfold on certain work.

The use of powerful workstations is evident in the need for systems to operate efficiently and quickly when requiring to work in large colour files of 300Mb or more in real time.

AppleMacs, since the first machines became available, have had a special relationship with, and been extensively used by, the graphics and print-related industries, expanding into multi-media and home use in recent years, although it still remains ostensibly a niche market product. PCs, on the other hand, are a mass market product, initially mainly for general business use but now, in addition, comprehensively covering multi-media, home use, games, etc, and increasingly impacting on the graphics marketplace.

Apple's market share has dropped considerably in recent years as PC versions of established graphics/DTP software have become more common and accepted, where once there was a great divide. With the vast majority of the market share currently held (and growing) by PCs, along with its high performance networking capabilities, cheaper pricing, use of more powerful processors, PCs are set to command more of the market currently held by AppleMacs and UNIX-based workstations.

three

TYPOGRAPHY

Typographical measurement

Although the printing industry in the UK, by and large, changed over to the metric system of measurement in 1970, one area that, in general, did not change but, in fact, retained its own separate and unique method of measurement, was *typography*.

The measurement of type generally bears no relationship to any metric or imperial system of measurement. In 1886 the Association of American Typefounders elected a committee to study and create a recognised system of type measurement and in 1898 the system was adopted in the UK.

Until then there was no mathematical relationship between different types and different *typefounders* (the manufacturers of metal type). It therefore was not possible to mix types from the irregular range available.

Different sizes were given distinctive names and the most famous that survived to form the basis of the new point system was the *pica*, which has become the standard 12 point measurement. Other old type names which have survived into the present time are *nonpareil* (6 point) and *long primer* or *elite* (10 point).

The system of measurement adopted by British printers is the *Anglo-American point system*. The basic unit is the *point system* with one *point (pt)* measuring 0.351mm (0.0139"). Small dimensions such as type body depths are stated in points, or fractions of a point. Larger dimensions such as type areas are stated in 12 point *ems* or *picas*.

Despite several attempts at metrication for modern typesetting systems, *the 12 point (pica) em is still the UK standard typographic unit*, measuring 4.217mm.

Similarly, continental systems such as the *cicero, didot, riga* and *aug* were independent of any metric system.

It must be acknowledged, however, that use of typographical measurement in mm is increasing in popularity - eg - column widths stated in mm rather than pica ems.

Sizes of type

When a type is described as being 8pt or 18pt, it is not the size of the letter which is being described, but the measurement of its own overall body size as shown in *Figure 3.1(a)* - eg - an 18pt solid type represents 18pt type on an 18pt body size, when measured from the base of one line to the next. Sometimes it is appropriate to increase the space between lines of type and this is called *interlinear spacing* or *leading* - eg - 14 on 18pt type represents a 14pt type on an overall 18pt body, as shown in *Figure 3.1(b)*.

Imagesetters are now available with output capabilities to suit most sizes of commercial printing machines eg outputting film from B3, B2, B1 to extra large format 2B0+.

(a) 18pt on 18pt body

Imagesetters are now available with output capabilities to suit most sizes of commercial printing machines eg outputting film from B3, B2, B1 to extra large format 2B0+.

(b) 14pt on 18pt body

Figure 3.1: (a) 18pt Stone Sans (b) 14pt Stone Sans on an 18pt body size

The most common sizes of type are 6, 7, 8, 9, 10, 11, 12, 14, 18, 24, 30, 36, 42, 48, 60 and 72pt, although the adoption of AppleMacs and PCs as the main input source of formatting DTP digital typesetting instructions has allowed a much wider range of available type sizes compared to previous dedicated typesetting systems - eg - Adobe PageMaker allows type sizes in tenth point increments.

The sizes up to 12pt are traditionally described as *composition sizes* with above 14pt described as *display sizes - see Figure 3.2.*

Type founts (or fonts)

The alphabet consists of capital and small letters. In typographic terms the capital letters are called *caps* or *upper case* and the small letters *lower case*. These terms derive from the early days of hand setting hot-metal type from cases of type, where the caps were kept in the upper case and the smaller letters in the lower case.

COMPOSITION SIZES

5 pt - ABCDEFGHIJKLMNOPQRSTUVWXYZ abcdefghijklmnopqrsuvwxyz

6 pt - ABCDEFGHIJKLMNOPORSTUVWXYZ abcdefghijklmnopqrstuvwxyz

7 pt - ABCDEFGHIJKLMNOPQRSTUVWXYZ abcdefghijklmnopqrstuvwxyz

8 pt - ABCDEFGHIJKLMNOPQRSTUVWXYZ abcdefghijklmnopqrstuvwxyz

9 pt - ABCDEFGHIJKLMNOPQRSTUVWXYZ abcdefghijklmnopqrstuvwxyz

10 pt - ABCDEFGHIJKLMNOPQRSTUVWXYZ abcdefghijklmnopqrstuvwxyz

11 pt - ABCDEFGHIJKLMNOPQRSTUVWXY abcdefghijklmnopqrstuvwxy

12 pt - ABCDEFGHIJKLMNOPQRSTUVW abcdefghijklmnopqrstuvw

DISPLAY SIZES

14 pt - ABCDEFGHIJKLMNOPQRST abcdefghijklmnopqrst

18 pt - ABCDEFGHIJKLMNO abcdefghijklmno

24pt - ABCDEFGHIJKL abcdefghijkl

30pt - ABCDEFG abcdefg

36pt - ABCDEF abcdef

42pt - ABCD abcd

48pt - ABC abc

60pt - AB ab

72pt- AB ab

Figure 3.2: Composition and display sizes using Stone Sans typeface

Caps or upper case	ABCDEFGHIJKLMNOPQRSTUVWXYZ
Lower case	abcdefghijklmnopqrstuvwxyz
Small caps	ABCDEFGHIJKLMNOPQRSTUVWXYZ
Figures aligning	1234567890
Figures non-aligning	1234567890
Punctuation marks	. , : ; ! - ' ' " " ( ) { } [ ]
Diphthongs	Æ æ Œ œ
Ligatures	fi fl ff ffi ffl
Reference marks	* asterisk, † dagger, ‡ double dagger, ¶ paragraph, § section mark, # hatch mark, © copyright mark, ® registered mark, ™ trade mark, etc
Special signs	£ pound, $ dollar, ¢ cent, & ampersand, mµ micron, ß beta, omega, etc

Figure 3.3: An example of some characters which make up a fount

A single piece of type is termed a *sort*. A *fount* (pronounced 'font' and increasingly spelt that way following American influence) of type is an assortment of type of the same size and design. Examples of these characters are shown in *Figure 3.3*.

Accented sorts in a wide range are generally available with most formats.

À Á Â Ã Ä Å Ç È É Ê Ë Ì Í Î Ï Ñ Ò Ó Ô Õ Ö Ø Ù Ú Û Ü
à á â ã ä å ç è é ê ë ì í î ï ñ ò ó ô õ ö ø ù ú û ü.

Type characters

The type characters of any fount include long letters which take up nearly the whole depth of their bodies - eg - J and Q, and short letters which are positioned near the centre of their bodies eg x, m, n, o. The height of the short letters is known as the *x-height* and *small capitals* are usually about this height. In addition, there are also ascending letters - eg - b, d, f, h, with *ascenders* extending above the *mean line;* descending letters - eg - g, j, p, q, with *descenders* extending below the *base line.*

Capital letters extend above the mean line and sit on the base line.

The width of a typeface is dependent on its design and character. The capital 'M' is wider than the capital 'I' and the *width* or *set* varies with each size and type design. The position of the face on the body and the width of each character are designed so that the correct amount of white space and balance will appear on each side of the character when set with other characters.

Figure 3.4: Different parts of type characters

Type size is measured by the body size of the type and *not* by the printed area appearing. From *Figures 3.1a* and *3.1b,* it can be seen that the body size of the type measures 18 points from top to bottom, while the space taken up by the individual letters varies considerably: this is especially the case with the difference between the two examples - (*a'*) which is 18pt solid and (*b*) which is 14pt type with 4pt *interlinear spacing* built-in - ie - 14 on 18pt overall. The letters vary in their position to the baseline, mean line, x-height, ascender, descender and cap line: as no individual character fills completely the body size, it is not possible to tell the type and body size by just measuring the appearing printed surface. The normal way to measure type and body size is shown in *Figure 3.1,* where the measurement is taken from the base line of one line in relation with another base line, so establishing body size. Type size is measured by including just above the ascender level to just below the descender level.

In modern setting systems, the *body* of a typeface, a term originating from the hot-metal, three-dimensional shape, is a purely abstract concept. Letters and figures, however, still have to fit correctly with each other. Letters are placed on a notional white space and the left or right edge of this space is called the *side bearing.*

Letterspacing is the adjustment of the standard space between characters to improve the visual appearance of a word / group of words, or to fill a given space.

Kerning is the adjustment of space so that one part of a letter extends over the body of another. The kern is that part of the letter which extends beyond the body, a feature most common with script and italic faces.

Ligatures are the joining together of certain letters *(tied or linked letters)* to form one grouped character, so reducing the unsightly and apparently unbalanced space which would otherwise appear between the letters.

Figure 3.5: Example of kerning/ligatures to create appearance of better letter fit, especially between 'f' and 'i'

Typefaces

A typeface is defined as a set of characters for printing intended to be used in combination and identifiable by its design and availability in a range of sizes.

Stone Sans 10 on 12 pt

Imagesetters are now available with output capabilities to suit most sizes of commercial printing machines eg outputting film from B3, B2, B1 to extra large format 2B0+: with modern working practices, through electronic imposition software and systems, the film can be prepared complete ready for platemaking. A further application for most imagesetters over a long period of time has been the option of producing polyester/Silvermaster plates direct from the computer-driven front-end. The most recent development in this area has seen the launch of imagesetters which have the ability to double up as a platesetter, exposing direct onto presensitised metal plates.

Stone Sans italic 10 on 12 pt

Imagesetters are now available with output capabilities to suit most sizes of commercial printing machines eg outputting film from B3, B2, B1 to extra large format 2B0+: with modern working practices, through electronic imposition software and systems, the film can be prepared complete ready for platemaking. A further application for most imagesetters over a long period of time has been the option of producing polyester/Silvermaster plates direct from the computer-driven front-end. The most recent development in this area has seen the launch of imagesetters which have the ability to double up as a platesetter, exposing direct onto presensitised metal plates.

Stone Sans bold 10 on 12 pt

Imagesetters are now available with output capabilities to suit most sizes of commercial printing machines eg outputting film from B3, B2, B1 to extra large format 2B0+: with modern working practices, through electronic imposition software and systems, the film can be prepared complete ready for platemaking. A further application for most imagesetters over a long period of time has been the option of producing polyester/Silvermaster plates direct from the computer-driven front-end. The most recent development in this area has seen the launch of imagesetters which have the ability to double up as a platesetter, exposing direct onto presensitised metal plates.

Stone Sans bold italic 10 on 12pt

Imagesetters are now available with output capabilities to suit most sizes of commercial printing machines eg outputting film from B3, B2, B1 to extra large format 2B0+: with modern working practices, through electronic imposition software and systems, the film can be prepared complete ready for platemaking. A further application for most imagesetters over a long period of time has been the option of producing polyester/Silvermaster plates direct from the computer-driven front-end. The most recent development in this area has seen the launch of imagesetters which have the ability to double up as a platesetter, exposing direct onto presensitised metal plates.

Figure 3.6: Some examples and variations of the Stone Sans type family

Typefaces are grouped into *type families,* each member of the family being derived from one basic design, but varying in weight, width or other treatment. Examples of the Stone Sans family are shown in *Figure 3.6,* covering Stone Sans, Stone Sans italic, Stone Sans bold and Stone Sans bold italic. Today there are several thousand different type designs in existence with printing companies (even trade typesetters or bureaux) having to be restrictive in the number of typefaces they possess - *see page 35, 'Fonts and working with fonts'.*

Traditionally, text faces were available with at least the *seven alphabet layout -* roman upper and lower case, bold upper and lower case, italic upper and lower case with, finally, small caps. Other variations, such as condensed or bold italic can of course be added, where available. Related typefaces in a family may be classified according to their *weight* - that is, their lightness or boldness - or according to their *width,* such as the degree to which they are condensed or extended.

Frequently the word *medium* is used to indicate the normal width and weight of the particular type family. Problems and confusion can arise, however, through different typefounders, manufacturers and stockists adapting or remodelling existing typeface designs, or designing a typeface which is only a subtle change from an established typeface. Apart from 'common' typefaces varying in name between different typesetting suppliers they vary in their set or width, also depending on the fount system being used the same amount of copy can occupy varying amounts of text depth.

The set of a typeface

• The width of standard typefaces varies in that their basic design can be even, narrow- or wide-set.

• An **even-set** face has the same width and type dimensions when set on a solid body - 8pt solid even-set, for example, is 8pt wide x 8pt deep.

• A **narrow-set** face is narrower in its width than its depth - 8pt solid narrow-set, for example, is 7pt wide x 8pt deep.

• A **wide-set** face is wider in its width than its depth - 8pt solid wide-set, for example, is 9pt wide x 8pt deep.

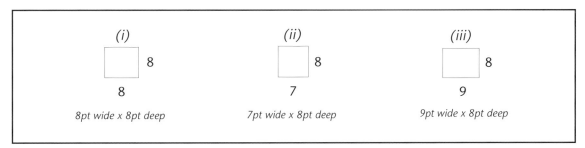

Figure 3.7: Representation of an 8pt type as even-, narrow- and wide-set

Page widths and depths

As previously mentioned, the *width* (or measure) and the *depth* of the page to be typeset may be expressed in either mm or 12pt pica ems.

Recognition of typefaces

The main differences between typefaces centre on the following areas:

(a) Length of ascenders, descenders and x-height

The size of the lower-case letters in proportion to the body varies according to the design. When the x-height is large, the ascenders and descenders are shorter than when the x-height is small.

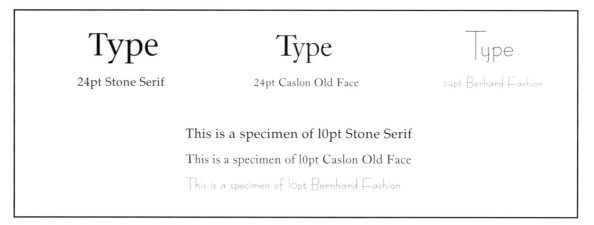

Figure 3.8: Examples of ascender, descender and x-height differences

(b) Serifs

Serifs are the small strokes or terminals at the top and bottom of the main strokes of letters and are to be seen on both capital and lower-case letters. Serifs are of various shapes, as shown below, and enhance aesthetics and the readability of the letters. Typefaces without serifs are classified as *sans serif* (without serifs) or, sometimes, *lineales*.

Figure 3.9: Examples of serif and sans serif faces

(c) Width of the various letters

Typefaces are designed with different sets or widths of letters. The 'm' or any other letter of one typeface may be wider or narrower than the same letter of another typeface. The lengths of the capitals and lower case do not always follow a predictable pattern - notice how with Times, the lower-case alphabet is fairly narrow-set in comparison to Stone Serif, yet the cap alphabet is fairly wide-set.

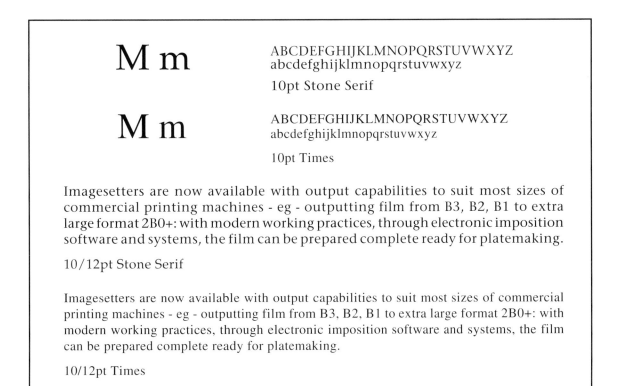

Figure 3.10: Example of the difference in set or width of letters between two different typefaces

(d) General weight and colour of the typeface

Most typefaces, with the exception of some sans serifs and slab serifs, have contrasting thick and thin strokes. The amount of contrast varies according to the design, with the result that, in body matter, some types produce a 'greyer' or 'blacker' page than others, although this also depends on the x-height and the amount of white space appearing between the lines.

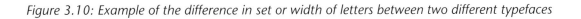

Figure 3.11: Typefaces of contrasting weight and colour

e) Design of the letters

Many typefaces, especially fancy display faces, can normally be easily recognised by the general shape and form of the letters, or by the characteristics of certain letters.

Bauhaus	Bernhard Fashion	*Brush Script*	**Chicago**	Courier
Klang	Monaco	Onyx	Old English	*Zapf Chancery*

Figure 3.12: Examples of different typefaces

Proof correction and standards

Capturing keystrokes

Traditionally, printing companies set a very high proportion of the typesetting element of their printed work with customers supplying manuscript as hard copy produced on a typewriter: this would then be rekeyed completely by the printer's typesetter, with varying degrees of errors creeping in, which would need further reading and correcting in a re-keying cycle until copy was perfectly clean and approved for reproduction.

Today, word processors are the main means of text capture/generating keystrokes in a transferable form - eg - formatted disks, as well as a hard copy record for reference purposes produced from a printer.

OCR software is now available which will 'read' and capture the hard copy through the use of a scanner - *see page 43*. A further development which avoids keying is the use of voice recognition software which allows the user to speak into a microphone, recording the words in digital form in the host computer - at present this only has a limited and specialist application.

Easy and simple access to typesetting preparation through DTP has brought the reward of cheaper setting, but with it the lack of skill and appreciation which is so necessary to produce good typographical standards. The printing company, although setting less and less copy, is still to a great extent the guardian of good quality typographic standards.

Proof reading

Reading and copy checking by printers is declining as customers are supplying electronic copy or film and so take responsibility for proof reading themselves, especially in the case of urgent work which is often expected to be turned round in hours.

With improvements in digital workflow now the focus of many changes in prepress systems, the use of 'Spell Check' and 'Thesaurus/Lexicon' programs will increase, so reducing the time needed for the proof reading process.

Proof correction marks

Proof correction marks have been standardised and BS 5261:1976 (part 2) (1995) adopted as the standard for making proof marks. Many BS marks are also included in a convenient folded-card form, BS 5261C, which outlines that each correction should be indicated by a marginal mark to signify or amplify the meaning of the instruction. In the British Standard all marks are indicated by internationally understood signs, rather than by words or letters.

Marginal marks are written in the left or right margins according to the position of the correction from the centre of the line. When there is more than one correction in a line, they are written in the order in which they occur, reading from left to right, and each correction is separated by a diagonal stroke (/). It is recommended that guidelines connecting the mark in the text with the correction should not be used, although some traditional proof readers and markers still retain this practice.

When letters or words are to be altered or deleted, these are struck through and the correction to be submitted or made is indicated in the margin, followed by a diagonal stroke. Letters or words omitted on the proof are written in the margin, followed by a *caret* mark (∧) and the position of the omission is also indicated in the text by a caret mark. It should be noted that the full stop, colon and leader are always encircled when marked on proofs to distinguish them from the comma, semi-colon and ellipsis, which is the mark indicating the omission of a word or words in a sentence (. . .).

Pages 32 and *33* show proof correction symbols taken from BS 5261:1976 (part 2) (1995) *'Copy preparation and proof correction - specification for typographic requirements, marks for copy preparation and proof correction, proofing procedure'*. These were devised by the British Standards Institution following discussions on an international standard for such symbols to replace the former British Standard which used several English words and letters unacceptable internationally.

In addition to the standards which have been introduced covering text, there have also been standards and recommendations issued for colour correction by the British Standards Institute *(BSI)* and International Standards Organisation *(ISO)*.

Figure 3.13 illustrates the use of marked-up copy with proof readers' marks.

INSTRUCTION	TEXTUAL MARK	MARGINAL MARK
Correction is concluded	None	/
Leave unchanged	- - - - - - - - - - - - - - under character to remain	⊘
Push down risen spacing material	Encircle blemish	⊥
Insert in text the matter indicated in the margin	⅄	New matter followed by ⅄
Insert additional matter identified by a letter in a diamond	⅄	⅄ Followed by, e.g. ◇A◇
Delete	/ through character(s) or ⊢—⊣ through word(s) to be deleted	ℒ
Delete and close up	⌶ through character or ⌒ through character e.g. charaȼcter charaȼȼacter	ℒ
Substitute character or substitute part of one or more word(s)	/ through character or ⊢—⊣ through word(s)	New character or new word(s)
Wrong fount. Replace by character(s) of correct fount	Encircle character(s) to be changed	⊗
Change damaged character(s)	Encircle character(s) to be changed	✕
Set in or change to italic	‾‾‾‾‾‾ under character(s) to be set or changed	⌿⌿⌿
Set in or change to capital letters	≡≡≡ under character(s) to be set or changed	≡
Set in or change to small capital letters	≡≡ under character(s) to be set or changed	═
Set in or change to capital letters for initial letters and small capital letters for the rest of the words	≡ under initial letters ≡≡ under rest of word(s)	≡
Set in or change to bold type	∿∿∿ under character(s) to be set or changed	∿∿
Change capital letters to lower-case letters	Encircle character(s) to be changed	≠
Change italic to upright type	Encircle character(s) to be changed	⌊⌿⌋
Invert type	Encircle character(s) to be inverted	↻
Substitute or insert full stop or decimal point	/ through character or ⅄ where required	⦿
Substitute or insert colon	/ through character or ⅄ where required	⦂
Substitute or insert semi-colon	/ through character or ⅄ where required	;

INSTRUCTION	TEXTUAL MARK	MARGINAL MARK
Substitute or insert comma	/ through character or ⋏ where required	,
Start new paragraph	⌐	⌐
Run on (no new paragraph)	⌒→	⌒→
Transpose characters or words	between characters or words, numbered when necessary	⊔⊓
Transpose lines	⇇	⇇
Centre	⌊enclosing matter to be centred⌋	⌊ ⌋
Indent	⌐	⌐
Cancel indent	⊢⌐	⌐
Move matter specified distance to the right	⌐enclosing matter to be moved to the right→	⌐
Take over character(s) word(s) or line to next line, column or page	⌐	⌐
Take over character(s) word(s) or line to previous line, column or page	⌐	⌐
Raise matter	↑ over matter to be raised / ⌞____⌟ under matter to be raised	⌞____⌟
Lower matter	⌜____⌝ over matter to be lowered / ↓ under matter to be lowered	⌜____⌝
Correct vertical alignment	‖	‖
Correct horizontal alignment	Single line above and below misaligned matter e.g. mis$_{alig}^{n}$ed	‗
Close up. Delete space between characters or words	linking ⌒ characters	⌒
Insert space between characters		between characters affected	Y
Insert space between words	Y between words affected	Y
Reduce space between characters		between characters affected	⌂
Reduce space between words	⌂ between words affected	⌂
Make space appear equal between characters or words		between characters or words affected	⋈
Insert space between lines or paragraphs	─(or)─	
Reduce space between lines or paragraphs	─) or (─	

33

Correction of typeset matter

In typesetting carried out by the printer, corrections on the first rough proof are known as *house corrections* or *literals* and are carried out to rectify errors and omissions. Amendments or alterations which are marked on the proof returned by the customer/author, other than those due to faulty setting/make-up - that is, literals - are called *author's corrections* and are charged to the customer, according to the amount of work involved.

The procedure adopted by many printers on receipt of digital data supplied by, or on behalf of the customer, is to print out the whole document again on their own equipment - eg - laser printer, and send it to the customer for approval. This is to highlight any differences or difficulties, which may occur from using the data on the printer's equipment and resources, rather than the customer's - eg - different word breaks, font clashes or problems, missing data, etc. Alternatively some printers will work direct from the laser proof received from the customer. Unless alternative arrangements are made, it is not the responsibility of the printer to correct even obvious errors in the work supplied to them, although the printer will often point out such areas to the customer, and request how they wish to proceed.

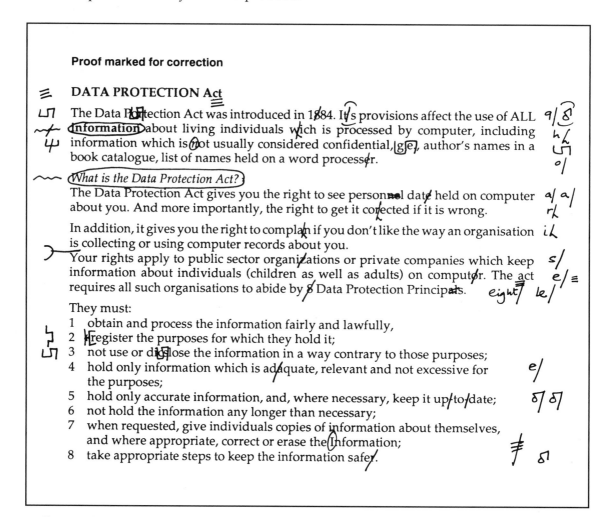

Figure 3.13: Example of typeset matter marked-up with proof correction marks

Fonts and working with fonts

Fonts (assuming the more-commonly used American spelling, rather than the older English spelling 'founts'), are now mainly available via CDs, where a large number of fonts are held - eg - there are nearly 4000 fonts on *Linotype Library Font CD 6.0.* The user or potential user of the CD is allowed to browse through the available fonts on the CD before making a choice as to whatever new typefaces they wish to purchase. As each font is selected, a list is normally prepared in the form of an order, which is sent to the supplier usually by fax or e-mail who in return provides 'unlock codes' so that the chosen fount(s) can be loaded onto the system being used and accessed as required. Most font CDs come compatible with Mac, PC/Windows, Sun and Silicon Graphics platforms.

PostScript Type 1 and TrueType fonts

There are two main kinds of fonts available for general use on Apple Macs and PCs - PostScript Type 1 and TrueType. Most fonts are available in PostScript Type 1 format which require users to run Adobe Type Manager *(ATM),* a facility for smoothing out ragged edges around the type when printing out.

PostScript Type 1 fonts, developed by Adobe, require two fonts, one covering the screen font at 72dpi and a further higher-resolution one for the output device.

Type 1 fonts are the industry standard for use on PostScript printers and are constructed as *object-oriented vector graphics - see page 43.* They are independent of the output device, retaining consistency and quality in the outputted product - eg - from low-resolution laser printer to high-resolution imagesetter.

TrueType fonts, developed by Apple and Microsoft, are not so readily available, with only a few type manufacturers offering their full range of fonts in TrueType format; in addition their use is primarily for PCs rather than Macs. The fonts also need to be converted to a PostScript outline when using a PostScript printer, and the output quality can suffer as a consequence: on the other hand, TrueType fonts were developed to reproduce smooth edged letterforms on non-PostScript printers, requiring only one font for both monitor/screen and printer use.

Adobe and Microsoft are working towards creating 'OpenType' fonts as one standard combining PostScript Type 1 and TrueType fonts.

Copyright and font licensing issues

Digital fonts are licensed software and are therefore covered and protected by law. The purchase of a font does not convey ownership to the buyer; it only sanctions the 'usufructuary' (restricted power to use another party's property by prior agreement) right to the digitised typeface and does not, for example, allow a font to be passed on to a second party such as an outputting bureau.

Fonts licensed by most type founders, including Adobe, are licensed for use on five computers/CPUs, but only one output device: if a font is to be used on more than five computers or one printer then a multi-user licence is required. This is a *computer-based policy* rather than the earlier system which was *printer-based*: some users may still retain font licenses based on printer-based agreement and in most cases this will remain valid, meeting the original arrangements. Even although copies of documents containing a given font or fonts are frequently passed to parties other than the originator, it is only legal to give them a copy of the font if they have already obtained a licence to use that font - this would include repro companies, bureaux, etc. Fonts are licensed for use within a single company, with special arrangements normally required for using fonts at multiple sites within a large company organisation.

Transferring fonts and work electronically to a second party

Certain typeface manufacturers permit embedding certain fonts into documents for the purposes of viewing and printing only: documents with embedded fonts may not be edited unless those embedded fonts are licensed to, and installed on to the computer doing the editing. In general, embedding certain fonts is legal if the fonts are embedded but cannot be used to edit documents or accessed as fonts for use in other documents. Printing to a PostScript language file and embedding fonts into formats like PDF *(Portable Document Format)* files - *see page 185,* are legal ways to embed fonts, but sending fonts via, for example, floppy disks or ISDN along with print jobs, is not legal, since they can be installed and used as fonts in other documents.

When a digital file is sent on to a second party such as an imagesetting/outputting bureau, several issues re the fonts used in the document require clarifying, such as: list of every font used, including version and date; manufacturer and/or supplier of the font; also if the fonts used are in PostScript Type 1 or TrueType format.

The list of fonts can normally be generated by the page layout program which produced the document; the font manufacturers and type of format will be established by noting the distinctive and descriptive type of screen icon displayed as TrueType, which only requires a single font file, and PostScript which requires both a printer font and a screen or bitmap font. It is also important to include any fonts which are nested in graphic files and not otherwise identified.

Font manipulation software

Font manipulation software, such as *Macromedia Fontographer, FontMonger, Typestyler* and *FontStudio,* can be used to create new fonts and/or modify existing ones, producing in some cases 'derivatives' of original fonts: it is legal for the original licensed font user to use derivative fonts for individual usage, but it is strictly illegal to assume ownership, to sell or give away, the created derivative fonts.

Other font-related software which is of benefit to the user in managing and using fonts more effectively are: *FontExpert* which is capable of recognising thousands of typefaces by name and manufacturer; *FontFitter* which automatically calculates the correct kerning and spacing of any typeface; *Font Gander* acts as a font manager, arranging for printed examples of fonts from a wide range of resources available to the user, as well as the facility to create font sheets and *Font Sneak* which reports font usage and collects fonts for prepress use. Several other software programs, such as *Font Box, Font Juggler* and *Suitcase,* are available to clean up and streamline the storage and use of fonts on a system.

The subject of the use (and unfortunately the abuse) of fonts, along with the creation and distribution of electronic files, is extremely complex and the reader is particularly directed to the following publications: *'Digital File Transfer Checklist'* and *'Guidelines for the creation and transfer of PostScript files'* published by the BPIF and *'Digital Advertisement Transfer Industry Committee (DATIC) Digital advertisement transfer guidelines and recommendations'.*

Acknowledgement is also due to FontWorks UK Ltd as at least part of this section on font licensing and handling owes much to font-related publications issued by the company, especially *'Guide to typeface licensing'.*

four

HANDLING TEXT

Having covered typography in *Chapter 3* across text-related areas such as typographic measurement, type sizes, fonts, type characters, typefaces, proof reading etc, this chapter covers the related area of handling text.

In recent years the procedure of creating and handling textmatter has changed dramatically, through the application of easy-entry computer-driven systems, which has allowed the customer to do work traditionally handled internally by the printer. Occasionally a trade typesetter would handle overflow work which could not be handled by the printer, or they would possess certain skills, expertise and facilities not held by the printer - eg - complex foreign language setting, plus a very wide range of expensive type matrices or photographic masters, which were required to cover a wide range of type fonts.

Over the centuries the process of handling text has been a 'physical' series of processes only moving to a digital workflow in the last decade or so. There have been many terms given to this area of prepress, including the main ones of letter assembly, composition and typesetting. The typesetting systems which cover up to the present time are hot-metal setting, phototypesetting and imagesetting: for further details, *see Chapter 9, 'Output media and preparation of printing surfaces'*.

Text input methods

There are several input methods available to create and/or capture text in modern computer-driven systems: these include direct keying, inputting text from other devices such as portable storage devices, scanning in from hard copy, voice recording and communication systems, via modem or ISDN link.

Direct keying

This is the most popular means of inputting text, especially for new work, using a word processor, IBM PC-compatible or AppleMac to capture the keystrokes in digital form. About 90% of text capture for printed work is undertaken by, or on behalf of, the customer, leaving only around 10% or less undertaken by printers 'in-house' or associated services such as bureaux.

Apart from capturing keystrokes, the keyboard is used to control and communicate with the host computer. Its complexity will vary with the model, but will typically have a dozen or more function keys aiding short cuts and carrying out specific tasks.

Most PC systems use a Visual Display Terminal *(VDT)* which utilises the WYSIWYG principle, where the terminal/monitor displays a relatively true facsimile of the required typeface, rather than a standard sans serif or generic serif face. In reality, some systems are not true WYSIWYG as the resolutions of the monitors are far too low to reproduce accurately the font information required, so special low-resolution screen font information methods have been devised for the WYSIWYG operation - *see PostScript Type 1 bit map screen founts on page 35.* Although the great majority of input/keyboard systems are PC-based, major prepress suppliers still market - albeit in a very restricted range - dedicated keyboard systems for their own specific equipment. The advantages of dedicated keyboard systems are: total compatibility with the purpose-built hardware and software produced by the manufacturer; also, in most cases, greater flexibility and complexity of integrated programs, plus generally higher quality typographic standards. The advantages of PC keyboards are that they are generally considerably cheaper than dedicated keyboard systems; also they do not require as extensive, or as long a level of, training for operators.

Since data capture today is done on PCs, compatibility and access is much easier. PC keyboards will continue to dominate in front-end prepress applications, but dedicated keyboard units are likely to be retained for some time, mainly for specialist, complex, high-quality image preparation and creation.

Manipulation and conversion of text data from one system to another

Conversion and transference of text data

Transferring text from modern storage devices such as floppy disks, Iomega Zip and Jaz, SyQuest EZ13, etc, prepared on IBM compatible PCs and Apple Macs will normally present few problems in importing into a host system for make-up and/or review. The main problems that arise come not so much from importing data into a system, but in trying to use/access the data for make-up and review. Examples of such problems, from data supplied, are: disks that cannot be read; file for which the printer/typesetter has no appropriate program; missing typefaces used in documents and encapsulated PostScript *(EPS)* graphics.

Optical Character Recognition (OCR)

OCR is a means of converting paper based - ie - hard copy documents, into editable text, by the use of a scanner and related software, avoiding the lengthy job of keying in and/or rekeying from existing copy. The two most popular types of OCR software are 'OmniPage' and 'TextBridge', where the hard copy is scanned and the data captured in a digital format. The newest and most advanced versions of the software are now capable of recognising documents with virtually any mix of text, numerals and graphics, creating files in word processing, spreadsheet, image or database file format.

Customisable zones allow the targeting of particular areas for improved accuracy. Accuracy levels (100% recording no errors) will vary considerably depending on the quality of the hard copy original to be scanned in: 80% to 90%, and up to 95% in some instances, is the target most OCR users are able to achieve. Automatic and manual editing will be used to achieve the 100% accuracy required. The initial accuracy level will obviously be heavily determined by the quality and condition of the available hard copy. The format and structure of the original document can be retained or a simple text file can be created depending on the result required. Many of the OCR programs can now be 'trained' to look for systematic patterns to match to, so identifying the particular characteristics of a typeface.

Most flatbed or small specialist scanning systems such as Visioneer 'Paperport' support 'OmniPage' and 'TextBridge' software. OCR software is available to run on PC compatibles, AppleMacs and on the Sun platform. The reader is directed to *Chapter 10, 'Computer-to-print and beyond'*, where OCR is covered in the production of electronic documents.

Automatic Voice Recognition (AVR)

This is another option of creating text, which works on the basis of capturing speech - ie - someone speaking into a microphone and through the appropriate software creating a digital copy which is introduced into an IBM compatible PC or AppleMac for text processing and formatting. The software often comes with a vocabulary of 60 000 words and above: as yet this type of system has still to establish itself as a major player in the text creation market. The speed of word capture has developed up to around 120 words per minute, and of the order of 95%+ accuracy.

Text transferring through telecommunications

Data which has to be transferred over a long distance can be transmitted by telecommunications using a modem or ISDN link.

Modem

A modem (*mo*dulator/*dem*odulator) is a device which allows computers to communicate with each other through standard telephone lines: it converts the purely digital signal from a host computer to the audio (analogue) signal needed for transmission over telephone lines. The first requirement for the machines at each end of the line is a serial connection, the basic standard of connection between computers, plus communications software which will allow the modems to communicate between each other without manual intervention.

The speed by which modems send and receive data is measured in *baud*, which approximates to bits per second: several modem speeds are currently available - 14 400baud or 14.4Kbps - normally used for faxes, 28 800baud or 28.8Kbps, 33 600baud or 33.6Kbps and 56 000baud or 56Kbps. To put this into context: it would take approximately seven minutes to transfer a text document of 1.5Mb using a 28.8Kbps modem (1 500 000 x 8 [bits in document] ÷ 28 800 [speed in bits per second of modem) = 416 seconds). These 'theoretical' speeds of transfer will, however, be greatly affected by how 'clean' the telephone line is at the time of transfer.

The advantage of using telecommunications, whether modem or ISDN, is that it is a relatively simple operation where sender or receiver could be using a wide range of host computers. The user of a modem will connect to a *server service* which receives calls and responds to them.

Server services vary from the simplest bulletin board used mainly to exchange messages between two parties: email (*electronic mail*) is a form of bulletin board - and in the case of the giant CompuServe concern has more than three million members. A modem is also used to connect to the Internet through an Internet Service Provider *(ISP) - see Chapter 10, 'Computer-to-print and beyond'*.

ISDN

Although modems are very popular, especially for low traffic data transfer, Integrated Services Digital Network *(ISDN)*, has become the *de facto* standard for sending and receiving large amounts of prepress data by telecommunications. ISDN is a dedicated digital telephone link-up working at very high speed: it is considerably faster than modem because all forms of communications are kept in digital form, rather than the *digital - analogue - digital conversions* necessary for modem operation, also digital communication lines have a higher bandwidth so allowing much faster transfer of data.

WAM!NET/4-Sight, the largest supplier of ISDN software and connections in the UK, offers a range of ISDN options, through British Telecom, ISDN2, ISDN8, ISDN30 with two, eight and 30 channels respectively. The time (when this book was published) taken to send and receive a 20Mb file would be 25 minutes using ISDN2, 7.25 minutes using ISDN8 and two minutes using ISDN30, against over four hours on some current modems - *see Figure 5.23*: these times are based on 'theoretical' maximum speeds. It should be noted that ISDN is too slow for some users, so new graphic networks are being set up by, for example, BT, MCI, Scitex and WAM!NET.

Software programs

Software programs used for document creation fall into three main areas - text capture and basic graphics, graphic generation and manipulation, and page make-up. Graphic generation and manipulation will be covered in *Chapter 5, 'Handling images/graphics'* and page make-up applications in *Chapter 6, 'Make-up, planning and assembly'*.

Text capture and basic graphics

Word processing software, as the name implies, is used to process words/text and to create text-based documents: it was initially devised to create letters and reports with facilities later added to introduce basic graphics, cut-and-paste, spell check, etc. From these relatively humble beginnings, so-called word processing packages have become very powerful, possessing a wide range of functions, with the ability to create and export text with typographic formatting/styles to DTP/page make-up programs. The more advanced word processing software will include most of the features found in dedicated, comprehensive DTP packages: missing might be master pages or multiple master pages in a document, guides for lining up page elements, crop, registration marks, and colour separation for output. The current most popular dedicated word processing packages include Corel 'WordPerfect', Nisus 'Writer', WorldSoft 'WorldWrite', with Microsoft 'Word' being the market leader.

One of the trends in software development would appear to be towards all-singing, all-dancing integrated software programs which offer the vast majority of facilities a user would require in just one program: in addition, relatively inexpensive integrated works software are available such as Claris 'Works', Microsoft 'Office' and CorelDraw 'Suite'.

Formatting text

In traditional typesetting, where this operation was undertaken by printers, including the keying or rekeying of text from hard copy, the formatting or encoding of the text matter would be undertaken by the typesetter. Specialist formatting codes would be used such as [h1] for main heading, [t1] for main text, [ ] for paragraph end, to be followed by indent or inter-paragraph gap.

Due to the fact that customers are now generally supplying text to printers as final pages, which have been mainly created on word processors, it is increasingly the case that most of the text encoding and formatting is prepared at this stage: a main exception to this would be the use of Standard Generalised Mark-up Language *(SGML)*, which is used mainly for preparing electronic documents - *see Chapter 10, 'Computer-to-print and beyond'.*

Style sheets

Most comprehensive word processing packages, and all DTP programs, will allow text to be entered into the application and structured in a defined way, even to the extent that existing templates are sometimes available for particular types of work, which can be changed to suit particular circumstances, but retaining as much of the original format as required.

Style sheets or formatting lists can be set up for each document, recording the coding required - eg - recording overall style for reference, typeface, type size, leading, tracking, and covering a wide range of predetermined elements such as main heading, sub heading, body text and captions. Features affecting document setup will also be included, such as paper size, page margins, column width(s), highlighting for bold, italic or underlined text, justified or unjustified setting, paragraph styles and tabulation, etc, will be included.

It is important that the customer and printer agree to follow a common working practice for formatting and coding text, so as to minimise, and eradicate if possible, the requirement for reworking any of the textmatter and format style supplied.

Vector and bitmap text and graphics creation

There are two main methods of creating and reproducing text and graphics: vector or outline form and bitmap or line-run data. In *vector form*, a character becomes an outline connecting a series of points, plotted wherever the direction of the character's outline changes, the position of each point being precisely located and defined digitally in the fount supplied: though vectors can be created from isolated points, they may also be formed by a joined-up succession of standard lines, curves and arcs to the exact shape of each line. In creating this kind of object-oriented form of lines and arcs, *Bezier curves* are used. Bezier was a mathematician who developed a set of equations to describe a curved line by its roundness or flatness value, a system which has been adopted by Adobe in creating PostScript fonts.

In *bitmap form*, a character is digitised to a grid and scanned, the resulting information being held in a fount store. Each character is scanned by a raster which makes a series of parallel sweeps across the face, recording details of the design in minute steps, every discrete dot or bit being identified as a 'signal' or 'no signal'. Line-run data is similar except that only changes from 'signal' to 'no signal' (or vice versa) are registered. Since less storage space is taken up by line-run data, more founts can be accommodated than with the bitmap system.

Once a letter has been input by either method, vector or bitmap, it is edited. In the case of a letter stored as a bitmap, editing and retouching will usually be on a point-by-point basis, the type designer going round the edge adding or removing single points or groups of points until the desired effect is achieved. Where, however, an outline has been plotted, individual plot points can be moved, added or removed and normally a Computer Aided Design *(CAD)* program will automatically 'elastic band' an outline. The typographer will then fix the side-bearings and base alignment of each letter and run tests to see that each letter fits acceptably with other letters in every conceivable combination.

Having created an acceptable typeface in digital form, the next stage is to convert it into a form usable for the imagesetter. This step often involves the conversion of bitmaps to line-run data or vectors - the latter being more useful as a vector can produce the whole range of sizes from one master. It is achieved by programs which read in the outline and then decide how many raster strokes need to be output to fill in the vector it has just scanned. Fonts stored in vector form are always output as rasters.

Returning to the topic of PostScript Type 1 and TrueType fonts covered in *Chapter 3, 'Typography'*, PostScript Type 1 fonts have two parts, a screen font which is of bitmap form, and a printer font which is in vector form: TrueType fonts come only in single vector form, which is used for both the screen and printer output.

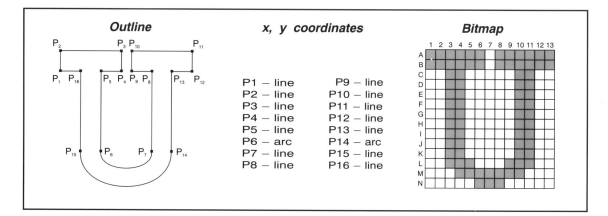

Figure 4.1: Letter form in outline and bitmap form

Page description languages and PostScript

Page description languages are a means of describing the appearance of a printed page in terms of its component parts. Computers can basically only communicate in their own language/operating system, thus making different types of computers incompatible with each other. Translators or interfaces are therefore required to connect the systems: page description languages perform this function of interpreter and operate by using a co-ordinate system through a set of mathematical commands to determine how the components - text, line, graphics and continuous tone - are to appear on the printed page.

PostScript was developed by Adobe Systems in the early 1980s and has to all intents and purposes become the page description standard for DTP, prepress and graphic arts industries: it is both a page description and a printer control language.

PostScript describes any printable image consisting of text and some page elements as a series of American Standard Code for Information Interchange *(ASCII)* computer codes, also enabling continuous tone *(CT)* to be embedded or referenced, as CT data is not usually in ASCII. These elements are then presented to an output device where the PostScript interpreter converts the basic ASCII codes into a bitmap for exposure to a relatively low-resolution laser printer, or via a RIP to a high-resolution imagesetter. PostScript, being device- and resolution-independent, easily accommodates outputting to both laser printer and imagesetter. As all computers use the standard ASCII characters it follows that, providing an appropriate operating software program/driver is available, then corresponding computers and printers can operate in PostScript format.

A PostScript file consists of the header, procedure definitions, document setup, pages detail and document trailer to describe all the necessary parameters and content to generate the required image(s).

Since PostScript was introduced as Level 1, it has undergone many developments and improvements. PostScript Level 2 included support for colour extensions, Display PostScript, composite fonts, compression/decompression filters, improved halftone algorithms for colour separations, device-independent colour, etc.

PostScript Level 3 has been especially developed to encompass the growing world of electronic publishing, networks and digital document creation supporting WWW, Internet, HTML and PDF documents - *see Chapter 10, 'Computer-to-print and beyond'*. Other features include supports for High-Fidelity *(HiFi)* and Hexachrome colour, plus enhanced image technology, which streamlines and speeds up image processing by sending reduced data to the RIP for outputting, etc.

Open systems, networks and network protocols, client/server principles

Open systems

These are computer-based systems where the hardware and software standard are specified independently of the supplier, allowing the purchaser to buy from any supplier, so enabling the building up of any type of configuration which suits their own particular requirements.

The opposite, or alternative, to open systems are proprietary systems which lock the user into host-based architecture, often through centralised, complex, stand-alone systems and dedicated software. It is a system that for many years has been heavily weighted on the side of the supplier but, with open systems now becoming the norm, users are being released from the often inflexible operation of a proprietary system.

Networks and network protocols

Ever since the first computers were introduced, there has been a great deal of time and effort expended on linking them together, so that they could communicate and exchange data with each other - ie - in creating computer networks.

Initially only proprietary/'closed' networks or protocols were available as each computer system had basically been developed in isolation. However, as computer systems improved and matured, open computer standards such as Transmission Control Protocol/Internet Protocol *(TCP/IP)* were introduced, opening up computer networks: its background owes much to military and academic use, but it has now been readily embraced by commercial undertakings.

AppleMacs, since their inception, have had the benefit of close association and relationship between software and hardware development - eg - Apple Computer, Inc. and Adobe Systems Incorporated. All Macs or IBM PC compatibles when linked to a printer for hard copy output perform information flow which is one directional - from computer to printer: when multiple computers are networked/combined together they exchange information and files, and share any facility or devices which is part of the network - eg - a server.

The communicating language used on networks is called a *protocol* and several protocols have been developed for different applications.

Network systems now in use with Macs include: AppleTalk, LocalTalk and Ethernet, Fibre Distributed Data Interface *(FDDI)* and SCSI.

Windows NT has developed as the market leader for PC LANs.

Workstations such as Sun and Silicon Graphics running the UNIX-based operating system are ideally suited to network environments and multi-tasking, through built-in hardware support. Workstations are also increasingly found as servers in client/server environments.

Client-server principles

A *client* is any AppleMac, PC or workstation on a network connected to a server.

A *server* is at the intersecting point of a network, providing shared resources through a communication link to network users - eg - input sources such as Macs, PCs, workstations, scanners, etc to output sources such as imagesetters, platesetters, etc - *see Figure 2.2.*

The server can be any computer, although it is normally a powerful workstation, which has software and applications, which allows it to respond to requests/instructions from client members of the network.

By using a client/server configuration, greater efficiency and productivity is achieved by considerably reducing the network traffic/transfer of data, assuming an OPI server is in use. This operates on the basis that when a client requests, for example, processing of information on the server, only that specific and relevant data will be returned to the client; whereas in networks working without a server, the whole amount of related data or file is transferred across the network, even although only a small part of the file was required by the client.

Small Computer Systems Interface (SCSI)

This is a means of connecting peripheral devices such as scanners, printers, hard drives, etc, enabling them to interface and link up with a single computer. A SCSI system can support up to seven devices: the connectors are either 25-pin, 50-pin or 68-pin at the end of the required length of cable which fits into the SCSI ports at the back of the Apple Mac.

The vast majority of Macs and workstations are fitted with SCSI interfaces and SCSI host adapters are available for PCs, although Integrated Drive Electronics *(IDE)* and Enhanced IDE are the most common interfaces for PCs: IDE supporting only two disk drives and enhanced IDE up to four devices.

PC to Mac and Mac to PC conversions/cross platform compatibility

There are two ways to emulate an IBM PC compatible on a Mac - ie - to get it to run as if it were a PC. Either hardware or software options can be used, both of which result in PC DOS and/or Windows operating systems running on the Mac.

Hardware option

The hardware-based option works through the use of a *PC or DOS card* which plugs into the Mac, so that it has the ability to work as if it was a PC. Examples of PC cards are Apple 'PC Compatibility', Orange 'Micro Orange PC' and 'Reply DOS on Mac'.

Software option

The software-based option creates a *PC window* on the Mac which allows PC software to be run on the Mac - 'Soft Windows' is an example of a software emulation option. MSDOS, Windows 3.1 and Windows 98 or later versions can be accommodated.

File exchange

As long as an operator has a the correct means of *file exchange*, a file can be read by either a PC or Mac, so allowing the user to work with PC formatted disks as if they were Mac disks.

When a PC floppy disk is inserted in a Mac running a file exchange utility such as 'PC Exchange', 'DOS Mounter Plus' or 'Access PC', the disk is accepted as if it were a Mac disk - for an explanation of *file formats - see Chapter 5, 'Handling text'*.

To open a file on PC (DOS) disk, or to save Mac files to DOS, so that a PC can read them, may require the use of a *file translation facility* such as 'MacLinkPlus', which allows PC files to be used on Macs and vice versa, without losing any of the files text formatting such as use of bold, italics, etc.

Compatibility between applications is also required - eg - Adobe 'PageMaker' version 6.0 files being used in the exchange between PC and Mac version, if the operator wishes to work on the converted file without incurring problems.

When files are to be transferred remotely - ie - by ISDN or modem, they should be converted/exported out in a file format suitable to the receiving system - ie - Mac or PC.

All software programs/applications tend not operate as efficiently on both platforms, assuming they are available on Mac and PC. The normal scenario is that the platform in which the application was first developed operates the most efficiently, and it takes some considerable time before the cross platform option is relatively trouble free.

Virus protection

A virus is a program which has been designed to malfunction with the intent of disabling certain items or operations in a computer system, resulting in damage to software programs, utilities and even the operating system. A virus, when introduced into a computer system, through an infected disk, or infected downloaded data, can spread very quickly, affecting everything in its path.

To avoid viruses being introduced into a computer system, anti-virus utilities such as 'Virex', Symantec 'AntiVirus for Macintosh', 'Disinfectant' and 'VirusScan' have been developed. The general operation of anti-virus utilities is that, when in operation, they scan and protect the storage media in the host computer by locating and destroying the identified viruses. As new viruses are being introduced all the time, this places the onus on computer users to be constantly alert to the danger of virus-corrupted data. Some anti-virus utilities such as 'Virex' can seek out previously unknown viruses by creating an outline or fingerprint of files in master uncorrupted form: comparing it on subsequent occasions with the 'masters' to detect any differences which may indicate a virus is present. Depending on the type of virus and virus protection used, the infected file can be deleted or repaired.

There are different sorts of virus, attaching themselves to selected programs and making use of various techniques to do so. Examples include: *resident file virus,* which remain in working memory after being invoked; *polymorphous virus,* which alters its appearance at each new infection; and *boot sector virus*, which attacks only the boot sector on floppy or hard disks.

HANDLING IMAGES/GRAPHICS

Graphic reproduction is the reproduction of graphic images by a printing process or other medium. Graphic images include pictorial illustrations and typematter consisting of letter and symbolic forms such as logos, symbols, etc.

Just as *Chapter 4, 'Handling text'* illustrated, there has been a blurring of the interface between what was traditionally known as text and graphics, with prepress equipment suppliers crossing over into what were previously separate and discrete areas. This chapter will concentrate on the traditional area of graphics with the integration of text; graphics on systems and workstations being covered in greater detail in *Chapter 6, 'Make-up, planning and assembly'*.

Images/graphics generation and manipulation

The traditional route

This would entail the designer or artist preparing the work on a large drawing board or tabletop working environment, with the images and graphics, or at least the base artwork, being prepared as camera-ready copy on special paper or board material. The initial stage is *preparing sketches or design ideas on paper* using pencils, pens, crayons and colour markers to create a visual, or group of visuals for presentation to the customer for comment and feedback. The next stage is *to prepare the layout, encompassing the customer's feedback and instructions on the initial sketches*: this entails drawing up the dimensions of the overall printed product, position of images, marking-up typesetting requirements, allocation of space for text, graphics and other images, commissioning of continuous tone pictures as transparencies and/or photographs. This forms the blueprint of the job and will often be sent to the customer to check, approve or amend as appropriate, before proceeding to the production of finished artwork. The final stage is *the preparation of camera-ready artwork* incorporating most elements of the job secured down onto a white art base board: additional elements such as photographs or transparencies, along with colour split and tint laying instructions, etc, are often included as overlay sheets, marked-up with corresponding reference and keys to the base artwork.

The desktop/digital route

This is by far the most common route for generating and manipulating graphics and has been for some considerable time: the traditional route has been included, not as a reflection of modern and common working practices, but as a brief overview of the conventional/traditional routines, from which have developed many of the desktop/digital terms and overall principles.

The whole area of generating graphics and their subsequent manipulation is now carried out on, or through, the centrepiece or focal point, of modern electronic systems - ie - *the desktop*.

Each of the stages outlined in the traditional route can now be carried out on the desktop-type base system, whether it be on a Mac, PC, workstation or combination of all three: all the elements of the digital route, from initial concept of a job to computer-to-plate, or computer-to-print, revolves around the host computer system, which links all the devices online, or imports from, and exports to, other systems.

The main component parts in the complete digital workflow are as follows:

Hardware

DTP main platform, Macs, PCs, workstations - covered in *Chapter 2, 'Changing role of prepress'*.

Digital cameras - covered in this chapter.

Scanners, flatbed and rotary-/drum-based - covered in this chapter.

Printers, monochrome and colour - covered in *Chapter 8, 'Proofing'*.

Imagesetters and platesetters - covered in *Chapter 9, 'Output systems and preparation of printing surfaces'*.

Digital presses - covered in *Chapter 10, 'Computer-to-print and beyond'*.

Software

Text and basic graphics - covered in *Chapter 3, 'Typography'*.

Graphics generation and manipulation - covered in this chapter.

Page make-up and associated areas such as imposition, trapping, etc - covered in *Chapter 6, 'Make-up, planning and assembly'*.

Periphery/external sources

Image and data libraries including electronic clip art, digital photographic and online image libraries plus Kodak Photo CD - covered in this chapter.

Internet, WWW - covered in *Chapter 10, 'Computer-to-print and beyond'*.

Originals

The process of graphic reproduction, whether through traditional or digital means, starts with an assessment of *originals*, a term which can include camera-ready artwork, drawings, paintings, photographs, transparencies, black-and-white or colour prints and even three-dimensional objects. Originals may be monochrome, for single-colour reproduction, or coloured for multi-coloured reproduction and fall into two main groups.

1   *Line originals* have no gradation of tone - that is, they possess no intermediate tones. The image is produced by clear distinct lines, dots, or other shapes of uniformly solid areas.

Examples of line originals include: paper paste-up from phototypesetters, typewritten or laser-printed line copy, dry transfer lettering; plus pen and ink effect drawings (in black ink on white paper or board): or their digital equivalent, produced electronically as described previously, using a word processing or similar-based program, also draw or paint software program on a host computer system.

2   *Continuous tone originals*, unlike line originals, consist of a variety of gradations between highlights (lightest areas), midtones (neutral/mid-way areas) and solids (darkest areas).

Examples of continuous tone originals include: photographic prints and transparencies: plus wash drawings, pencil, charcoal and crayon sketches - all of which are increasingly prepared and reproduced by electronic means.

Figure 5.1 below, shows an example of continuous tone and line originals.

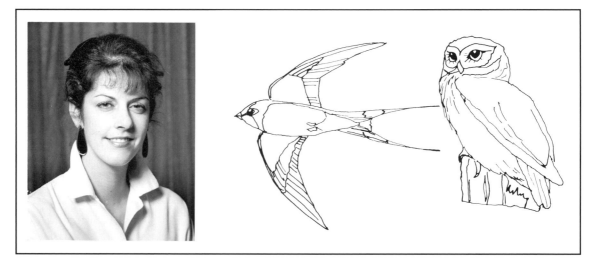

Figure 5.1: Example of a continuous tone and line originals

Monochrome line originals

When produced traditionally, it was generally accepted that flat artwork should be prepared in a size larger than that of the finished size, probably 1.5 to 2 times, as photographic reduction gave a sharper result and any minor irregularities tended to be lost. Excessive reduction was wherever possible avoided, since this caused loss of detail. For example, fine lines can fill in on thin type reversed out of a solid area.

Line originals will now commonly be reproduced using graphic software packages and/or word processing software, which allow relatively simple and straightforward graphic forms to be created: an alternative is the use of *clipart* or similar systems - *see page 80*. These software packages allow the operator to view originals on screen, at for example 200% and 400%, and thus ensure at least relatively fine definition and correct butting up of line edges, etc. These can then be checked and adjusted, so that when reproduced at the correct size, the desired results are achieved without visible imperfections.

Colour line originals

Line illustrations may be produced for printing in two, three, four or more colours, with a separate colour split for each colour - called a *colour separation.*

Different techniques are used to isolate, or separate, the original into the required number of colours.

Traditionally, using flat artwork, this would take the form of a coloured original, or a key drawing with the different colour areas indicated on an overlay or series of overlays.

In computer-generated illustrations, the illustrator/operator will simply highlight or mask off the coloured original by use of the cursor, or pressure pen and pad system, tracing around the required areas, and instructing the software program in use to split for colour as requested.

Continuous tone originals

Transparencies are still one of the most popular mediums for colour reproduction of continuous tone originals, although digital media such as Photo CD and digital picture libraries are increasing in popularity and use - *see pages 79* and *80*. Ideally, transparencies should be sharp and with a fine grain structure - that is, free from excessive grain - without colour bias or cast, and with good tonal and density range (from 1.8 to 2.8).

Photographic colour prints, paintings, wash drawings and the like, are termed *reflection copy*. If they are to be reproduced on a colour scanner, ideally they should be of an overall size small enough to fit comfortably on the desktop flatbed platen or drum scanner's analyse unit; and flexible enough to bend, when a drum scanner is used.

Cleanliness in handling continuous tone originals is even more important than in line originals because smudges and stains, like tones, will be reproduced.

Originals with uneven surfaces, such as drawings or paintings on heavy grained paper, board or canvas, require careful lighting and in such cases it is often worth getting a commercial photographer to produce a transparency or photograph, which will constitute a more suitable original for reproduction.

For traditional reproduction flat originals known as *flat copy* are placed on the copyboard of a camera, or fitted around the analyse drum of an electronic scanner.

Flat copy is viewed or illuminated by reflected light - that is, the light is shone on the surface and reflected back to the recording or imaging system.

Transparencies are recorded by transmitted light - that is, the light is shone or transmitted through the original.

It is no longer true, as once was the case, that a printed copy can only be as good as the original it is taken from. With new digital techniques and the application of new technology we can change, retouch in small dot or 'pixel' form, in fact recreate an original in any way required. However, this does not detract from the fact that there is no substitute for a good original, which should be fit for its purpose - that is, possess the properties for good reproduction and be a suitable and accurate representation of the chosen subject. Retouching of any kind will normally involve additional time and cost.

Traditional keyline artwork is where the base artwork is prepared on a flatboard, with black lines or keylines prepared where images or colour should appear: sometimes the black lines will actually print, but more often they are only used for position.

Traditional camera-ready copy is defined as copy that can be reproduced without further preparation, except possibly tint-laying and the inclusion of any illustrations when supplied separately.

Reproduction of line and continuous tone

The reproduction of monochrome line illustrations, being of a black-and-white nature, normally presents problems no different to those of reproducing type. The reproduction of continuous tone, however, is somewhat different.

In nature we are presented with an infinite variety of continuous tone images. Due to the limitations of the printing processes we cannot print a true continuous tone image. Printing can only cover parts of a substrate with a layer of ink, so reproducing areas of solid *(image areas)* and clear, non-inked areas *(non-image areas)*. Midtone areas *(grey/neutral areas)* are an illusion created by a printed halftone dot formation, or stochastic/FM screen pattern - *see pages 81 and 82.*

Halftone screen

In the major printing processes, continuous tone originals are traditionally reproduced by the use of the *halftone screen*, which breaks up the whole printing area into dots or shapes of varying sizes: the centres of the dots are spaced an equal distance apart but, as the dots vary in size, the amount of substrate, paper or board, etc, showing between them also varies. In the lighter tones, the dots are minute, allowing a large amount of the substrate to show through, producing a light tint effect, and conversely as the white spaces become smaller, the tone darkens.

Printed screened dots vary infinitely in size but, for practical reasons, it is not usually possible to retain the white space between dots when they go over about 97%, or to retain the dot itself, when it goes below 3%.

Figure 5.2 shows a very coarse screen halftone of a man drinking beer. The area in the top left- or right-hand corner is a fairly solid area, with a very small white dot surrounded by a large black area; the head of the beer gives the opposite effect, with parts of the cheeks illustrating a neutral grey area of 50% black/50% white.

Figure 5.2: Varying sizes of black dots produce the gradation of tone in a halftone picture; the smaller the dot, the more white is shown

However, examination of any traditional halftone print under a magnifying glass will reveal the screen pattern of dots - *see pages 58 to 60, for further details on screen rulings.* Dot patterns can also be seen by examining large posters on outside advertising hoardings from a few feet, or on a picture printed in a newspaper on coarse newsprint. Line and halftone are, therefore, distinguished not only by the form of the original, but by the presence or absence of the halftone dots in the printed result.

Reproducing the original

Graphic arts cameras

After inspecting the originals to ensure they are suitable for reproduction, the next stage in conventional graphic reproduction is to produce negative or positive films, which are normally the intermediate step to ultimately producing the printing plates or other means of print surface preparation. Graphic arts cameras are now practically redundant in most printers' workflows as they lock the printer into traditional film planning and reproduction.

Generally they are now only retained to handle the odd piece of flat artwork in conjunction with existing analogue film. When an original is exposed to light in front of a graphic arts camera, the light is absorbed in the black areas of the original, and reflected back by the white areas, through the lens onto the photosensitive material held in the camera. After development of the material, say film, a negative is obtained on which the white or clear areas of the original appear dense and the black areas transparent. The negative is, in fact, the opposite form of the original, and normally must be contacted and re-exposed to another light-sensitive film to produce a positive: there are processes, however, which give positives from positives without an intermediary negative, with such processes using rapid access autoreversal duplicating film.

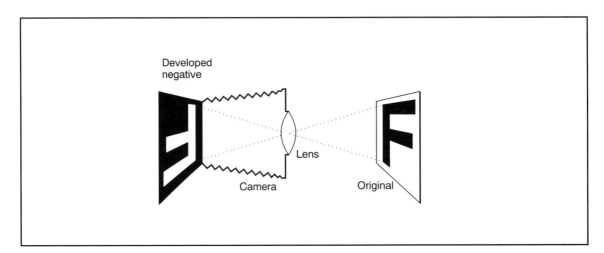

Figure 5.3: Production of a line negative using a traditional graphics arts camera

To avoid confusion, processed film for reproduction should always be described in terms of 'viewed from emulsion side-up' - for example, right-reading or wrong-reading emulsion side-up. Figure 5.3 illustrates the basic procedure of producing a line negative. Film produced on a graphic arts camera, scanner or imagesetter, for *offset litho,* needs be in the form of *wrong-reading, emulsion side-up film,* where printing from the plate is offset onto a rubber-covered blanket cylinder, before being transferred onto the substrate. For all the other major printing processes, which are forms of *direct printing,* the opposite is the case - ie - *right-reading, emulsion side-up film* is required. *Figures 5.4* and *5.5* illustrate the principle of 'offset' and 'direct' printing, using a film-based route - the tint example representing emulsion side-up film. The film type selected is a negative, although a positive could just as easily have been chosen to illustrate the process. Although the exception, there are occasions when the above convention for offset litho and gravure film is incorrect - eg - on clear plastic or other transparent/translucent materials where the printed images on the 'underside' of the printed material as viewed are reversed to normal, so appearing right-reading from the non-printed top side.

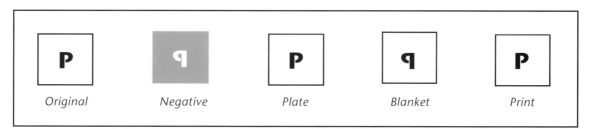

Figure 5.4: Reproduction reflecting 'offset' printing

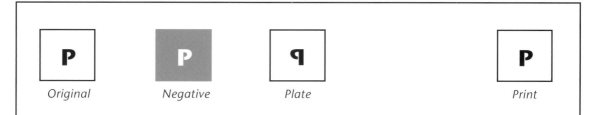

Figure 5.5: Reproduction reflecting 'direct' printing

Contact screens

Contact screens, used to create the illusion of continuous tone in film-based work with graphics arts cameras, has a pattern of grey or magenta dots separated by other dots of lesser density. In traditional film-based reproduction, the contact screen is held in close emulsion-side to emulsion-side contact with the light-sensitive material being exposed to create the halftone pattern required. Manufacturers produce a variety of contact screens suitable for different purposes - coarse, medium or fine screens, special effects, grey or magenta, etc, to suit different circumstances. Contact screens are less used today due to the decline in traditional working practices.

Dot patterns

Many different dot patterns can be produced by halftone screens. Traditionally, the midtone dot (50%) is square, so that each dot becomes joined to its neighbour at four points. This pattern is easy to assess for reproduction properties but it can lead to a jump in the tonal range in the midtones - a disadvantage which may be avoided by using a screen giving an elliptical dot; this variety of screen produces a chain of dots at 50%, forming in one diagonal before 50%, and in the other after 50%, so giving a more even transition. Round dot screens are also available - *see Figure 5.6.*

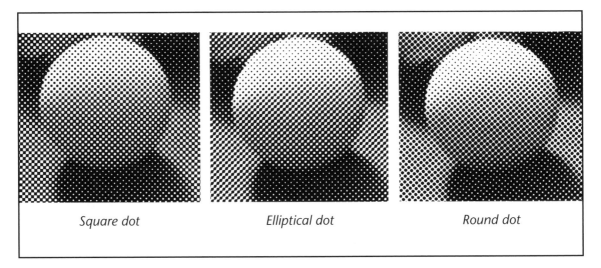

| Square dot | Elliptical dot | Round dot |

Figure 5.6: Examples of different halftone dot patterns

It is generally accepted that the round dot is best for high-speed presses and is used extensively for web-offset printing. The square dot results in sharper printing, and is used extensively in sheet-fed offset litho printing. The elliptical dot, since it allows more gradual transition and better detail on the midtones, is used extensively when printing flesh tones and very fine subtle colour blends or changes. For monochrome work, screen positions are such that the line of halftone dots falls at an angle of 45° across the processed image and the printed sheet. At this angle, the screen pattern is less apparent to the human eye than if it were vertical or horizontal. Other angles used for four-colour process are discussed on *page 70.*

Screen frequencies/rulings

Screen frequencies or rulings can be specified in lines per cm or lines per inch. Screens with 25, 34 and 40 rulings per cm are classed as *coarse (Figure 5.7)* and those with 48, 52 and 60 rulings as fine *(Figure 5.8)*: other very fine screens such as 80 and 118 per cm are available. With coarse screens, the size of the dot is larger and, while they are easier to print without, for example, filling in, more detail is lost than when fine screens are used.

Several factors have to be considered when choosing the screen ruling but, generally, a coarse screen is more suited to rougher, uncoated papers, whereas a fine screen is more suited to a smooth, coated surface. Ideally, originals should be reproduced to suit the method of reproduction.

In traditional reproduction, the screen reduces the original to a pattern of dots in the following manner: the light reflected by the original varies in intensity according to its tonal values, with the lighter tones reflecting more light than the darker tones; the rays of light of varying intensities pass through the screen and, where the light is strong, the area affected on the film is larger than where the light is weaker.

On development, the light-affected areas appear dense on the negative, varying in size according to the strength of light reflected by the various tones of the original. The transparent areas between the dense areas vary in size inversely, and it is these transparent areas which become the dots on a positive.

Figure 5.7: Examples of coarse screens measured in rulings per cm

Figure 5.8: Examples of fine screens measured in rulings per cm

lines per inch	lines per cm
300	118
200	80
150	60
133	52
100	40
86	34
65	26
50	20

Figure 5.9: Comparison of screen frequencies/rulings as number of lines per inch and per cm

It should be noted that due to the rounding up or down conversion between inches and centimetres, the actual figures shown below may differ slightly.

sheet-fed offset litho - eg - general commercial colour	40 -	60
sheet-fed offset litho - eg - very fine screen/fine art work	80 -	118
cold-set web-offset - eg - newspapers	34 -	52
heat-set web offset - eg - magazines	40 -	80
screen - ranges from	20 -	52
flexography/letterpress - ranges from	26 -	52
gravure (equivalent of screen rulings) - ranges from	34 -	60

Figure 5.10: Average screen frequencies/rulings per cm used by the different printing processes

Monochrome scanners

Most monochrome scanners, like their modern camera counterpart, have an on-line densitometer facility and are widely used in newspapers, monochrome magazine and book printers, where high-volume capacity and quick turn-round is essential.

In the monochrome scanning operation, the original is normally placed on a glass copy holder to be scanned and digitised into the system. The potential image can often be displayed on a monitor for interactive control of highlight, midtone and shadow dot; also displayed is the gradation/density curve which can be adjusted to different printing requirements. The operator has access to an array of control buttons, where a considerable amount of correction and adjustment can be carried out relatively easily and quickly.

When the operator is satisfied that the desired quality has been achieved, the scanned images are linked up to a Mac, PC or workstation, for image manipulation; alternatively they are output on bromide paper or film for conventional make-up and reproduction.

Photographic film and other light-sensitive materials

Most traditional photographic material is based on chemical compounds of silver-producing light-sensitive materials in two main types - paper-based, known as *bromide,* and film-based, as *negative* or *positive.* When film is processed, it becomes transparent in the unexposed areas, whereas paper remains opaque, or translucent, at least.

Almost all traditional photography depends on silver-based emulsion, which requires the unexposed areas to be developed away, leaving the exposed silver salt areas to turn to opaque silver, with the process of development halted by stabilisation or fixing, depending on the emulsion type. Films are made up of light-sensitive emulsion, consisting of silver halide salts and gelatin coated on a stable base. Silver-based film emulsions are colour-sensitive, reacting normally to the ultra-violet, blue-violet and blue regions of the spectrum. In order to extend this colour sensitivity, colour dyes are added. The two most common films of this type are orthochromatic and panchromatic.

Orthochromatic film has an extended colour spectrum, going from blue-violet, blue, green, yellow through to orange, but not including red. As it is insensitive to red, it can be operated under 'red' safelights in the darkroom. Orthochromatic film is used extensively for black-and-white reproduction, and with electronic colour scanners.

Panchromatic film is sensitive to the whole visible spectrum, from blue-violet through to red. It, therefore, can only be operated in total darkness until the exposed material is fixed, when a dark-green safelight can be used.

The newer generation of colour scanners and laser imagesetters use red sensitive film, which require a cyan safelight. Unlike the film used in conventional cameras, which reproduce the whole tonal range, *lith* and *rapid access* films deliberately offer a steep transition between clear film and solid image.

Lith film is a high contrast, high quality film, usually with orthochromatic dyed emulsion. It is one of the oldest of the current film technologies and its use is declining due to the complex bath processing required in the process, especially in controlling the correct strength of the developer.

Rapid access film has become much more popular than lith, due to the fact that keeping the chemicals in balance is less critical in rapid access than in lith processing. It is also a single chemistry system but does not produce as high quality results as lith.

New film technology has seen the introduction of *third-generation film and daylight-operated film*. Third-generation film is an attempt to combine the processing speed of rapid access with the quality of lith, if not improve on it. Daylight films are normally insensitive to all areas of the colour spectrum other than blue. It can, therefore, be safely handled with red, orange or yellow safelights which offer nearly as good operating conditions as normal daylight.

Fourth-generation film has been developed to improve on its predecessors, to the extent that higher and more consistent results are obtained through a more stable developing process, along with sharper and higher intensity dots and a reduced consumption of chemicals. It is available as a conventional camera-based option or for imagesetters and scanners depending on the exposure source used - eg - HeNe, IR laser, etc.

Many proprietary systems use a lith-based silver-emulsion process first developed by Agfa-Gevaert known as Diffusion Transfer *(DT)*, Chemical Transfer *(CT)*, or often Photo-Mechanical Transfer *(PMT)*. All are essentially the same process, involving the exposure of an intermediate photosensitive surface in the normal way (with a screen if required), followed by its processing in contact with the final image carrier, or receiver. During development, the image transfers from one sheet to the other, with the first being discarded. The final image may be on paper, film or metal, and in negative or positive form. The process can also be used for the production of litho plates with a paper, plastic or metal base - these are mainly used in the area of small offset.

Film processors

The light-sensitive material is processed to develop and fix the image, with most material now processed in automatic or semi-automatic processors. These vary from the simple desktop machines, used mainly in silver diffusion processes, to the highly sophisticated machines, used in bulk lith, or increasingly third or fourth generation film processing. In the latter cases, the chemical balance in the machine is automatically restored, by monitoring the amount of material, say film, being processed, and a constant temperature is maintained. Film is usually transported through the processor by rollers, which take it from bath to bath to develop, fix and wash it before final drying. Processors may be programmed to provide the correct processing times for particular films and types of image, and may be connected on-line to the equipment producing the exposed light-sensitive material, or provided with daylight loading facilities.

Development of dry film processing

Several dry film systems have been and are being developed using selenium, carbon, or laser dye removal/laser ablation instead of silver, although other developments include silver processing by heat rather than chemical processing - *see IR plate processing* in *Chapter 9, 'Output systems and preparation of printing surfaces'*.

The Heidelberg Prepress Drysetter imagesetter uses Polaroid's Dry Tech film based on dry-carbon laser-sensitive imaging technology: due to the evolving technology of dry film processing, along with the highly controlled working conditions required, partnerships or alliances between film suppliers and output device manufactures of imagesetters, for example, are becoming common.

The Polaroid film works through very high thermal imaging of the material, which causes the transfer of carbon particles on the base material to transfer to a redundant carrier sheet, so creating a negative dry processed film.

There is a considerable environmental improvement associated with dry film processing as it does away with the water and silver-halide processing: conventionally based film processes can, however, hold a wider range of output resolutions, whereas with dry film it is limited to narrow, but high resolutions such as 2540 and 3386dpi.

Many printing companies have chosen to delay going into dry film processing and to wait until direct-to-plate technology has become more established, so missing out the film-based intermediate altogether - *see Chapter 9, 'Output systems and preparation of printing surfaces'*.

Principles of colour

Colour is a very complex issue and there are many factors which need to be considered in order to understand how we perceive and reproduce it.

Colour as a wavelength

We can see the visible wavelengths between 380 and 760nm (one nanometre equals one millionth of a millimetre). If one particular wavelength dominates or, more specifically, the spectral power distribution is unequal, we see a particular colour - if there is a balanced distribution of all wavelengths we see white or grey - ie - neutral. Light with a wavelength of 380nm appears as violet, 760nm as red and 570nm as green.

Colour, as we know it, can be in the form of a 'physical' solid, such as printing ink or coloured toner; or in the form of an energy light source, such as with a TV or computer colour monitor.

The human perception of colour

The sensation of colour is the effect of light upon the eye interpreted by the brain. White light is composed of a mixture of all colours of the rainbow or spectrum, and most objects are visible by the light reflected or transmitted from them, depending upon whether the object is opaque or transparent - *see Figure 5.11.*

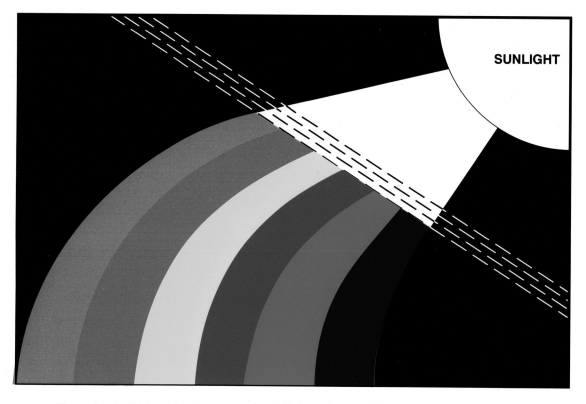

Figure 5.11: White light is composed of all the colours of the rainbow/visible spectrum

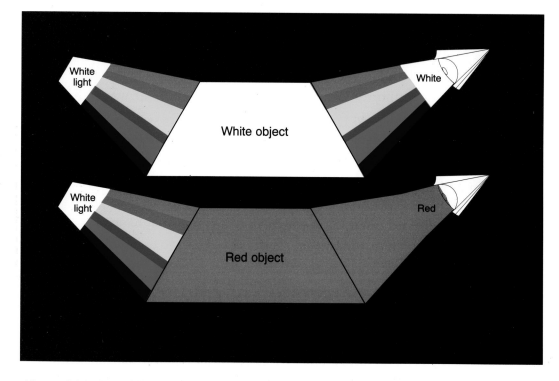

Figure 5.12: How different coloured objects filter out and reflect different colours - thus a red object reflects only red

Objects appear coloured because they reflect or transmit some parts of the spectrum and absorb the others. For example, a red object appears red as it reflects the red light and absorbs most of the violet, blue, green and yellow lights. White objects reflect or transmit almost all parts of the spectrum, while tones of grey absorb equal proportions of all its constituents and black absorbs almost the whole of it - *see Figure 5.12.*

The properties of colour

Colours have three main properties - hue, saturation and brightness:

• **Hue** is the name given to a specific colour, to differentiate it from any other. The hues blue, green and red; yellow, magenta and cyan form the familiar colour wheel - *see Figure 5. 14.*

• **Saturation**, similar to **chroma**, indicates the purity of a colour. It refers to the strength of a colour, - ie - how far it is from neutral grey.

• **Brightness**, similar to **lightness, luminance** or **value**, describes how light or dark a colour is, indicating whether a colour is closer to white or to black: brightness does not affect the hue or saturation of a colour. Grey is a neutral 'colour' between white and black - to lighten a colour the brightness or lightness element is changed.

• **Neutral colours** do not possess the properties of hue or saturation but are described according to their lightness - white, black and grey are neutral 'colours'.

A simplified illustration of how *hue, saturation* and *lightness* operates is shown opposite:

four different hues or colours - yellow, red, green and blue

four different saturations of one colour - cyan as 100%, 50%, 25% and 0%

four different levels of lightness - black, 50% grey, 25% grey and pure white

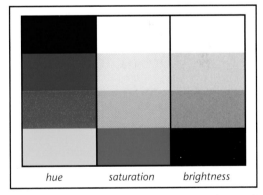

Figure 5.13: Variations of hue, saturation and lightness

• **Neutral subtractive 'colour' -** when yellow, magenta and cyan printing inks or toners are present in equal amounts, the coloured result appears *grey* or *black.*

• **Neutral additive 'colour'** - when blue, green and red lights are present in equal amounts, the coloured result appears *grey* or *white.*

• **Opposite colour pairs -** colours which appear opposite each other when combined together, form a 'neutral' colour - eg - red + cyan, green + magenta, yellow + blue (blue/violet).

Reproduced below is a *colour wheel*, showing the additive primary colours of blue, green and red as well as the subtractive primary colours of yellow, magenta and cyan - note blue, green and red; yellow, magenta and cyan appear *opposite* each other on the colour wheel.

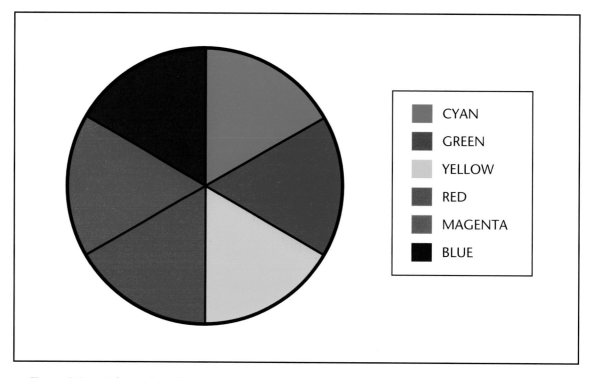

*Figure 5.14: Colour wheel illustrating **b**lue, **g**reen, **r**ed, plus **y**ellow, **m**agenta, **c**yan and their relationship/position to each other on the wheel*

Colour models

Due to the perception of colour being reliant on properties which can vary over time and circumstances, colour and the interpretation of colour by the observer can be highly subjective - *see Chapter 8, 'Proofing'*. Colour models have therefore been developed to define colour in an objective and standardised manner.

The *RGB model* as the letters imply is a colour model based on the additive colours of red, green and blue; it is typically the model used for colour interpretation/manipulation on monitors and scanners, etc, right up to the major output stage of printing, when the *CMYK colour model* based on the subtractive colours of cyan, magenta, yellow and black is used.

Colour management systems

These are systems which have been developed to respond to the need to provide true colour portability and device independence across an increasing array of colour output systems and host colour input sources. Examples of colour management systems are Apple 'ColorSync', Agfa 'FotoFlow', Kodak 'YCC' (used on the Kodak Photo CD systems) and Kodak 'Colour Management System'. There are now over 100 companies offering software and hardware that supports the current ColorSync standard. In colour reproduction it is essential to control and predict the results from the initial stage of scanning the originals, through the colour monitor used to manipulate and view the work, followed by the intermediate reproduction stages of film, proofs and finally the printed result. Colour management systems set out to perform this function, with the result that we achieve a constant and consistent view of colours - regardless of which device it's viewed on - so that front-end systems are calibrated to match proofs and press outputs. This subject is dealt with in more detail in *Chapter 8, 'Proofing'*.

Colour reproduction

Originals in full colour, such as transparencies and colour photographs, are mainly reproduced by four-colour process, using yellow, magenta, cyan and black printing inks. A separate screened negative/positive, printing plate, cylinder or stencil is required for each colour, so that the printing combination of colours reproduce the full effect of the original. For the most faithful reproduction possible, *special colours* may be necessary, particularly in packaging and labels, where they may be used for overall solids or house colours. These are often specified as a PANTONE Matching System *(PMS)* reference - *see the companion publication - Introduction to printing and print finishing, Chapter 3, 'Printing inks, toners, varnishes and coatings'*.

There are two types of colour reproduction - *additive* and *subtractive synthesis*.

Additive synthesis

As previously mentioned it is possible to divide the spectrum of white light into three broad bands - blue/violet, green/yellow and orange/red - which appear essentially *blue, green* and *red* to the eye: these are in effect the *additive primary colours*. If these colours, in the form of beams of coloured light, are in similar proportions upon a white screen then white light is created. With the overlapping primary colours of blue, green and red, the secondary colours of yellow, magenta and cyan are produced - *see Figure 5.15.*

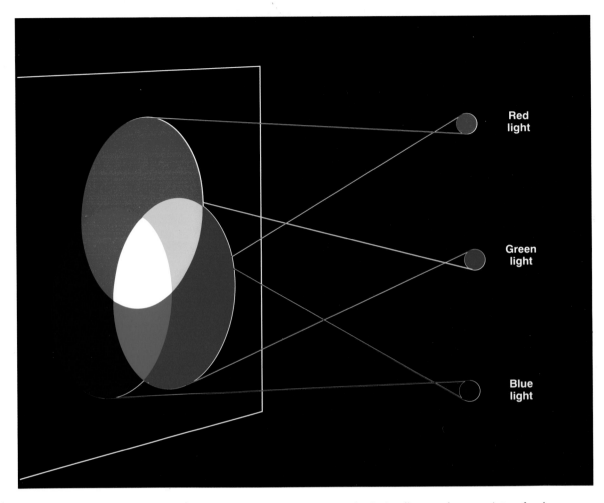

Figure 5.15: The three broad bands of the spectrum can be 'mixed' to make a variety of colours

Subtractive synthesis

In applying colour pigments to the substrate to be printed, the effect generated by additive synthesis cannot be obtained because, starting with the white light reflected by the substrate, the addition of colour inks to it *subtracts* portions of the spectrum in the white reflection so that yellow, magenta and cyan which form the *subtractive primary colours* are used.

The majority of commercial work is printed in four, rather than three colours, adding black to the process set. This is included to compensate for deficiencies in the yellow, magenta and cyan pigments, and to allow type to print in only one dense, high contrast colour. Although the way in which the black separation is made can radically affect the final result - *see page 76,* the theory of subtractive reproduction relates to the three primary colours of yellow, magenta and cyan.

Figure 5.16: The three process colour inks, each of which subtracts one-third of the spectrum

In ideal subtractive colour behaviour, each of the primary colours would subtract one third of the spectrum.

The yellow ink would absorb the blue portion and reflect a mixture of red and green light appearing yellow to the eye, which cannot analyse it into its component parts; the magenta ink would absorb the green portion and reflect blue and red; with the cyan ink absorbing the red portion and reflecting blue and green.

Process colour separations

To produce a set of four colour separations the original is scanned/input on an electronic colour scanner using RGB *(red, green, blue)* light sources and output for printing purposes as CMYK *(cyan, magenta, yellow, black)* separations.

Figure 5.17 below, illustrates the use of BGR colour lights/separation filters to produce YMC separations or printing plates; K *(black)* is reproduced from a yellow/orange combination-type filter.

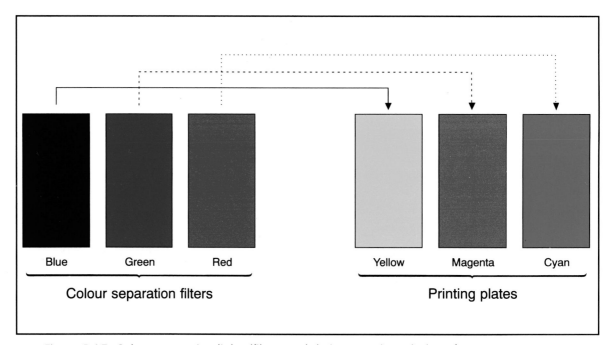

Figure 5.17: Colour separation lights/filters and their respective printing plates

The principle of colour separation is probably best considered from the traditional method, where the blue filter is dense in the areas of the image representing the parts of the original reflecting or transmitting blue, less dense where there is less blue light and transparent where there is none; the printing plate therefore produced from the blue filter is the yellow plate. On the same basis the green filter produces the magenta plate and the red filter the cyan plate.

The angle of the conventional halftone screen used in four-colour separations, must be different for each colour, to prevent the dots of successive colours becoming superimposed upon preceding ones, so forming an undesirable screen clash pattern or moiré effect when printed. Screen angles frequently used for sheet-fed offset litho are: black 45°, magenta 75°, yellow 90° and cyan 105°. In web-offset printing angles are often changed to black 15°, magenta 45°, cyan 75° and yellow 90°, although other permutations of screen angles are used. The objective is to achieve a 30° angle of separation between the colours where possible.

Electronic colour scanners

Electronic colour scanners, and the related electronic engraving machines for producing gravure cylinders and flexographic plates, dispense with the graphic arts camera and many of its related processes. Modern scanners have an interface connecting it to the host computer where scanning operations are controlled by software linking the scanner and host computer: this can take the form of, for example, an Adobe Photoshop plug-in or the scanner supplier's proprietary software.

Colour scanners have developed into a wide range of different options based on the following : high-end drum scanners and vertical or desktop drum scanners, plus entry-level, mid-range to high quality CCD flatbed scanners.

Drum- or rotary-based colour scanners

The large high-end drum scanner is still the yardstick against which all colour scanners are measured in terms of the ultimate in quality and productivity, possessing the highest resolution and dynamic range, as well as being less susceptible to reproducing dust or scratch marks on the original. It must be acknowledged, however, that the gap with other scanning systems is narrowing all the time.

From the original to be reproduced, the modern high-end drum colour scanner can generate a halftone *screened,* or *continuous tone (contone)* colour-separated digital file, which can be introduced into a DTP or workstation environment, or the analogue equivalent *(film)*, output in negative or positive form, right- or wrong-reading, depending on the requirements. The special needs of each of the printing processes will also have to be taken into account with the colour sets produced.

An electronic drum colour scanner consists essentially of two main components linked together - an *analyse unit* and an *output unit.*

Originals are sorted into separate groups of transparencies or flexible reflection copy for scanning. The first stage of preparation after sorting is determining the various values of the originals - density range, necessary colour correction, masking and undercolour removal - *see page 76.* This may be done off-line on a scan data programmer where the operator uses a separate peripheral to store settings for future jobs on a floppy disk, or it may be done on-line by using the calibrating system on the machine. This information, together with the scaling instructions, is entered by keying in or calibrating dials on the machine.

The originals - transmission or reflection copy (which must be exposed separately) - are mounted to the analyse drum, and the unexposed film, on which the separations are to be produced, is mounted onto the exposure or output drum.

During the operation of the scanner, the two drums revolve in unison, though on some systems they may be in separate units or even at separate locations.

Figure 5.18: Example of a high-end drum scanner - ie - Heidelberg Prepress ChromaGraph S 3400 and tower drum scanner - ie - Heidelberg Prepress Tango

At the analyse unit, the original is scanned by a recording head moving along the rotating drum. This takes the form of light illuminating the original to be scanned via a small spot imaged through the lens onto a pinhole. The light passes through the pinhole and is collected by three photomultiplier tubes *(PMT)* and colour separation optics to generate blue, green and red outputs. The data is then passed to the expose unit which records the image at the size and resolution frequency required onto the film mounted on the output unit so producing four-colour process separations. After scanning and exposing is complete, the exposed film is processed as required. Although earlier scanners used contact screens to produce halftones, modern scanners are programmed to convert the signals received from the analyse unit into appropriate dot formations for the production of screened negatives or positives.

Most high-end drum scanners in today's mainly digital and streamlined workflows will not operate as a stand-alone scanner producing separated film for manual planning. The high-end scanner will interface with a host computer workstation, creating initially digital scans which are transferred into a software application producing composite images/files as required to be output as planned film using the scanner as an output device, or alternatively, an imagesetter. A further option would be for the composite digital file(s) to be used on an entirely digital workflow.

Mid-range desktop drum scanners, along with the tower/vertical drum scanners, are basically a scaled down/smaller footprint version of the larger traditional drum version, while not having the full productivity of the high-end scanner, along with losing the ability to scan large format originals, they nevertheless offer a high standard of scanning using basically the same scanning principles as the traditional drum scanner. One of the major advantages they share with the high-end flatbed scanners is the built-in ease of operation, intuitive software and simple interfaces to host computers.

Flatbed scanners

Flatbed scanners have been developed to meet the growing DTP-led market requirements represented by originals being scanned in a form suitable for retouching, manipulation and make-up on an AppleMac, PC or workstation system and available in greyscale (black-and-white) and colour versions.

The simplest direct-entry form of desktop scanner is the *hand held type*, such as the 'Logitech Scanman', where the scanning head is guided over the original to be reproduced: use of such devices is normally confined to home users. A further example of a relatively simple scanning device is the *sheetfed type*, such as the Visioneer 'Paperport', where the hard copy document is fed through a system of rollers while the sensor and light sources remain fixed. Both the hand held and sheetfed scanners are commonly included with OCR software - *see page 40.*

The component parts of a CCD flatbed scanner are platen, scanning mechanism, light source, lens and CCD:

The *platen* supports and retains the originals in position as well as establishing the overall area that can be scanned: this will often vary from entry-level at around A4, to mid-range and high quality flatbed scanners in excess of A3.

The *scanning mechanism* controls the movement of the scanning operation where the platen remains stationary during the scanning process with the light source and associated components moving along the platen, or alternatively with some entry-level models, the platen moves the original past the stationary 'camera' unit of CCD and lens.

Drive mechanisms are either based on a belt design which, is most commonly used on entry-level scanners, or on higher quality flatbed scanners, leadscrews are often used with a precision servo drive, so achieving a much smoother and quieter scanning motion.

The *light source, or sources*, used in flatbed scanners are mainly fluorescent tubes illuminating the originals from above or below the platen depending on whether transparent or reflective copy is being scanned. The light source can be applied in a *single pass* of the original as white only, or on a *three pass* basis as blue, green and red lights. The quality of the light source has a significant bearing on the quality of scan that can be produced - eg - a double bank of tubes and a stabilised power supply will provide a more even distribution of light and more consistent results.

Light from the source, or sources, is reflected from the original, via a series of mirrors and lenses, onto a CCD sensor held in the scanning head. The light is then converted to analogue electrical charges varying in proportion to the intensity and wavelengths of the light received by the CCD, which in turn are converted into digital signals (analogue to digital conversion) to produce a digital file which can be accessed and reproduced on a computer system. Most modern flatbed scanners use a linear CCD array, made up of a row of thousands of charge-coupled photosensitive elements, contained on a silicon chip.

The combination of the *lens* and *CCD* determine the maximum optical resolution which defines the smallest detail the scanner can reproduce.

This can be seen from the following examples:

- where a flatbed scanner has a maximum scanning width of 300mm, single lens mechanism with 8000 element CCD array. Assuming the lens is focused across the whole of the 300mm then the maximum resolution would be 8000 ÷ 300 = 677dpi;

- if, however a second lens was brought into play which focused a 60mm strip onto the CCD array then the maximum resolution would be 8000 ÷ 60 = 3378dpi.

Flatbed scanners are available with either fixed focus single lens or variable multiple lens systems. The fixed focus single lens scanners are suited to work requiring enlargements up to around 400%, as well as scanning reflection copy and pre-printed material; whereas the variable multiple lens systems allow a much higher magnification/scaling range from, for example, 20% to 3000%.

The facilities available on high quality flatbed scanners include performing image analysis, selecting the appropriate settings to suit each original as well as guiding the operator through each process or step, with the option on some machines of a split screen on the monitor allowing 'before' and 'after' adjustments to be compared. A further facility is the opportunity to retain the customised tables created on a job for future use. Prompts and guidance for the operator is generally highlighted by descriptive icons.

One of the major drawbacks associated with flatbed scanners has been the limitation that high resolution could not be achieved over the whole area of the platen surface, only the central band, so severely restricting the number of originals which could be scanned in a batch. The development of what is termed *XY scanning* has overcome this problem where the CCD array is able to move up and across the platen in both dimensions of the originals - ie - length and width (X and Y axes) so that every original can be scanned at the maximum resolution possible, regardless of its size or position on the platen with, finally, the process of stitching the scanned strips together into a single file or image if and when required.

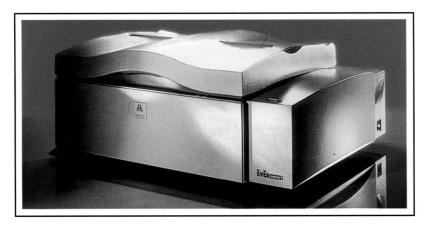

Figure 5.19: Example of a high-end flatbed scanner - ie - Scitex Eversmart

For many years large drum- or rotary-based colour scanners have been recognised as capable of far higher quality and productivity than flatbed types: this is now being seriously challenged by the new breed of desktop-type small drum and flatbed scanners, which are generally much less expensive than their larger counterpart, with an increasingly high level of quality and suitability to the modern desktop-based systems. Flatbed scanners also have the advantage of being able to reproduce relatively thick, rigid and in some cases three-dimensional originals, which is not possible with drum-based scanners.

Colour reproduction properties of process printing inks

Although process printing inks have been improved in terms of printing qualities, they are still imperfect in terms of their reproduction properties, and therefore process colour sets need *colour correction* to compensate for these 'impurities'. It is the accepted modern practice for the colour separation and colour correction to be done on an electronic scanner, where previously it would be done on a colour camera using a photographic masking technique.

Yellow process ink is a comparatively pure colour, but performs as if it were contaminated with a little magenta ink: colour correction reduces this to compensate. Magenta process ink performs as if it were contaminated with yellow and cyan ink and this must also be allowed for in colour correction. Cyan process ink performs as if contaminated with magenta and some yellow ink so again this must be corrected on the separations.

Colour printing

The printing sequence of four-colour process inks often differs depending on whether the printing is on single-, two-, four- or more multi-colour presses, and therefore whether it is wet-on-dry, or wet-on-wet printing.

The most common sequence of printing four-colour process colours *wet-on-dry* on single colour machines is cyan, yellow, magenta, black, whereas the most common sequence of printing *wet-on-wet* on multi-colour presses, four units and above, is black, cyan, magenta, yellow. Different sequences to those suggested can, of course, be used, but it is important to establish a set sequence for particular applications, and not to deviate from this other than for exceptional circumstances. Inks in general use for offset litho four-colour process printing are formulated to a British and European common standard, BS 4666:1971 (1981), also ISO 2846 which is a related but not equivalent standard. As colour separations and printing plates are processed to conform to these standards, the results of using the relevant standard inks should be uniform wherever printed, provided, of course, that the material being printed is the same. Standardisation in colour printing is covered in *Chapter 8, 'Proofing'*.

UCR *(undercolour removal)* and other means of colour adjustment

The fact that much colour printing is now done on presses printing four or more colours means that each colour is applied while the previous colour is still wet, unlike the procedure on single-colour machines, or on the second run of two-colour machines, where colours must be allowed to dry between printing runs. There is a limit to the ink film thickness that can be applied by *wet-on-wet printing*, without set-off.

Single-colour presses can cope with solid areas overlapping in all four printings, giving a combined print area of 400%, but this is simply not possible with wet-on-wet printing, the maximum range being between 240% and 300%.

To reduce the total ink weight, the computer in a colour scanner can automatically lower the amount of colour to be printed in each of the three primaries - yellow, magenta and cyan - while strengthening the black printer, a technique called *undercolour removal.* Though the same intensity of colour is not possible when printing wet-on-wet, it is to a certain extent compensated for by the high pigment content of modern printing inks.

Extended UCR (commonly referred to as *achromatic reproduction*) is offered under various different names by major scanner manufacturers such as Screen's Integrated Colour Removal *(ICR).*

Conventional process colour sets rely on the three subtractive primaries to supply almost all the detail in a subject in the shadows as much as in the highlights. The conventional black separation is *skeletal,* and contributes no more than the finishing touches.

With UCR, more work is transferred to the black printer: instead of using it only when the three primaries prove inadequate, the computer strengthens the black printer in heavily inked areas containing all three primary colours, at the same time making an appropriate reduction in the yellow, magenta and cyan.

Extended UCR/achromatic reproduction, or Grey Component Replacement *(GCR)* as it is also referred to, takes this a stage further and, in the extreme, involves the total replacement of yellow, magenta and cyan in the grey component of any tone by black.

Individual colours are, therefore, reproduced by two primaries plus black - for example, if an area was to reproduce conventionally as 20% yellow, 30% magenta, 60% cyan, then with extended UCR this would be altered to 20% black, 0% yellow, 10% magenta, 40% cyan.

As colour inks are more expensive than black, extended UCR can produce savings, with other advantages including a more consistent balance in neutral areas such as flesh-tones and generally greater ease in maintaining colour balance during the print run.

A criticism often levelled at extended UCR is that only a limited maximum density is achieved by the removal of the combined three-colour primary grey. In very dark areas, two primaries plus black sometimes do not produce the depth of density required. This may be rectified by using a very high intensity black ink or Undercolour Addition *(UCA)*, which works on the principle of allowing measured amounts of the complementary colour in the neutral areas only.

It is imperative with any type of colour adjustment that the scanned sets are produced to a set of standards approved and agreed by the printer. Achromatic sets require different treatment from conventional colour sets - for example, more black is carried and a printer must take this into account.

Creating and processing digital images

Graphics generation and manipulation software programs

There are basically two different software program types used to generate and create digital graphics - object-oriented and bitmap - *see vector and bitmap text creation* in *Chapter 4, 'Handling text'*.

Object-orientated/vector form programs

These are often referred to as 'draw' programs where each graphic is prepared as a complete form or outline, applying mainly geometrical shapes to create the image or images required with the use of straight lines, rectangles, Bezier curves, circles, angles, etc. The result is often a geometric-shaped graphic which lacks real creativity, but in the hands of an experienced and skilled designer the results can be excellent and highly creative. A major benefit of an object-oriented graphic is that it will use considerably less data space than its bitmapped counterpart.

The most sophisticated and popular object-oriented illustrative programs, including Adobe 'Illustrator' and Macromedia 'Freehand', have features such as a wide range of smooth curved shapes through the use of anchor points and direction lines; auto trace facility, which allows scanned bitmap images to be created or imported and traced, creating simpler and more easily processed graphics; gradients palette, which creates smooth graduated blends between two or more colours or tints; built-in colour separation; comprehensive tools palette, as well as edge roughen and blend features.

Bitmap form programs

These are often referred to as 'paint' programs, manipulating images which have been scanned into bitmap or pixel form. The mouse or pressure sensitive tablet is used to paint or fill-in pixel areas as directed by the artist or designer.

'Photoshop', 'Painter', 'Live Picture', 'Dabbler', 'Sketcher' and 'XRes' are amongst the most popular paint software programs.

Several drawing tools are available on the professional bitmap programs, including: pencil, chalk, charcoal, ink, crayon, airbrush, watercolour and oils simulated effects; flood fill for filling in selected area with a chosen effect; range of different brush strokes; frisket and mask facilities to restrict painting to selected areas; 3-D and textured effects; cloning tool which creates a copy of a bitmapped image as if it had been painted; wide-ranging colour palettes, plus some paint programs offering animation and multi-media presentation facilities.

Image editing and manipulation software programs

This group of software programs have been developed to retouch, enhance, amend and manipulate graphic images. The main programs that fall into this category are 'Photoshop', 'Live Picture', 'Artisan 6' (part of Corel Draw) and 'Color It!'

The range of features normally available, in at least some of the programs outlined above, include: converting RGB to CMYK; support for a wide range of file formats; painting tools; image transformation, including rotating, stretching, skewing and distort options; filters for image sharpening, softening, special effects; creation of duotones, tritones and quadtones; on-screen CMYK editing; monitoring and collaging of images; 3-D and 4-D (animation, video) links. Paint and image edit software are now virtually interchangeable.

Digital cameras

Digital cameras are a means of creating colour halftone originals in first generation electronic image form; they are akin to a high quality conventional film-based camera, only instead of having a film holding unit they have a CCD-based storage facility recording digital images. The quality and cost of digital cameras vary dramatically. At the lower end, costing a few hundred pounds, are camera systems suitable only for reproducing small images at relatively low- to medium-resolution, typically around 640 x 480 pixels, used for house or car sale ads in newspaper or similar publications. The higher resolution, more professional digital cameras, reproduce up to 6000 x 7500 pixels and above, and cost in the range of £8000 to £40 000.

Some cameras are of a hybrid or dual role, in the sense that they can be adapted from a traditional film-loaded camera to a digital camera by the fitting of a digital back unit. A further variation is the creation of still images from video cameras, or recorders, which can be introduced into a host computer system by using some form of freeze frame digital recording service.

Kodak Photo CD

Photo CD is a technology developed by Kodak aimed at bridging the worlds of silver halide and silicon imaging. Photo CD images are created through the scanning of photographic film, either positive or negative, to create a photographic-quality digital image. The image file size is compressed from its original file size - 18Mb to 72Mb, depending on film size - eg - 35mm transparency or 5"x4" photograph, down to between 5Mb to 18Mb through a virtually lossless compression routine.

The resultant image file is converted to the *Image Pac format* where it is reproduced in five or six resolutions, with examples shown below, as follows:

type	general usage	image size			data file in RGB	CMYK
base/16	(thumbnail resolution)	128	x	192 pixels	72kb	96kb
base/4	(low-res/positional resolution)	256	x	384 pixels	256kb	340kb
base	(TV resolution)	512	x	768 pixels	1.1Mb	1.5Mb
base x 4	(high definition TV resolution)	1024	x	1536 pixels	4.5Mb	6.0Mb
base x 16	(photographic/repro)	2048	x	3072 pixels	18Mb	24Mb
base x 64	(photographic/high-end repro)	4096	x	6144 pixels	72Mb	96Mb

The picture information is stored in *Photo YCC*, a Kodak-devised encoding system which optimises Photo CD images for display on TVs, monitors and for printing applications. The image file is written by a dedicated writer to a CD *(compact disk)*: more images can be added until the CD is full, but it is important to note the CDs cannot be overwritten and revised. Thumbnail sketches of all the images on the disk are printed out as an index/point of reference. Up to 670Mb of data can be stored on one CD. Kodak has created a series of Photo CD formats to suit different purposes: including Photo CD Master, Pro Photo CD Master, Photo CD Portfolio and Photo CD Catalog: in addition, associated software is available to assist in manipulating and enhancing the Photo CD images, such as Access, PhotoEdge, Shoebox and Renaissance.

Image and data libraries

An increasingly popular means of obtaining images, covering a wide range of topics and subjects, is the use of clip art and photographic/online image libraries. The benefit of such a system is that the user is using 'stock' images, so avoiding the high cost and time it takes to commission and/or create the images required from scratch.

Clip art

Clip art is available in many digital forms - ie - on disk, Photo CD, or accessed via the Internet, often as 'shareware' in a number of file formats to suit the use and type of images available such as bitmap, object oriented, low- and high-resolution, PostScript and non-PostScript in EPS, PICT2 and MacPaint file formats: it is also available in hard copy book or folder form, for use in conventional paper-based systems. The user of clip art needs to note and abide by the restrictions and regulations applied by the owners or vendors of the clipart system. Many clip art packages come with paint- and draw-based software programs such as 'CorelDraw' covering a wide range of monochrome and colour, line and tone images, which are listed by category and use.

Photographic and online image libraries

Stock photographic libraries have existed for some considerable time where the potential user chooses an image from a printed catalogue and in return the selected transparency or photography is supplied - the photographic original then being scanned to generate a digital file for subsequent processing. The simpler, more direct digital route is the selection of photographic images chosen from a *photo CD library system.*

Most photo libraries on CD are royalty-free and contain 20 to over 100 images per CD: some photo CD libraries cover specific subjects and areas, where others are more general and multipurpose. Some examples come with added features such as clipping paths, which allow the easy highlighting and selection of different parts of the overall image. The quality of images on the photo CDs is, on the whole, excellent as most will have been scanned on high-end scanners, with retouching and colour balancing, if required. Examples of photo CD libraries are 'PhotoDisc', 'Digital Stock' and 'ArtBeats'.

Online image libraries are now being offered on the Web where registered users can download low-res images (in RGB TIFF format) at no cost, to be used as positionals/image visuals and high-res pictures ordered subsequently on CD. Some large photographic/media studios, prepress companies and printers have built up a large photo and/or media library for specific customers, or as a general facility which companies can access if they use their services. As with clip art, users need to note and work within the licence agreements of the host companies.

Trapping, spreads and chokes

Even with perfectly prepared colour separated artwork, digital or conventional, slight misregister between colours will often take place if only a dead fit is allowed between the colours. This is due to stretch or shrinkage occurring to the paper or board during the printing process, also slight misregistration between the different printing units.

The result is the appearance of a white line or gap between colours, which are planned to butt up to each other.

The process of *trapping* helps to overcome this problem by *spreading* or enlarging the foreground colour, alternatively *choking* or shrinking the other colour or colours, so that they overlap each other slightly, avoiding any unwanted gap between the colours. Trapping, in the form of spreads and chokes, can be performed in a number of ways - manually, photomechanically or digitally through the use of appropriate software.

New screening developments

One of the major problems found when PostScript-driven DTP was first introduced for process colour work, was the enormous size of file which had to be created, stored and manipulated, even for a relatively simple continuous tone picture - eg - a full A4 picture in four-colour process will require a file size of around 34Mb for a 300 dots per inch *(dpi)* resolution - *see Figure 5.24.*

Initially, a major problem was the very slow processing speed but this has been improved considerably by the new, much faster RIPs where four-colour pictures can be output in less than five minutes. A further problem which can arise with conventional halftone screening is screen clash patterning, such as moiré, which can be very severe in some cases: this is particularly prevalent on pictures with chequered-type patterns such as on clothing or other garments; also patterned products such as interwoven fencing and roof tiles.

Traditional screening methods used on scanners are based on the Amplitude Modulation *(AM)* approach, where the variation in signal (electrical) charge is used to create dots of different size. Some new screening methods are based on the Frequency Modulation *(FM)* approach, where the dots are all the same size ('first order' version), but more or less of them appear in each area as required - *see Figure 5.20.* There are, however, developments in what has been termed 'second order' FM screening which results in variable dot sizes. FM screening is also often referred to as *stochastic*, or *irrational* screening.

New developments in screening technology such as *stochastic*, break down continuous tone originals into small 'microdots', resulting in much smaller file sizes and therefore faster processing; a further benefit is improved printing detail, often approaching the appearance of continuous tone/screenless printing from high quality originals on high quality coated substrates, plus the eradication of the screen clash pattern problem. The microdot sizes used in FM screening, vary from around 14 to 20 microns, going down to seven microns: a 20 micron FM dot equates to about the smallest highlight dot on a 150lpi screen.

To obtain the benefits offered by FM/stochastic screening, several tightly monitored working practices should be put in place, including the use of high contrast film capable of holding a sharp hard dot, a tightly calibrated imagesetter, correct film and plate exposure in terms of time and processing, and a dust-free working environment as dust specks will show up more alongside the small microdots. Some suppliers, such as Scitex, have developed a screening system - in this case Scitex Class Screening - which allows users to choose the best type of screening application appropriate to each particular job.

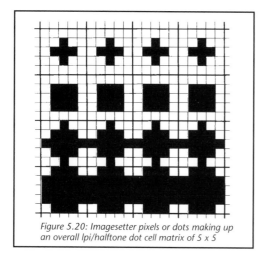

Figure 5.20: Imagesetter pixels or dots making up an overall lpi/halftone dot cell matrix of 5 x 5

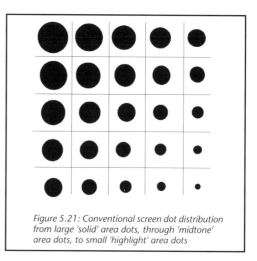

Figure 5.21: Conventional screen dot distribution from large 'solid' area dots, through 'midtone' area dots, to small 'highlight' area dots

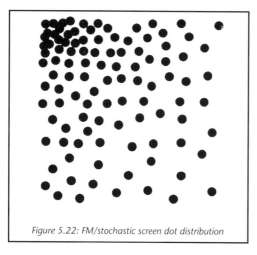

Figure 5.22: FM/stochastic screen dot distribution

Figure 5.20 illustrates the way 'pixel squares' build up the desired halftone dot shapes in lpi, through the use of an imagesetter

Figure 5.21 illustrates the dot tonal range from small dot highlight areas through to large dot solid areas, created by conventional halftone screening techniques, such as use of the contact screen

Figure 5.22 illustrates the scattered, irregular pattern of FM/stochastic dot distribution, where the clustering together of the microdots create the illusion of different tonal patterns

Figure 5.8 (two pictures) on page 72 has been reproduced using an FM/stochastic screen pattern which can be identified by viewing the pictures under a magnifying glass. All the other pictures in this publication have been reproduced using conventional dot pattern screens - again this can be detected with the use of a magnifying screen.

Halftone reproduction

The terms, 'halftone screen' and 'screening originals', stem mainly from the original glass screen and contact screen used along with screen frequency/ ruling and screen angles, in camera-based systems as previously described in this chapter. The major modern digital route for producing halftone screened images suitable for printing, is via an imagesetter, which converts the digitally created pixels into controlled varying dot sizes and shape as required - *see Figures 5.18*. When an original is scanned, it is recorded in picture elements *(pixels)*: the scanning resolution is then described as the number of pixels per unit of length - eg - inches, millimetres or centimetres.

In modern graphic reproduction terms the most important factors that affect the print quality of continuous tone originals reproduced using halftone screening are:

- grey levels
- input or scanning resolution
- output screen frequency/ruling
- output resolution.

Grey levels

It is a common convention that the eye can only detect a certain number of grey levels with 256 grey levels being used as a convenient level for calculation purposes, so this is taken as the maximum required to reproduce a high quality printed halftone.

The formula to calculate the number of grey levels that can be reproduced from a known output resolution and screen frequency is as follows:

$$number\ of\ grey\ levels = \left(\frac{output\ resolution\ of\ printer\ (dpi)}{screen\ frequency\ chosen\ (lpi)} \right)^2 + 1$$

The doubling of the screen frequency has been calculated from the fact that in the transformation from pixels to halftones it has been found that four times as many pixels are required to represent each halftone. Sampling theory has been applied to establish this quality factor in practice: the factor of 2 is often used up to 133lpi or 150lpi, then a factor of only 1.5 above these figures for finer screen frequencies.

Example 1

Imagesetting output resolution of 2400dpi and screen frequency of 150lpi.

$$\left(\frac{2400}{150}\right)^{2} + 1 \quad = \quad \textit{257 grey levels}$$

Example 2

Laser printer resolution of 1200 dpi and screen frequency of 85lpi.

$$\left(\frac{1200}{85}\right)^{2} + 1 \quad = \quad \textit{200 grey levels}$$

- 200 is still a relatively high greyscale level for a laser printer which cannot match the high resolution of an imagesetter - see pages 143 to 145

Input/scanning resolution

The formula to calculate the input/scanning resolution from a desired output screen frequency is as follows:

Input/scanning resolution = screen frequency (lpi) x 2 x % size/scale factor

Example

An imagesetter, reproducing a s/s original, set to a screen frequency of 120lpi.

120 x 2 x 1 (s/s) = *240dpi*

- 240dpi represents the minimum input scan resolution to achieve an output screen frequency of 120lpi

A further useful formula involving scanning resolution is in calculating this factor from the existing original to the print size required.

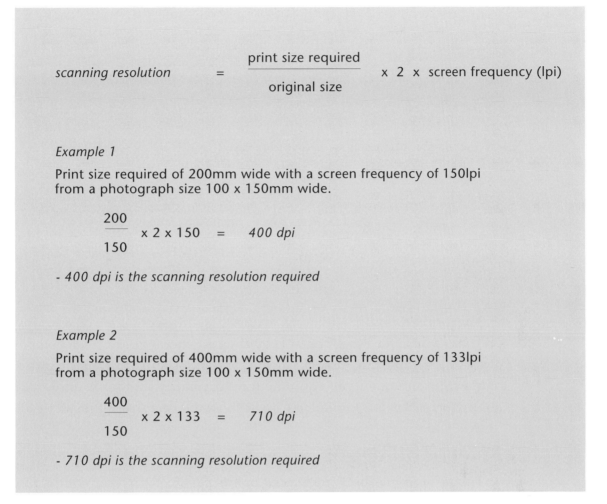

$$\text{scanning resolution} = \frac{\text{print size required}}{\text{original size}} \times 2 \times \text{screen frequency (lpi)}$$

Example 1

Print size required of 200mm wide with a screen frequency of 150lpi from a photograph size 100 x 150mm wide.

$$\frac{200}{150} \times 2 \times 150 = 400 \text{ dpi}$$

- 400 dpi is the scanning resolution required

Example 2

Print size required of 400mm wide with a screen frequency of 133lpi from a photograph size 100 x 150mm wide.

$$\frac{400}{150} \times 2 \times 133 = 710 \text{ dpi}$$

- 710 dpi is the scanning resolution required

Output screen frequency/ruling

This area has been covered previously in the chapter - *see pages 58 to 60*. It should be noted, however, that most printer and imagesetter manuals will instruct the user to the most suitable/default halftone screen frequency for the particular model in question - eg - 106lpi for the Apple LaserWriter 630 Pro and 200lpi for the Apple Color LaserWriter 12/600.

Output resolution

The formula to calculate the output (printer) device resolution in dpi can be achieved by applying the '16 rule' (16^2 giving the maximum 256 grey levels) is as follows:

output printer resolution = required screen frequency (lpi) x 16

Example

Screen frequency of 150lpi to be used.

150 x 16   =   *2400 dpi*

- 2400 dpi output resolution on the imagesetter is required to create a 150lpi screen frequency

The formulae and calculations included in this section are commonly used in prepress work and are aimed at providing a general guide. Each company will, over time, establish its own 'best fit' calculations and working practices, based on the type and quality of equipment used, quality standards undertaken, plus quality of originals supplied, etc, to achieve the best overall results possible.

Pixel or bit depth

The pixel or bit depth, measured in bits per pixel, determines the number of tones or colours each pixel in a bitmap can possess. This will be determined during scanning of the original - reproduced in *Figure 5.23* are examples of a range of black-and-white, plus colour originals, along with their corresponding pixel or bit depth: the greater the pixel depth the higher the quality of greyscale or colour that will be reproduced. A pixel is the smallest part or dot a picture on a computer screen is broken down into - the eye mixes the pixels collectively into continuous tone. The pixel or bit depth is also established by the number of binary digits required to reproduce the level of one scanned pixel.

The number of pixels in an existing image or area cannot be changed except by interpolation, although the overall image area can. This then results in the following scenario: to increase the resolution *(ppi)* the image size needs to be reduced, and conversely increasing the image size will reduce the overall ppi. An example would be an image size 6"x4" with a resolution of 300dpi - if the image is enlarged to 12"x8" it would then possess 150dpi at that size, if it was to be reduced to 3"x2" it would then have far more detail at 600dpi.

Pixels per inch *(ppi)* is a measure of the resolution of an image.

image type		bit depth
black-and-white line art	(1^2)	1 bit per pixel
black-and-white basic greyscale	(2^2)	2 bits per pixel
black-and-white continuous tone greyscale	(2^8)	8 bits per pixel
full colour - RGB	(2^{24})	8 bits per colour x 3 colours = 24-bit depth
continuous tone full colour - CMYK	(2^{32})	8 bits per colour x 4 colours = 32-bit depth

Figure 5.23: Range of image types with corresponding bit depths

Line art is an image scanned to a bit depth of one bit, with each pixel having two states - black-and-white (or in computer terms, 0 or 1).

Basic greyscale is an image scanned to a bit depth of two bits, with a range of two grey tones, plus black-and-white.

Greyscale is an image scanned in one colour, often to a maximum bit depth of eight bits, with a range of 256 levels, black-and-white with 254 grey levels in between.

Full colour in RGB represents an image scanned to a bit depth of 24 bits (Rx8, Gx8, Bx8) giving 256 levels per colour - ie - a maximum of 16.7 million colours in total (256x256x256).

Continuous tone full colour in CMYK represents an image reproduced to a bit depth of 32 bits (Cx8, Mx8, Yx8, Kx8).

An 8-bit computer monitor is capable of displaying 256 (2^8) colours or shades of grey.

A 24-bit computer monitor is capable of displaying 16.7 million (2^{24}) colours and is also known as 'true colour'.

A 32-bit colour system is capable of displaying and processing 24-bit colour, with the 8 extra bits used for creating masks or transparency effects.

	File sizes - values in Mb			
Colour scans - scanning resolution and screen frequency				
image sizes	A6	A5	A4	A3
CMYK				
300 dpi (150 lpi)	8.27	16.50	33.20	66.40
266 dpi (133 lpi)	6.50	13.00	26.10	52.20
72 dpi (positional)	0.49	0.98	1.91	3.83
RGB				
300 dpi (150 lpi)	6.20	12.40	24.90	49.80
266 dpi (133 lpi)	4.88	9.75	19.60	39.20
72 dpi (positional)	0.37	0.73	1.43	2.87

Figure 5.24: Different file sizes, derived from a range of image sizes, scanning resolution, screen frequency and colour type

Dpi and lpi

Dots per inch *(dpi)* is a measurement of input and output device resolution covering the number of dots created or generated by the scanner, laser printer or imagesetter. Dpi is quite different to lines per inch *(lpi)*, which is a measurement of screen ruling, representing the frequency of the horizontal and vertical lines per inch to be used in the final printed result.

Lpi will be made up in different dot sizes and shapes within the same screen ruling crossline pattern, either generated by conventional contact screen or digitally by an imagesetter - *see Figures 5.20* and *5.21*.

Dpi, when referring to the resolution of a laser printer or imagesetter will be fixed, within the same setting, whereas lpi screen frequency will vary depending on the requirements - eg - 100lpi, 150lpi, 200lpi etc, as well as the different dot sizes within the set screen ruling. The relationship between dpi and lpi can be seen from the fact that the quality of the halftone cell will be influenced by the overall cell size *(lpi)* and the resolution of the dots *(dpi)* required to create that cell: for an explanation of *ppi - see page 86.*

File formats

When transferring images between different applications and users it is important to choose, wherever possible, a recognised standard file format.

A few major examples are as follows:

- **Tagged Image File Format** *(TIFF),* developed originally by Aldus, has become one of the industry standard file formats, supporting black-and-white line art and continuous tone greyscale, plus RGB and CMYK colour. A TIFF file specifies the level of grey/brightness associated with each dot of the image: they are in bitmap form and cannot be altered.

- **Encapsulated PostScript** *(EPS)* is more complex and comprehensive than TIFF, consisting of two parts - the PostScript code that describes the boundary box and any vector elements and a 72dpi low-resolution screen preview image which is ideally suited to the DTP prepress environment. It has been developed to encompass drawings, images and complete layouts, in vector and bitmap form, which can then be placed/embedded into other documents.

- **Desktop Colour Separations** *(DCS)*, also often referred to as *EPS 5*, have been developed with the specific purpose of reducing the amount of CMYK data handled by predominantly page layout programs. It is an image file format where five files are created for each colour image - one PostScript file for each of CMYK and a low-resolution PICT preview file. To keep storage memory requirements to a minimum during use, only the PICT file is used with the DTP program: when the file is finalised as required, the linked high-resolution files are automatically called up to replace the low-resolution PICT file.

- **PICT** is a graphics file format developed by Apple for use on the Mac platform. Most object-oriented drawing programs and page layout programs can create and/or read PICT files - they can also be interpreted by PostScript output devices to print out at, say, 300 to over 1200dpi depending on the resolution available on the output device. The PICT format can also contain just bitmapped images.

Portable Document Format (PDF) is covered in Chapter 10, 'Computer-to-print and beyond'.

Data/file compression

The apparent insatiable demand for more and more colour reproduction and complex design, has led to bigger and bigger file sizes being created and exchanged, between two or more parties. Although larger media storage, faster networks and communication systems have been developed, the option of file compression has become popular.

Compression techniques use complex algorithms to search for redundant data, which is then removed: after use, through storage or transmission, the compressed data is restored to its original form via a complementary decompression algorithm.

Compression techniques fall into two main types - 'lossless' and 'lossy':

- **Lossless data compression** retains all the information in the original data, so that it can be reconstructed without any apparent deterioration in the data, but the compression ratios are relatively modest from 2:1 to 8:1.

- **Lossy data compression** does lose some of the original information but can compact data by as much as 100:1 - ie - 1% of its original size.

Joint Photographic Experts Group (JPEG), is an example of a very popular compression picture file format using the lossy technique. The most popular compression utilities are 'Stuffit' and 'Disk Doubler': in addition compression applications such as High Water 'Interchange Pro' have been developed for high-end colour use.

An example illustrating the use of 'Interchange Pro' is the reduction of a 20Mb TIFF colour file with results as shown in *Figures 5.25* and *5.26*. Timings were achieved using the following equipment - PowerMac 9500 running Interchange v3.0 software, with default RAM allocations: 10Base-T transfer times from PowerMac 9500 to PowerMac 8100 under normal network traffic conditions: PowerMac printing to Harlequin RIP from QuarkXPress v3.3.2 with resolution 2348dpi and halftone screen frequency 133lpi: ISDN transmission from PowerMac 8100 running ISDN Manager and controller in twin (turbo) mode. *Figure 5.26* illustrates two versions of the picture - ie - as the original 20Mb file and 1.8Mb compressed version.

	20Mb original file	1.8Mb highly compression file
Compression to DCS/PEG	N/A	16 secs
Mac to RIP clear screen	3 mins 26 secs	18 secs
10Base-T transfer	1 mins 29 secs	8 secs
ISDN transmission	22 mins 59 secs	2 mins 5 secs
Time to RIP	2 mins 52 secs	2 mins 5 secs

Figure 5.25: Transfer times of original file and highly compressed file

Figure 5.26: Reproduction of original 20Mb file and 1.8Mb highly compressed file

Open Prepress Interface *(OPI)*

OPI is a development which allows two copies of an image to coexist in low-resolution *(low-res)* and high-resolution *(high-res)* format, with the objective of utilising the most efficient handling and processing of the data.

The raison d'etre for OPI is that at the initial DTP stage only a low-res image (taking up a small amount of memory) is required to position images in a page document. This is then replaced by the high-res file for final colour separations and outputting, which can be handled much more efficiently by powerful workstations and servers.

A common use of OPI is where the printer or bureau with an OPI operating system and server scans and processes the images in low-res and high-res form: the low-res is supplied back to the customer, designer or DTP operator to make up the job, with the high-res images retained by the OPI provider.

When the finalised and approved files are returned to the OPI provider, the OPI server automatically substitutes the high-res images for the low-res, before final outputting as required - *see Figures 2.2* and *2.3*.

It is essential that the low-res and high-res images are linked by OPI comments identifiable to the OPI system, otherwise the operation will not perform automatically.

SIX

MAKE-UP, PLANNING AND ASSEMBLY

Make-up, planning and assembly involves the correct positioning and arrangement of the various print-related elements in the chosen medium - for example, digital, or analogue/conventional, such as bromide paper, negative or positive film, to form the required finished result as made-up pages or planned images in single units, imposed or multiple-image laydowns, for subsequent reproduction and printing.

As established in previous chapters, there are two main routes for make-up, planning and assembly - *traditional.* and *desktop/digital.*

Traditional systems by their very nature are labour intensive, leading to major bottlenecks in the processing of prepress work and forward planning for subsequent printing and print finishing. Electronic make-up, planning and assembly across a wide range of work has been found to be at least 50% quicker than manual working, with the gap widening all the time, due to improvements in the quality and speed of digital systems: to a great extent software applications have now replaced craft skills and the desktop/workstation replaced the light table/work bench.

It should be acknowledged, however, as has been raised elsewhere in this publication, that entirely digital workflows have still to be adopted by the vast number of printers - ie - creation, manipulation and management of digital data direct-to-plate or direct-to-press. At least some part of their prepress processes - eg - film planning and/or platemaking, therefore, have still to be carried out using manual conventional methods: additionally, mixed media workflows - converting analogue elements to digital data - are a further practice undertaken by printers and their service suppliers - *see pages 147* and *148.*

A further point to be borne in mind is that generally print customers like the assurance of something physical, like film, plus suppliers can more easily justify charges for a physical product, such as film, compared with digital.

Desktop/digital systems

Just as with traditional systems there are two different types of digital make-up, planning and assembly systems - DTP and Electronic Page Composition (*EPC*), also often referred to as Digital Artwork and Reproduction (*DAR*).

In the mid to late 1980s, electronic/digital make-up was established on expensive high-end EPC and DAR systems, installed mainly in medium- to large-sized repro companies, using proprietary hardware and software. Initially these systems were developed as 'stand-alone', relatively closed proprietary environments.

At the same time as EPC systems were achieving a strong position in prepress, especially in complex, high-end colour work, AppleMacs and PCs were establishing themselves, especially in the single colour field, but quickly moving into the era coined 'good enough colour' in the late 1980s/early 1990s.

The 1990s has seen a phenomenal growth, accelerated from the mid 1990s up to the present time, in work undertaken on AppleMacs, PCs and workstations, as developers and suppliers have launched software and hardware, which has revolutionised the way printing and other media is created and disseminated, examples of which are highlighted throughout this publication.

EPC systems have had to adapt to finding a niche area mainly around complex colour image manipulation, montaging, handling extremely large files, where multi-tasking facilities are desirable; even still, EPC systems are under threat as AppleMacs and PCs become more powerful, linked with multi-tasking work-stations and improved networks.

EPC systems

EPC/DAR systems have now developed in most cases as 'open' and flexible systems where they can accept files from DTP systems in the form of digital storage media or conventional originals, covering continuous tone images, text and line art. Once imported, the data, whether in a mixed format or not, can normally be modified and amended as required, using tools and facilities which, for example, allow PostScript files to be edited and layouts and designs altered, along with retouching and colour correction.

Further features commonly include low-resolution images generated from high-resolution scans which can be sent back to DTP users, so maximising the speed of the page make-up facility on the DTP system.

Being an open, but still a proprietary-based system, there is the opportunity to have 'seamless' links to electronic imposition software, colour retouching, design, illustration and image manipulation software, also proofing systems.

Most EPC systems are based on Silicon Graphics or Sun Sparc UNIX-based workstations and support PostScript, producing very high quality vignettes and montages which, until recent years, were unachievable on most DTP systems.

An example of a high-end creative EPC system is Quantel 'Printbox' which has been developed out of Quantel 'Paintbox', a system originally developed for TV and other multi-media image-based systems.

The full Printbox system is based on on-line page production, an interactive page make-up environment, where every facility and element is on-line at all times, editable, interactive and simultaneous. The production process is never halted by any other operation within the system; for instance, scanning can take place at the same time as colour correction, page make-up and output.

The system consists at the initial input stage of a Scan Manager, which controls communication between the user and the Printbox scanner, followed by the Printbox workstation, controlling and amending data sent to the Layout Manager which integrates images and text, using QuarkXPress data, where appropriate. Data after proofing and approval is held in storage media, or directed to a server and RIP for outputting in the form required - ie - to planned film or computer-to-plate.

EPC/DAR systems are particularly popular in the generation of packaging and label work, as well as high-end complex colour work.

Figure 6.1 indicates a flow diagram covering the use of an *EPC/DAR system*, producing multiple-image work such as cartons, labels and direct response marketing work, with tint blocks highlighting areas of make-up, planning and assembly.

Desktop publishing systems

At the heart of DTP systems are the page make-up software programs. The software programs perform the function of combining all the elements of typematter, tints and graphics into complete made-up pages and/or into complete images, with a wide ranging format shape and size such as labels, cartons, or point-of-sale *(PoS)* work.

As covered in *Chapters 5* and *6, textmatter* can be input into the host computer by direct keying, OCR, or from remote sources such as a floppy disk, or other suitable media.

Line charts and graphics can be created from scratch, with the operator producing the required result by scanning in from a previously prepared hand-drawn or photographic original; alternatively, direct digital data is available via a clip art system/picture library, generated from drawing, or office-type integrated software.

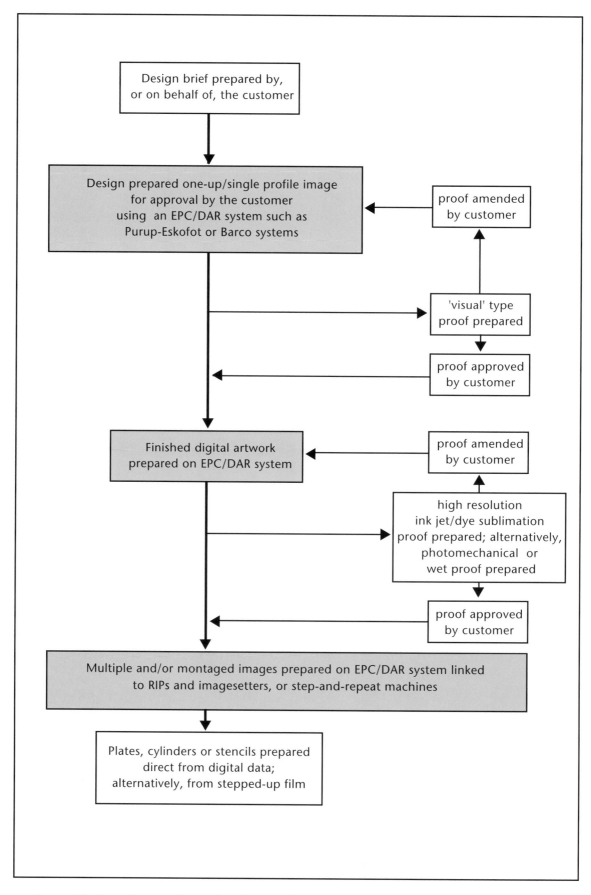

Figure 6.1: Flow diagram illustrating the use of an EPC/DAR system producing multiple-image work such as cartons, labels and direct response marketing

Continuous tone originals are introduced into the DTP system by the use of a scanner, reproducing conventional originals or direct digital data, via digital camera, Kodak PhotoCD, clip art, on-line image libraries, plus images created and/or manipulated with the use of graphics generation and manipulation software programs such as Adobe 'Illustrator' and 'Photoshop'; alternatively, images can, of course, be imported as a finished graphic which has been prepared and created on a completely different system.

The component parts of a DTP system consist of:

- A **host computer**, such as an AppleMac, PC or workstation.
- A **monitor,** with keyboard and mouse connected to the host computer, allowing a WYSIWYG working environment on screen.
- **Software programs** to perform the functions of page make-up, planning and assembly.
- **Peripheral devices**, such as external storage media, laser printers, scanners, imagesetters, etc, connected to the host computer on an on-line or off-line basis, linked up only as required.

DTP page make-up software

A wide range of DTP software programs is available, from the relatively limited examples aimed mainly at the home and leisure market, to the professional programs developed for business and especially the graphic arts industries: as a result DTP software programs have, at least initially, been designed to run on a particular platform and perform to a certain level of functionality.

Some programs have developed into narrow or 'niche' markets, with particular suitability to a certain type of work, others have developed to offer an extremely comprehensive range of facilities and functions which literally cover every conceivable requirement of a DTP program working on an AppleMac, PC, workstation or all three platforms. However, there can be no question that the professional end of DTP packages, especially in graphics print related areas, is dominated by two highly successful software programs - Adobe 'PageMaker' and 'QuarkXPress'.

PageMaker was the first major DTP application and has held a dominant position ever since DTP was developed: it is currently reputed to account for over 50% of all page make-up software program sales, being most popular in corporate publishing, but less so in design and typographic rich areas, such as high-end publishing and repro-related areas, where QuarkXPress is dominant.

PageMaker works on the basis of copy and images being pasted onto drawn up grids, whereas QuarkXPress uses frames for handling text and graphic elements allowing designers more freedom in layout.

Both systems on each subsequent upgrade and new version appear to play catch-up with each other, offering features which were previously available on the rival product, plus introducing new features which improve their functionality.

The main features offered by most high quality professional DTP packages are as follows:

- handle a wide range of page sizes, orientation and measurement systems - eg - inches, millimetres and point system
- create left and right hand pages, plus facing master multiple pages and templates
- record number of pages, and highlight page(s) in use
- create page layout grid, with column and ruler guides
- edit and spell-check facilities
- page views in reduction and enlargement increments - eg - from 25% to 400%
- control over choice of typeface, style, size, letter and line spacing, kerning, alignment and rotation
- control over hyphenation and paragraph style
- basic drawing tools and facilities - covering lines in different thicknesses and patterns, shapes and circles, ovals, rectangles and hexagons, fill and line, tints
- tabulation facilities and controls
- import and edit text, line and graphics from a wide range of sources, plus export of files in recognised formats suitable for other applications
- crop, scale and rotate images
- cut, copy, paste facilities
- control over halftone images covering brightness and contrast, screen frequencies and angles
- import, process and output colour separations
- export/print to a wide range of output devices such as laser printers and imagesetters
- control palettes and icons providing user-friendly working practices and guidance.

Brief overview of PageMaker DTP package

Adobe PageMaker is a powerful page layout program which has become the market leader, along with QuarkXPress, through its relative ease of use. Initially it was accepted by 'traditional' printers, typesetters and others, wishing to create documents quickly, easily and economically. This was due to its simple approach of creating a 'pasteboard' frame around the screen page and dropping in or 'pasting-up' type and graphics onto the page and placing into position.

PageMaker is a page-oriented make-up program, which has also been referred to as 'an import - then position' application. As text is entered, or flowed onto a page set up in PageMaker, by direct keying or imported from other sources, such as a word processing program, the program operates by filling the predetermined shape of the columns set up on the master page.

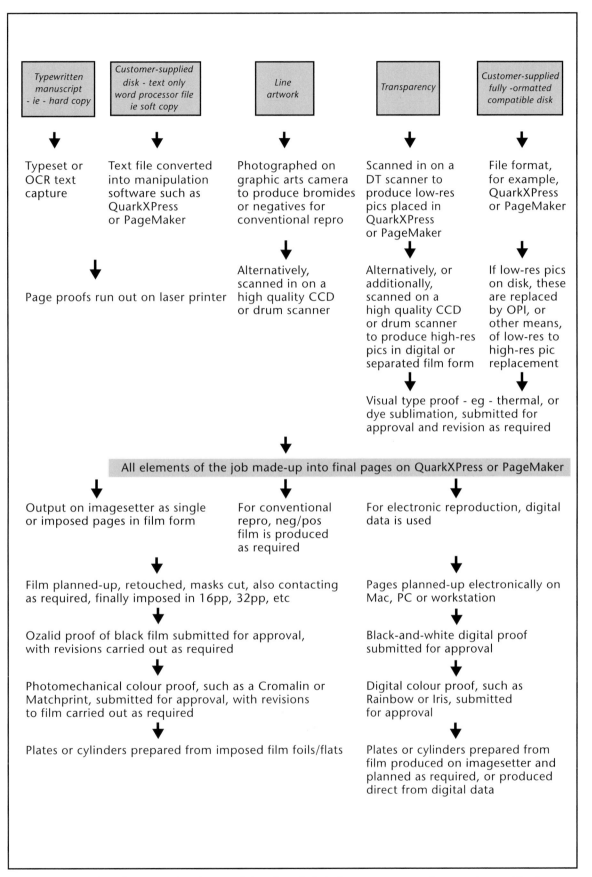

Figure 6.2: Flow diagram showing traditional and digital prepress routes frequently used in the production of magazine, periodical or catalogue prepress operations - with tint blocks highlighting the use of DTP page make-up software, represented by QuarkXPress and PageMaker

Text can be placed as separate unconnected blocks, or more commonly as blocks which link automatically, with subsequent changes or alterations rippling through the document or story.

Text blocks can be repositioned and/or resized in width and depth by selecting the area(s) required; graphics are handled in the same way. The program works with all the common text and graphic file formats. On selecting an element for placement, a text or graphic icon appears, indicating the status of that object: the icon is placed at the selected point and loaded/positioned with a click of the mouse.

Figure 6.2 shows traditional and digital prepress routes, frequently used in the production of magazine, periodical or catalogue prepress operations - with tint blocks highlighting the use of DTP page make-up software, represented by QuarkXPress and PageMaker.

Brief overview of QuarkXPress DTP package

QuarkXPress is a frame-based program, offering a high control over typographical matters, alongside the ease and flexibility of running text around graphics, aimed at making up a document on a page-by-page basis. This approach is one of the major reasons why the program is so popular in the production of shorter, mixed media publications containing text and graphics, such as brochures and magazines, rather than high pagination, structured documents and reports.

The facilities offered by the program add up to a very comprehensive, creative, colour, and feature-rich DTP package. The acceptance of QuarkXPress by the 'heavyweights' of the prepress industry can be gauged by the way that it has been built in as practically the standard DTP program on EPC/Colour Electronic Page Setting *(CEPS)* systems.

As stated above, QuarkXPress is a frame- or grid-based page orientated system, where text and graphics are placed in pre-defined frames or boxes.

In the early versions of the program, a fixed relationship between frames was established - eg - a second level of frames containing graphics, text or both, could be created or nested within the main or first frame level, but once established, the relationship could not be altered.

It was not possible, for instance, to drag the second level box outside the main parent frame. With developments from version 3.0 onwards of the program, the facilities were made more flexible by allowing the frames to be independent, or remaining linked as required.

The system has a pasteboard facility, where objects can be taken off the page, to allow amendments and changes to the parameters of the object - eg - to add bleed to an image.

Control over typographical features is considerable with minute adjustments over letter spacing/tracking, kerning, letter widths, as well as hyphenation parameters.

Master default pages are used for establishing page layout and format, with over a hundred left and right default pages, represented by icons to assist identification, location and selection as required.

The system of default pages is very flexible in that, for example, a default page layout can be selected and dropped into a selected page completely unrelated. There are also powerful lining tools holding the text blocks in a structured form, as well as tools which can be used to create irregular shapes to graphics with corresponding text run-rounds.

Full process and spot colour support is available and, in fact has always been a strong point of the program, creating, manipulating and retouching images, along with links to high-end systems.

QuarkXPress uses comprehensive style sheets to set up frames of text blocks, founts, type style and spacing, allowing up to seven documents to be opened at any one time.

Corel Ventura

Ventura, after PageMaker and QuarkXPress, is the next most popular DTP package and is one of the most popular page make-up software programs used by publishers. It is a frame-based software program where text is created in frames, separate for text and graphics - the page format is automatically setup when the page is created. In terms of alterations to page layout, Ventura is not so easy and straightforward as PageMaker, but has always been recognised as being particularly suited to the production of lengthy documents with a standard format. One of Ventura's most powerful features is the use of *style sheets* to automatically control the entire format of a document. The design and style of the pages can be changed simply by loading a different style sheet. Ventura's style sheets offer a wide array of functions including page size, number of columns, line spacing, type sizes and styles. Ventura is used most effectively in the production of technical manual and reports, where fixed page formats are used.

Extensions, add-ons, plug-ins

The above refer to a selection of terms covering utilities which enhance and expand the capabilities and functionality, as well as to often provide productivity boosts, in areas such as DTP packages, by taking on, or extending, specific tasks not available, or not adequately, covered on the basic program.

Programs such as QuarkXPress, PageMaker, Photoshop and Freehand are well established in this area with the growth of add-ons, plug-ins and extensions set to continue in these areas.

Some extensions are available from the manufacturers of the software program, but most are available through third-party developers.

A few examples of PageMaker 'plug-in' utilities, previously known as 'additions', are as follows:

Bullets and numbering providing the facility to add bullets and number at the start of paragraphs.

EPS font scanner facility which scans EPS graphics for fonts and checks the computer for corresponding screen fonts.

Guide manager allows baselines of text columns to align.

Hypertext mark-up language (HTML) author defines the location of graphics in relative terms for use in electronic documents and use.

Open template provides access to a library of existing templates covering a range of different types of job.

Whereas most 'extensions' to PageMaker are mainly included as 'plug-ins' with the current version of the software, QuarkXPress is very different in its approach in that there are over 300 'XTensions', some available direct from Quark, although the vast majority are from third-party developers.

A great deal of the success of QuarkXPress, especially in the prepress world, is due to the diversity and quality of the XTensions, which continue to expand, increasing its overall capabilities.

An example of QuarkXTensions is 'Thing-a-ma Bob' for fractions and shortcuts, and typical of third-party XTensions are DK&A products 'INposition' and 'INposition Lite' automating the imposition process, plus 'Trapper' providing manual or automatic trapping, OPI support, post-production editing and workflow routines.

Traditional systems

Paper make-up, planning and assembly

Paper make-up as a process has all but been replaced by DTP systems, although it is still practised by some printers, albeit on a much reduced scale.

The process involves attaching bromides, or other suitable material, from an output device such as an imagesetter onto a predetermined laydown sheet which indicates the position for the different elements of the job - eg - text, graphics and illustrations. Each of the elements which have been prepared for same-size reproduction *(s/s)* are then placed into position, so creating camera-ready copy.

The prepared flat artwork is then photographed on a graphics arts camera to produce a negative or series of negatives which are then planned up in position ready for further processing - *see film make-up, planning and assembly* on the following page.

Film make-up, planning and assembly

Unlike paper make-up, film make-up is still used extensively by printers: unless a printer is able to produce or have access to single pieces of complete, composite film to fit the full size of his presses, or works in a completely digital workflow, then film planning will have to be undertaken prior to platemaking.

Film planning can either be in *negative* or *positive* form. It is a more demanding task than paper make-up, requiring a high level of skill. Film output from the imagesetting system (or still very occasionally from a graphics arts camera) needs to take account of the requirements of the printing processes involved - *see page 57*.

In the UK, most negative-working planning is used for single, two-colour and spot-colour work, whereas positive-working is mainly used for four-colour process work. In other parts of Europe the situation is often the reverse with negative-working popular for four-colour process planning.

Negative film planning tends to be a more difficult operation for complex and intricate work as the planner finds it more difficult to see through the reversed dense black areas to position the various elements onto the layout; the use of punched pin register systems overcomes the problem to a great extent.

Preparing layouts or laydown sheets

Layout sheets are produced to indicate the positions of typematter, graphics, page imposition, register and trim marks, gripper allowance and the like. Negative film layout and assembly work, especially for small-offset work, can be produced using a dimensionally stable paper such as goldenrod, where the layout is drawn onto the material and windows are cut away to receive the negative image areas. More intricate and complex work, along with positive working, uses a clear plastic acetate sheet or *foil* for planning.

The plastic acetate sheet or clear foil is precisely placed over the layout sheet, or other appropriate work sheets, and illuminated from below on a special planning light table. The layout or other sheets are used as a guide when attaching the film in position onto the foil with adhesive tape. In the case of multi-colour work a separate planned and assembled foil is produced for every colour.

Figure 6.3 illustrates in sequence an eight-page laydown on a punched pin register foil, followed by a black type and process planned foil, process colour planned foils and clean-up mask for process pictures.

Mixed media

For mixed media working - ie - digital and conventional and/or conversion from analogue film to digital data - *see Chapter 9, 'Output systems and preparation of printing surfaces'*.

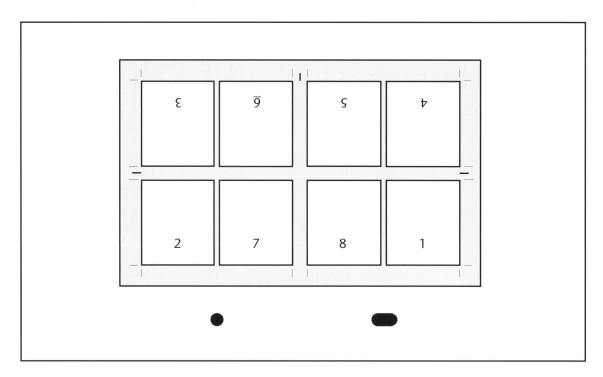

Figure 6.3a: Diagram illustrating a clear acetate foil superimposed on the layout and impostion scheme of an eight pages-to-view job prior to film assembly

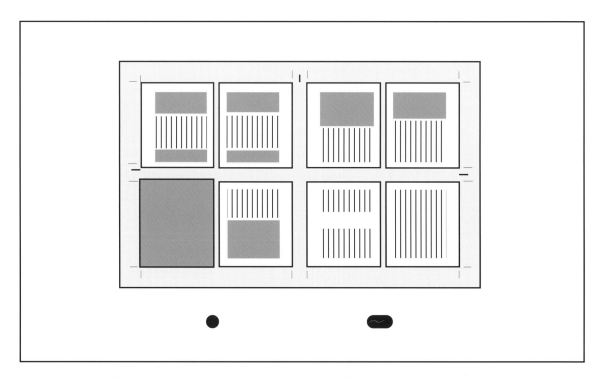

Figure 6.3b: Diagram illustrating the stage of black positive process separation and type, represented by heavy tint and thin lines, laid in position on the foil

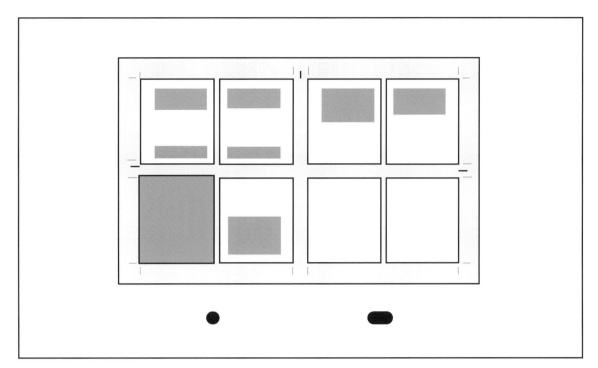

Figure 6.3c: Diagram illustrating the stage of assembling one of the three process colours on the foil - yellow, magenta or cyan: with each process colour appearing in exactly the same areas, the foils would be alike apart from each representing a different colour

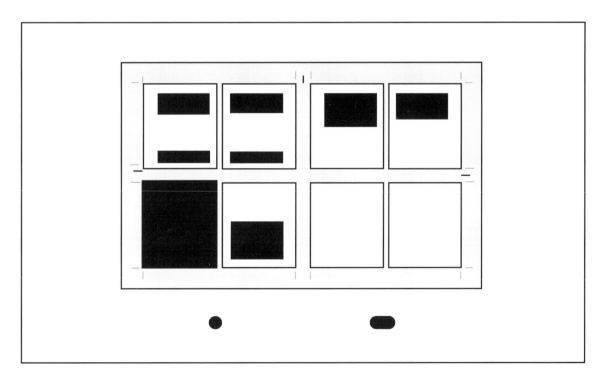

Figure 6.3d: Diagram illustrating the stage of preparing a clean-up mask for the squared-up four-colour pictures: this mask will be under-size to the scanned picture area so that the mask will clean up the edges of all the four-colour film uniformly - in addition there will be a further mask cut to protect the black type area and burn away film edges, etc, as required

seven

METHODS OF WORKING AND IMPOSITIONS

This chapter has a very close connection and relationship with the previous one. Having created, planned and assembled the text and graphic images into the desired finished form, the next stage is to work out the most economical way of producing each job, taking account of the various parameters related to it - ie - how each job is to be printed, in terms of position/number of images on each plate, cylinder or stencil.

Methods of working considerations

When deciding on the preferred method of working for any job, several factors need to be considered:

• **The quantity to be printed** - leading to considerations of multiple-image printing (where appropriate) on long runs

• **Working size of jobs** - for example, overall size(s) required for jobs, with appropriate allowances for trims, grips, die cutting, margins, etc, as single- or multiple-image working. A closely related and influencing factor, as indicated below, is available press sizes.

• **Printing press sizes and number of units available** - for example, a possible selection of small offset, B2 or B1 sheet-fed presses in one, two, four, five and more colours. Alternatively, heat-set web offset presses in eight-, 16- and 32-page configurations in four, five and eight units, or other reel/web-fed configurations.

• **Types of printing press to be used** - for example, printing one side only, perfector or convertible.

- **Colour 'fall' of printed pages** - for example, whether a booklet or brochure is printed in four-colour process throughout, or whether the publication is a mixture of monochrome and four-colour process pages, so that grouping of common colour pages can be used cost-effectively.

- **Method of finishing** - for example, insetted sections as used in saddle-stitching have half the pages (lower half) on one side of the centre spread, and half the pages (higher half) on the other side. Gathered sections, for example, as used in thread sewing and perfect binding, break the pagination down into sections of consecutive numbering - *see Figures 7.6 to 7.13.*

The finishing operations on bound publications which have greatest impact on the method of working, and hence imposition, are *cutting, folding* and *binding*.

The laydown of the pages on the printed sheet or web must be capable of being cut or slit and/or subsequently folded into the correct sequence by the equipment available. In the case of reel-fed label printing, the main considerations are the size of available cylinders, width and circumference, also the related finishing equipment such as flat-bed or rotary cutters.

Imposition

Imposition is the arrangement and assembly of printed images into a predetermined format, so that, when bound, each printed page will appear in the correct sequence and position; alternatively it relates to the laydown of multiple-image work. The approach to imposition applies equally to all the major printing processes, apart from recognising the fact that offset litho requires a right-reading offset litho plate, whereas conventional letterpress, flexography and gravure require wrong-reading printing plates or cylinders. Screen printing operates from a right-reading stencil mesh, emulsion-side down.

All imposition schemes work backwards from the finished printed product. As there are considerable practical differences between sheet and web printing, these are dealt with separately in this chapter.

One of the first considerations when planning how a job is to be printed, is to ensure that the available finishing equipment can complete the work in the desired way, because once a job is printed, a mistake in the imposition and laydown is difficult, if not impossible, to correct.

If in doubt about any job, the finishing department of the printing company needs to be consulted, especially if an outside supplier is to be involved.

When an imposition/laydown scheme has been supplied by a customer, it should be checked with the finishing department, unless it is a scheme with which all are thoroughly familiar.

Multiple-image printing

Work which is not to be bound in any way, such as a carton, label or leaflet, and printed on one or both sides, presents few complications in terms of how the laydown of images is decided.

Large print quantities, to be most effective, will normally result in *multiple-image printing*. *Figure 7.1* illustrates a carton which is to be printed nine-up: if the quantity required is 360 000, this would result in a print run of 40 000 plus overs, times the number of required press passes to complete the job.

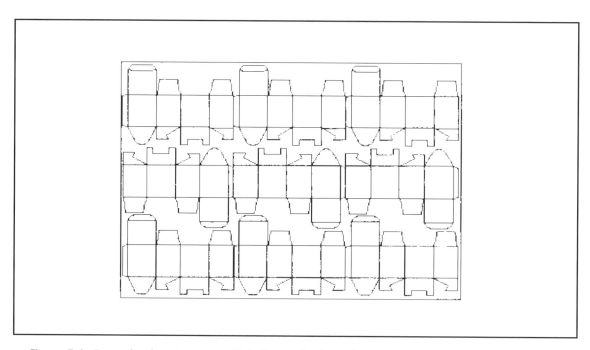

Figure 7.1: Example of a nine-up multiple-image laydown for a carton

Sheet-fed presses

There are various methods by which paper/board may be printed, or worked, on sheet-fed printing machines and these depend on:

- **Printing on one side only or both sides** - ie - perfected or backed (also sometimes referred to as duplexed).

- **Imposition scheme or laydown** - ie - the arrangement of the pages so that they appear in the correct sequence when the sheet is printed and folded, or the number of images to view in the case of multiple-image work.

When paper or board is required to be printed on both sides and bound, different impositions will be used for printing the sheet, depending on whether the imposition is for half-sheet work or sheet work. These terms are applicable to any size imposition of two pages or more, and the methods of working are explained on the following pages.

Half-sheet work

In the method of working known as *half-sheet work,* all the pages in a section are arranged in one imposition: by printing one side of the sheet from the imposition and then turning it over at the end of the run to print the other side - *two identical copies, times the number of sets, are obtained from one sheet.* One set of images - ie - one-up, will give two copies out, whereas four sets of images - ie - four-up, will give eight copies out. Two examples to illustrate this are as follows: 30 000 copies printed one-set half-sheet work of an eight-page A4 portrait booklet would require 15 000 sheets plus overs of sheet size SRA1 (640 x 900mm) or equivalent; whereas 60 000 copies printed two-set half-sheet work of a four-page A4 portrait folder would also require 15 000 sheets plus overs of sheet size SRA1 (640 x 900mm) or equivalent.

A sheet to be printed eight pages on one side with eight pages on the other would be arranged as a 16-page imposition, and the working size of the sheet would be twice as large as the complete sheet required. After printing, the printed sheet is then slit, or cut in half, each half of the sheet producing one complete copy. Half-sheet work may be either *work and-turn* or *work-and-tumble,* depending on whether the sheet is *turned,* or *tumbled,* prior to perfecting. These impositions are naturally suitable only for single-side press working, rather than perfecting on perfector or convertible presses - ie - presses which print on both sides of the sheet in one pass. When reference is made simply to 'half-sheet work', work-and-turn is normally implied.

With half-sheet work, only one imposition is used and there is therefore only one make-ready per set of plates, but the size of the plate(s), and the working size of the sheet and press, have to be large enough to accommodate all the pages that are to appear on both sides of the sheet.

Work-and-turn

In this method, the sheets are *turned* on the axis of the short side, which ensures that the long edge of the sheet, gripped when printing the first side, is also presented to the grippers for the second printing - *see Figure 7.2.* In this type of imposition, the plate or set of plates backs itself. In order to ensure correct register of pages during backing-up, the side lay is changed from left to right and, in this way, the same edges of the sheet are fed to the lays each time the paper or board passes through the machine.

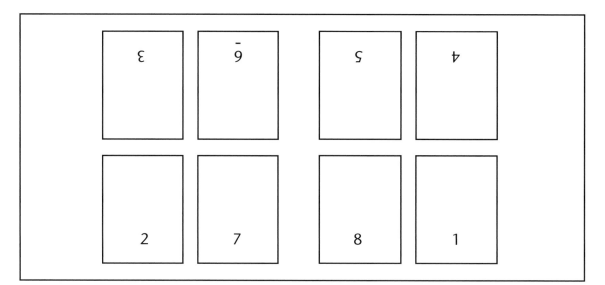

Figure 7.2: Eight-page work-and-turn imposition, covering pages 1 to 8

Work-and-tumble

As with work-and-turn, both the inner and outer pages of the sheet are imposed together. All the paper or board is printed on one side, and then tumbled from front to back, before the reverse side is printed from the same imposition - *see Figure 7.3*. Unlike the procedure in work-and-turn, the sheet is turned on the axis of its long side - that is, *tumbled* - where the two long edges are fed to the grippers in turn. For this reason adequate gripper margin has to be allowed on both long edges, and the paper or board has to be perfectly square or centred, before printing, in order to ensure register of pages in the back-up. Thus a tumbled sheet produces two complete printed copies for single-image working, as does a turned sheet, the size and number of working sheets being the same for both methods.

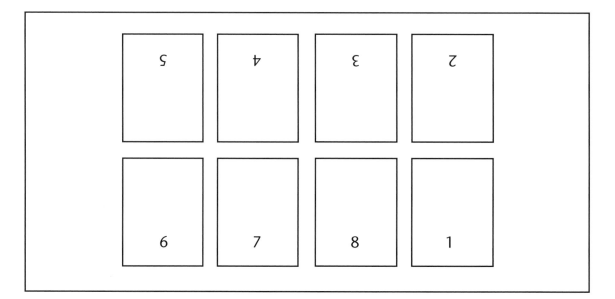

Figure 7.3: Eight-page work-and-tumble imposition (roll folded), covering pages 1 to 8

Work-and-tumble is frequently used for six- and 12-page jobs, and other instances, such as an eight-page roll-fold, which would tend to result in an elongated or awkward-shaped sheet, if printed by work-and-turn. *Figure 7.3* is an example of an eight-page work-and-tumble imposition, suited to roll-fold finishing.

Sheet work

In full sheet work, the pages to be printed on each side of the sheet are arranged in two separate impositions, *inner* and *outer.*

The outer imposition always contains the first and last pages of the section, and prints one side of the sheet, while the inner imposition always contains the second page of the section, and prints the other side.

Whereas half-sheet work produces two copies of a section from one imposition printed twice, sheet work produces one copy printing two sets of plates (*inner* and *outer*) once each, as shown in *Figure 7.4.*

The paper or board is printed on one side from one imposition, and is then printed from the other imposition on the reverse side, the same edge of the paper being fed to the grippers for each working. Thus, two sets of plates are needed to complete the sheet, and a separate make-ready is required for each. As each imposition contains the pages for one side only, the working size of the sheet is the same as that required for folding. In this way each perfected sheet produces one copy, and therefore the same number of sheets as completed copies are required.

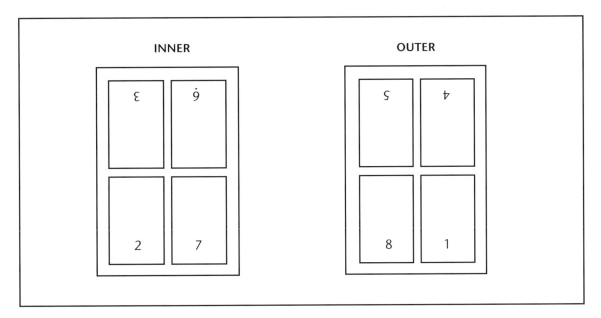

Figure 7.4: Eight-page sheet work imposition (inner and outer), covering pages 1 to 8

Apart from some small offset machines, the longer dimension of the sheet is fed to the front lays in sheet-fed printing - this ensures better register and greater accuracy, since dimensional changes, due to the effects of the press on the paper or board, are obviously less, the shorter the dimension being used.

For jobs consisting of several sections, such as bookwork, sheet work often produces economies in finishing, as previously stated, by eliminating the need for guillotining after printing, which is required with half-sheet work. Long run, multiple-section jobs made up of sections of the same number of pages are generally printed sheet work, the sections sometimes being produced on pairs of machines.

A useful reference publication on imposition for bound work is the BPIF's *Standard Folding Impositions* which contains 27 different impositions, in diagrammatic form with text commentary, varying from an eight-page section to 4 x 16-page sections.

The booklet sets out imposition schemes suitable for most all-buckle and combination folders, plus some for all-knife machines.

Choosing the method of working

Location of colour pages and a steady flow of printed sheets to the finishing department usually govern the method of working.

Sheet work helps to overcome the problem of having to keep a machine idle while waiting for the ink to dry on the first side before printing on the other. This is because the first imposition (say *outer*) can be lifted as soon as the first side has been printed, and the reverse side (say *inner*) need not be put on until the sheet is in a fit condition for backing-up. In half-sheet work, the machine may have to be kept standing before the sheet can be backed-up from the same plate, especially on short runs, and also where heavy solids have to be run.

For four-colour process work, printed both sides, the preferred method of working is mostly half-sheet work as only one set of plates is required - assuming, of course, that there is a press available, large enough to run the job, front-and-back together. If, however, the job in question involves a very short run, including, for example, printing heavy solids on difficult drying stock where the time spent waiting for wet work to dry could be considerable, then sheet work would be the preferred method of working.

An example where sheet work would always be chosen is when one-sided material is used: if half-sheet work was used in this instance, half of the job would be printed on the correct side of the material, and half on the 'unfinished' reverse side. A further example where sheet work would always be used is with the use of convertible/perfector presses, for example: a five-colour press printing 4:1 (four back one colour) or a six-colour press printing 5:1 (five back one colour) would automatically use sheet work as the job would be completed in one press pass.

Flat plans

When producing periodical publications such as magazines, journals and other structured format work, it is common practice for the publisher/customer to supply the printer with a *flat plan*, indicating the required pagination for editorial and advertising pages, or other matter: on the other hand, it can be used simply to indicate the sequence of copy or colour to be used on a publication such, as an annual report. As an alternative, a *production dummy* may be supplied as a made-up copy or series of folded sections. The dummy will normally be produced from plain paper folded to the finished bound size, with details marked-up of page numbers, copy, illustrations, numbers of colours, etc.

The publisher, designer or customer has the task of juggling and manipulating the overall contents into a coherent and cost-effective publication.

The printing of most periodical publications is produced under contract, where the printing company quotes various options of colour usage within certain cost parameters - for example, the contract for a monthly magazine of 96 pages plus cover may state that the publication is saddle stitched, and that the text is to be printed in 12 x 8-page sections, as 6 x 8 pages in four-colour process, and 6 x 8 pages in black only, split evenly throughout the publication.

Figure 7.5 illustrates a flat plan for the centre 16 pages of the text - ie - pages 41 to 56 colour process, blank areas indicating the pages planned in black only. A careful study of the flat plan will show that the outer section pages are planned to be in four-colour process, with the inner section in black.

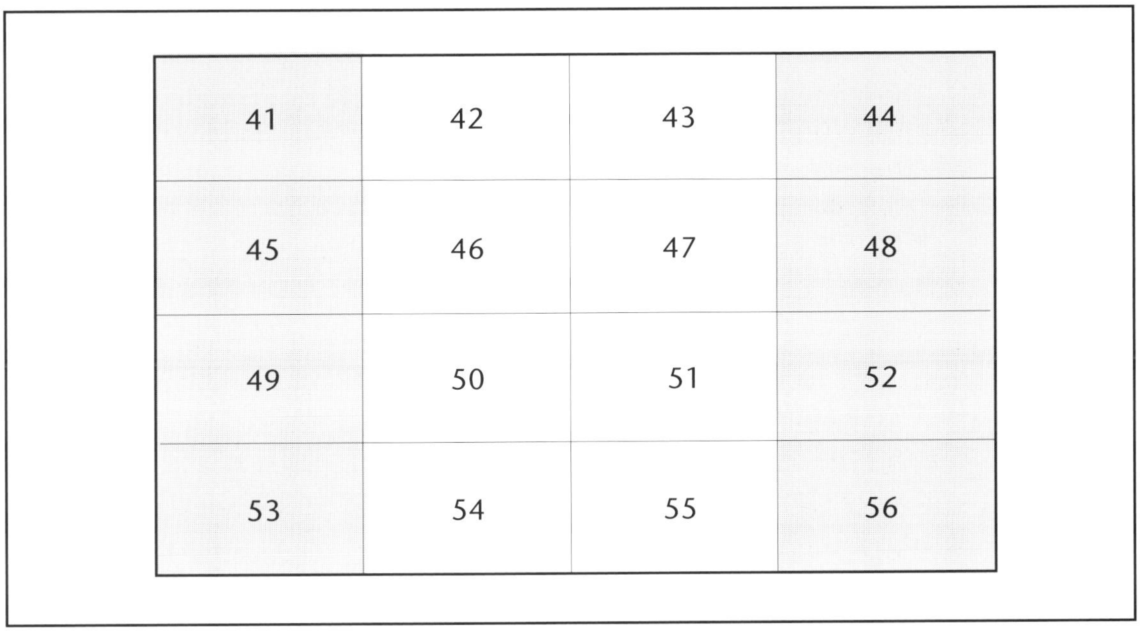

41	42	43	44
45	46	47	48
49	50	51	52
53	54	55	56

Figure 7.5: Flat plan covering colour fall of 16-page section - pages 41 to 56

Any deviations from the specification, including the use of colour outside the agreed flat plan, will incur extra costs. The flat plan is used by the printer as a guide to the colour fall of pages, which has a major impact on deciding the method of working.

Insetted and gathered forms of binding sections

Flat plans, or production dummies, need to take into account the method of binding for a publication. For periodical type work such as magazines, journals, catalogues and more general type work, such as brochures, parts lists and manuals, etc, there is the option of using *insetted sections* for *saddle stitched binding*, or *gathered sections* for mainly *adhesive or thread-sewn binding - see Figures 7.6 to 7.13*.

In bookwork-type work, where pagination is normally well over a hundred pages on bulky stock, gathered sections is the chosen method of binding: publications thicker than 7mm are unlikely to be suitable for insetted, saddle stitched work. The method of calculating the pagination (page numbers) in the two types of bound sections are quite different and are outlined below.

Insetted sections

*Figure*s 7.6 to 7.9 illustrate four examples of insetted bound work, covering 16-, 24-, 32- and 64-page publications, split up into eight-page sections as follows:

16-pages - 1-4 and 13-16, 5-12;
24-pages - 1-4 and 21-24, 5-8 and 17-20, 9-16;
32-pages - 1-4 and 29-32, 5-8 and 25-28, 9-12 and 21-24, 13-20;
64-pages - 1-4 and 61-64, 5-8 and 57-60, 9-12 and 53-56, 13-16 and 49-52,
17-20 and 45-48, 21-24 and 41-44, 25-28 and 37-40, 29-36.

The main rules of insetted imposition (where right angled folds are adopted) can be established from these examples, these are:

• *the sequence of pages run down to the 'half-way figure', and back again*
• *pairs of pages add up to one more than the total number of pages*
• *on each section the pages are linked across the fold, so that, for example, the first* four, *eight or 16 pages, etc, are 'paired' with the last four, eight or 16 pages respectively.*

Gathered sections

*Figure*s 7.10 to 7.13 illustrate four examples of gathered bound work - note the imposition rules as established for insetted work do not apply to gathered work. It can be seen from the figures that the pagination of gathered sections is much easier to establish - 1-8, 9-16, 17-24, 25-32, 33-40, 41-48, 49-56 and 57-64 respectively.

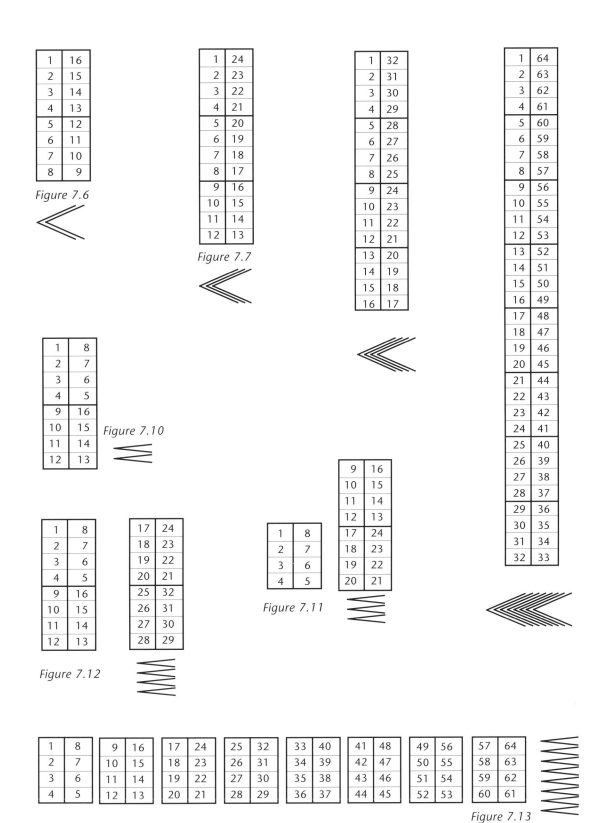

Figure 7.6

Figure 7.7

Figure 7.10

Figure 7.11

Figure 7.12

Figure 7.13

Figures 7.6 to 7.13: Examples of insetted and gathered section laydowns, covering 16-, 24-, 32- and 64-pages

Web-fed presses

Large-width web-fed presses

All conventional web-fed printing for periodicals, catalogues and newspapers is printed on perfectors, where the method of working and imposition terminology is fundamentally different to sheet-fed printing. Web perfectors always operate on a similar basis to sheet work, although instead of inner and outer impositions, web printing relates to *top side of web* and *bottom side of web*. A facility which is peculiar to web-fed printing is section/signature delivery as *collect* or *non-collect.*

Collect is where the finished folded product is insetted into one set as it is delivered off the press; whereas non-collect is where the delivery is split into two sets or separate folded sections.

Imposition for a web-fed press is governed largely by the folding equipment fitted at the end of the press. The main exceptions occur if a sheeter or a reel-up unit is fitted in place of a folder. In such cases a sheeter will cut the printed web into sheets which can be finished in the same way as sheet-fed jobs, while a reel-up unit will re-reel the web for further processing: alternatively, in the case of narrow-width presses, used extensively for business forms, the printed reels are re-reeled to be collated and made up on reel-fed collators.

There are many differences in the workings of web folders compared with sheet folders. In particular, while only one sheet of one section can be folded at a time in conventional sheet work, several webs (which may be of varying widths) containing different sets of pages can pass through the same web folder at the same time. Thus for example, a five-unit web-offset press, capable of printing 16 pages size A4, five colours on each side of the web at once, could produce a collect 32-page section.

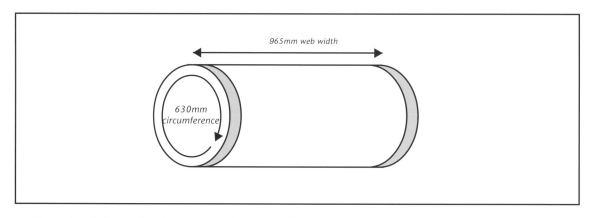

Figure 7.14: Example of a '16pp' web press with a 630mm circumference and 965mm maximum web width

This would be done by running one web through four perfecting units to produce 16 pages in four colours and running a second web through one unit to produce a further 16 pages in monochrome - *see Figure 7.15*. It is normally possible to arrange for the colour or monochrome pages to fall at the outside or towards the centre of the section as desired.

Figure 7.15 indicates the colour availability options on a five-unit, twin-web 16-page heat-set web-offset press, producing 32 pages as 2 x 16 pages in the option of four-colour process (1 x 8 pages) backing four colours (1 x 8 pages), and one colour (1 x 8 pages) backing one colour (1x 8 pages).

(A) represents the top side of the web, the equivalent of the outer form in sheet work printing, with (B) representing the bottom side of the web, the equivalent of the inner form in sheet fed printing.

Page	1	four-colour	(A)	Page	32	four-colour	(A)
Page	2	four-colour	(B)	Page	31	four-colour	(B)
Page	3	mono		Page	30	mono	
Page	4	mono		Page	29	mono	
Page	5	mono		Page	28	mono	
Page	6	mono		Page	27	mono	
Page	7	four-colour	(B)	Page	26	four-colour	(B)
Page	8	four-colour	(A)	Page	25	four-colour	(A)
Page	9	four-colour	(A)	Page	24	four-colour	(A)
Page	10	four-colour	(B)	Page	23	four-colour	(B)
Page	11	mono		Page	22	mono	
Page	12	mono		Page	21	mono	
Page	13	mono		Page	20	mono	
Page	14	mono		Page	19	mono	
Page	15	four-colour	(B)	Page	18	four-colour	(B)
Page	16	four-colour	(A)	Page	17	four-colour	(B)

Figure 7.15: Example of the laydown of pages for a five-unit, twin-web 16-page heat-set web-offset press, producing 32 pages as 2 x 16 pages, one in four-colour process and the other in mono

Narrow-width web-fed presses

Narrow-width web-fed presses are available in a wide selection of formats capable of producing a very comprehensive range of printing and print-related products.

The two main areas for this machinery are *continuous stationery/business forms* type products and *self-adhesive label* type products.

Continuous stationery and business forms can be either single part or multi-part, reel-to-reel or reel-to-pack. The machines can either be fixed-cylinder size presses or variable-cylinder size presses. On the larger size presses the most popular cylinder sizes are 24.75", 24", 23.5", 22", 20" and 17" circumferences.

There are also the less popular sizes of 28", 26" and 18". A 24" cylinder press would be able to produce forms in derivatives of 24" - that is to say 24", 12", 8", 6" and 4" deep: a 22" cylinder press could produce 22", 11", 7.33" and 5.5" deep forms. Cylinders widths are up from around 12" to 30" wide.

The main reason that business forms, and other related work, is still designated in imperial measurements (inches), is that computer stationery still relies on sprocket holes half an inch apart, and half-inch tear-off stubs.

Figure 7.16 illustrates a 26" wide x 24.75" circumference cylinder, printing six-up of an A4 form, 11.75" (297mm) x 210mm (8.25") - ie - 2 x 11.75" across the cylinder and 3 x 8.25" around the cylinder.

Narrow-width reel-fed self-adhesive type machines are normally available in up to 250mm widths. Labels are often delivered one-wide-to-view on the web. If printed more than one wide, a slitter unit is used to cut between the labels.

The number of, for example, labels, business forms or pages, which can be obtained from a narrow- or large-width web press, is determined by the number out from across and around the cylinder, as illustrated by *Figure 7.16*.

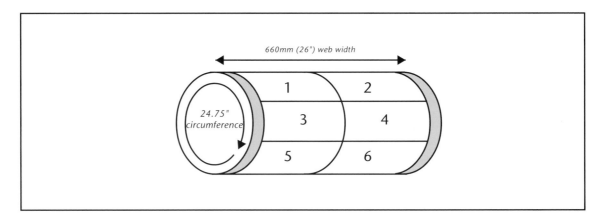

Figure 7.16: Example of a printing cylinder illustrating six-up A4 forms from one cylinder

Designers'/publishers' spreads and printers' spreads

The 'customer', when organising internally or externally, through a graphic designer or bureau, finished artwork, film or digital data to be sent to the printer, needs to consider having the 'hand-over work' prepared in *printers' pairs*, rather than designers' pairs; better still, if multiple pages such as four- or eight- pages are to be supplied, these should be in line with the imposition agreed and supplied by the printer, with appropriate margin allowances.

The figures below illustrate pairs of pages appropriate to an eight-page saddle stitched booklet as *designers'* and *printers' pairs.* When designing and laying out pages, the designer will naturally lay pages out in pairs, as they would appear in the final printed copy - ie - appearing double page spreads. The printer, however, lays out pages to the required imposition, so that when printed, folded and bound, the pages will fall into the correct sequence.

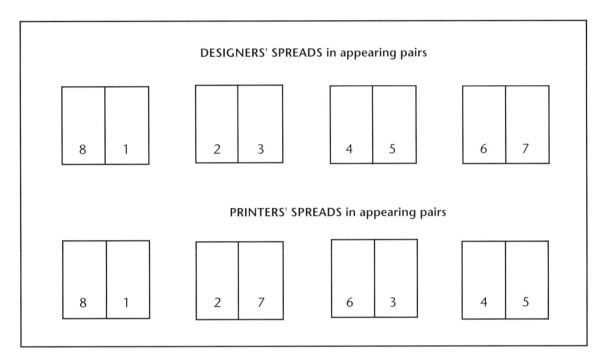

Figure 7.17: Example of designers' and printers' spreads - note two pairs are the same and two different between the two examples

Electronic imposition

As we move closer to an all-digital prepress workflow, electronic imposition becomes an increasingly key player in generating selected impositions and multiple-image laydowns within a Mac, PC or workstation environment.

Electronic imposition is the process of arranging electronic files into the selected planned format, and placement for subsequent outputting in analogue form - ie - planned film, or digital form - ie - direct-to-plate.

Briefly, the process consists of the operator calling up the electronic files created on DTP, or dedicated proprietary make-up software, alternatively importing them from other sources such as disk, cartridge, ISDN, modem, etc. The files and images are then placed into an electronic imposition software programme, where the operator selects the facilities required to create the desired finished result - accessing imposition, OPI and trapping options as required.

On some electronic imposition software, several versions have been developed to suit the circumstances and requirements of the user - eg - simple/light version or higher feature/heavyweight multi-licence client-server version.

Even when handling small files it will be necessary to undertake electronic imposition on a powerful Mac or PC: for large files, workstations will be required, configured either as stand-alone, or networked configured. Often the configuration will take the form of a workstation server handling all the heavy processing, run on a client/server basis link to less powerful and expensive Macs or PCs - *see Figure 2.2*.

Electronic imposition comes in two main options - stand-alone/standard and proprietary/bespoke:

- **Stand-alone/standard** - this option allows the user to install software, which will normally link into their current equipment and workflow with relative ease, based on a reasonably- sized self-contained prepress set-up.

- **Proprietary/bespoke** - this is a specialist option, where dedicated or proprietary electronic imposition/job management systems are built into an automated workflow system, or powerful alternatives are configured into the comprehensive networked workflow.

Margin allowances in imposition

When preparing an imposition allowances/margins must be included to ensure the job can be trimmed or cut-out to the required final size.

With electronic imposition this often means laying the images or pages out in such a manner that complete plate-ready film or computer-to-plate planning is carried out.

Apart from determining the margins around an image, an extra allowance is required for final trim - the standard is 3mm. In bound work, such as saddle stitched or thread sewn, this means 3mm on head, tail and foredge - ie - three sides only - *see Figure 7.19*. With perfect bound work, 3mm on all four edges is required - ie - head, tail, foredge and back: this is due to the backs being ground down to reduce the bound sections to single leaves and to aid adhesion of the glue applied to the backs - *see Figure 7.21*.

Non-bound work, such as labels, leaflets and posters require 3mm on all four sides - *see Figure 7.18*, although to ensure a smooth, sharp edge on all sides, double cuts need to be allowed for, as in *Figure 7.21*.

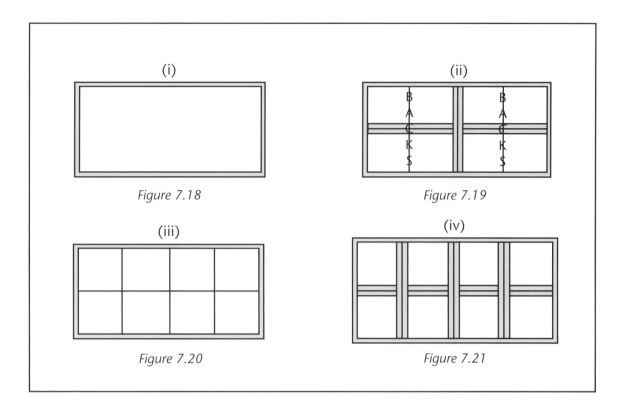

The single tint areas in the above figures represent a 3mm trim allowance.

Figure 7.18 represents an example of a single image, such as a label, leaflet or poster, with 3mm trim all round.

Figure 7.19 represents an example of a saddlestitched, or thread sewn portrait section, printed eight pages-to-view, with 3mm trim on head, tail and foredge only.

Figure 7.20 represents an example of a label or leaflet printed eight-up, with 3mm trim on outside edges only and single cuts to reduce to final size.

Figure 7.21 represents an example of a perfect bound portrait section, printed eight pages-to-view, with 3mm trim on head, tail, back and foredge; alternatively as a label or leaflet printed eight-up, with 3mm trim on outside edges and double cuts to reduce to final size.

Outside of the working size of a job which includes trim, the printer needs to make allowances for positioning the images precisely on the film or plate carrier (in the case of computer-to-plate) to be output on the laser printer (normally only used for text or relatively coarse halftone single-colour small offset type work), imagesetter or platesetter. These additional allowances will include gripper margin and colour bar (on colour work).

eight

PROOFING, PRINT SPECIFICATIONS AND STANDARDISATION

Proofing

Proofing is the term used to describe the making of a copy of the proposed printed image(s), or part of the printed image(s) to check content and/or reproduction quality before the job is printed.

Proofs have two main roles:

1 *for submission to the customer as a preview* for checking, amendment as necessary, and approval.

2 *for use as a working guide and aid for the printer*, establishing the requirements of the job, before proceeding to the next stage of the printing process, up to the final print run.

There is no such thing as an all-purpose proof - ie - one that suits every need and circumstance: therefore, the types of proof available are many and varied. They are produced in a specific form, at a particular time in the printing cycle to allow the customer and the printer to judge at that stage if the indicated result is going to be satisfactory.

In the initial stages of a job, proofs such as digital black-and-white laser proofs, or conventionally generated proofs such as galley, page and ozalid proofs, are used for checking the accuracy and position of the printed elements on a page. Later, quality standards and colour registration are checked by the production of a wide variety of digital- and analogue-based colour proofs. The objective is to produce a proof which is appropriate at each stage of the prepress workflow.

Monochrome/spot colour proofs

Digital route

With the vast majority of prepress work now being carried out on DTP-driven front-ends, the *black-and-white laser printer* is now the most popular means of producing monochrome and colour split proofs.

Laser printers, which are connected to DTP/workstation terminals, have advanced considerably since they were first introduced as an A4 format size with output resolution of 300dpi: they are now available in 600, 1200 and 1800 dpi up to A3 plus and above. The operator, having created and viewed the image(s) required on a WYSIWYG terminal/monitor, will instruct the printer to print out the number of copies x number of pages required, etc.

If colour splits are required, the normal procedure would be for the operator to carry this out on a DTP software program, so that the proofs can be generated as separate colour overlay-type sheets with a master composite proof, which could be marked-up with highlighter for colour split as an alternative.

If a larger proof size than is available from the laser printer is required, then large format printer/plotters can be used which are available in up to B1 size and above - this system is particularly suitable for proofing out electronically imposed signatures for magazines and other bound publications, or multiple-image laydowns such as for sheet-fed flat labels or cartons. An alternative is to produce large size proofs on a small format printer by 'tiling', where the overall image is created in 'tiles', or segments, which when butted together in the correct position, make up the full montaged proof.

Traditional route

Some printers, especially specialist book and small circulation magazine printers, are still working, at least in part, using traditional paper make-up procedures - *see Figure 2.1* and *page 102*.

Page proofs are generally proofed using a photocopier in up to A3+ spreads, allowing for the addition of trim and other printers' marks.

When larger format proofs are required, working from planned and imposed film, diazo/ozalid dyeline proofs are commonly used.

Diazo/ozalid (dyeline) proofing systems, similar to those used for producing drawing office plans and blueprints, may still be used to produce proofs of film matter consisting of line and halftone work of a high quality. The light-sensitive compounds of the copying paper when processed are diazonium salts and stabilisers which decompose, becoming inert and colourless when exposed to ultra-violet light, through using a positive-working paper, with the opposite result occurring with negative-working paper.

Development in ammonia vapour causes a reaction giving a strong visible image. A modern equivalent of the ozalid which avoids the ammonia processing is DuPont's 'Dylux' proofing system, which requires no processing and produces a high quality monochrome proof. It is used extensively in newspapers, catalogues and magazines. The system is used with a variety of film, including colour separations, black-and-white line or halftone. It can be used with positive or negative film. The imposed film assembly is contacted face-to-face with the Dylux paper and exposed using a special filter in a conventional vacuum frame. The image area is formed in blue or black.

Overlay film proofs

Overlay film colour proofs are created by superimposing exposed and processed emulsion overlays. The benefit of their use lies in the ability to easily separate the films again into separate colours for comparison: in some ways they can equate to a progressive film proof.

An example of this type of proof is DuPont's 'Cromacheck', which is a dry proofing system for negative, line and halftone coloured film laminates, in four-colour process colours, plus a range of other colours, bronze, silver and gold. The coloured film is exposed to the negative film in an exposure frame, producing the desired result without further processing. It is produced, as most overlay proof systems are, as a layout and register proof. The proof is used as a check on film assembly work, showing the exact positions of illustrations, colour areas and text. 3M 'Color Key' and Agfa 'Copycolor' are also examples of overlay film proofs with a finished product similar to that of 'Cromacheck'.

Colour proofs

Pre-production-run colour proofs are produced to represent and equate as closely as possible to the finished printed result. Colour proofing is now accepted as part of the control process essential in producing a predictable print quality.

Digital colour proofing systems

A great deal of the lower-cost DTP proofing options fall into the *visual proof type - see page 132,* as colour rendition can only be described as fair: where for example, the greens are 'greenish' and the browns are 'brownish' - ie - colours are represented only on a broad basis. In colour rendition terms, it is really more accurate to refer to this type of product as a *colour visual,* rather than a visual proof, although it is used frequently on this basis for short-run general commercial printing of leaflets, booklets, etc.

Medium- to higher-cost proofing systems tend to fall into the *target* and *contract type* proofs, where the systems lend themselves to controllable and accurate colour rendition. It is only when a high quality, carefully calibrated proofing system is used, incorporating some means of colour profiling and colour management, that the proof result can accurately reflect and replicate the required high quality colour printed result.

The different types of technology used for producing digital colour proofs include the following - dye sublimation, laser copier/printers, thermal wax and inkjet in its various forms:

Dye sublimation produces a high sheen, continuous tone, photographic type of proof. It operates by the application of heat, generated through a thermal print head, consisting of thousands of minute heated heads, acting upon yellow, magenta, cyan and black coloured laminates: as the laminates are heated, the coloured dye sublimates/vaporises onto the paper carrier to form the proof.

Examples of dye sublimation proofing systems are DuPont Cromalin '4Cast', Imation/3M 'Rainbow' and Kodak 'DCP 9000'.

Dye sublimation is an increasingly popular option for medium-cost colour proofs, falling mainly into the target proof quality range; although depending on the quality of the system, along with the calibration set-up and accuracy, it also covers the full range from colour visual to contract proof.

Colour laser works through the use of a charged photoreceptive drum or belt, used in conjunction with a laser light, which selectively dissipates the charge in the non-image areas; the coloured toners contained in four separate cartridges of yellow, magenta, cyan and black are attracted onto the drum or belt in the still-charged image areas, which are then transferred and fused onto the paper carrier. Colour laser printers are basically colour copiers with a RIP interface which allows the machines to produce digital prints, rather than copies of a hard copy original, receiving instructions from an onsite or remote controlled computer network.

Examples of colour laser machines include the wide range covered by Canon, Hewlett-Packard, Kodak, Xerox and Ricoh, etc. Colour laser printers are a popular option for low-cost colour visuals.

Dry laser technology is used on the high quality Kodak 'Approval' system, through transferring the laser-exposed image carrying coloured laminate sheets onto a donor sheet, then onto actual production paper stock to produce the proof: it is a form of thermal dye sublimation which requires no further processing. The system produces a high quality, halftone digital proof, much favoured by many print-buyers and printers, so avoiding the resistance encountered with most digital proofs which do not have the conventional halftone structure. The Optronics 'IntelliProof' is another high quality laser-based system which produces halftone screen digital colour proofs; Screen's 'TrueRite' is a further example.

Thermal wax/thermal transfer creates the printed image by heating coloured wax panels and forming them into minute wax dots which fuse onto the paper: four passes for yellow, magenta, cyan and black colours are required to produce the full colour proof. Examples of thermal wax/thermal transfer printers include Tektronix 'Phaser II PXe, II Pxi, 200e and 200i', and Agfa 'Duoproof'.

Inkjet printers fall into two types - *liquid* and *solid (or phase change)*. Liquid inkjet can then be further broken down into *drop-on-demand* and *continuous flow:*

Drop-on-demand breaks down into two further types - *piezo* which operates on the basis of a pump action to force droplets of ink onto the paper, and *thermal jet* or *bubble jet* which, through swift alternate heating and cooling, creates a gas bubble which forces ink out as directed droplets again onto the paper to form the proof.

Continuous flow operates by the printing head continuously directing ink droplets towards the paper carrier: the ink droplets are given an electric charge, so that the image-forming droplets are directed onto the proof paper, with the unwanted/non-image area droplets deflected away into a recycling reservoir. Four nozzle heads create the four process colours.

Solid inkjet printers operate through the use of solid ink sticks of yellow, magenta, cyan and black which change to a liquid state when heated: the liquid ink jets are then directed onto the proof paper and as the ink comes into contact with the paper, it returns to its original solid state.

A variation of the solid wax technology is the Polaroid 'DryJet', which works from a system of multi-density, eight CMYK-based wax nugget colorants which are heated to a liquid state and held within ink wells: the colorants are then sprayed through two, multi-nozzled inkjet heads with the ink solidifying on contact with the paper.

Fuji has developed a digital version of its analogue-based' ColorArt' proof, under the name 'ColorArt FirstProof', which uses a proprietary system of *thin layer thermal transfer/thermo-autochrome*, with four toner layers of yellow, magenta, cyan and black.

These toners are coated onto a base and exposed to a thermal print head, transferring the print image coloured toner onto a donor material and then the actual proof material - in some ways the system combines solid inkjet with drop-on-demand, through the use of piezo-electric heads generating the ink droplets.

Large-format colour printers operate mainly using an inkjet process and have proved popular for short-run posters and for proofing large format colour images.

Two-in-one digital proofing systems

The reasoning behind the two-in-one proofing machines is to provide simplicity and compactness in one desktop proofing machine. The machine offers a combination of thermal wax and dye sublimation options where the user can produce a thermal wax *initial colour visual cum layout and content type proof*, followed by a higher quality photographic effect continuous tone dye sublimation proof, which falls into the *target proof range* - a combination which suits a great deal of the work undertaken by small- to medium-sized general commercial printers. Examples of such machines are: Agfa 'Duoproof', Fargo 'Pictura' 310e' and Seiko 'ColorPoint 835PS'.

Most digital proofing systems produce continuous tone proofs, but a few systems have been developed which produce halftone digital proofs.

DTP-based colour proofing systems are linked via a RIP controller to the AppleMac, PC or workstation front-end, along with their own or proprietary colour profile and control software, enabling adjustment and fine tuning to suit the particular requirements of any job. To ensure the highest level control of the digital proofing process, it is important that exactly the same digital file and RIP is used to produce the proof and final print.

It is generally accepted an unintentional benefit of digital over conventional proofing that, through highly developed software, incorporating flexible profiling and colour tables, digital proofs can replicate the desired proof and print match much closer for gravure, screen, flexo and letterpress printing processes than their analogue counterparts. DuPont claims particular success in this area with the wide adoption of the Digital Cromalin in cold-set web-offset newspapers and rotogravure-printed catalogues. Increasingly, calibrated digital proofs will also be used for offset litho printing, in order to achieve a totally digital workflow from receipt of data through to press.

Further advantages of digital proofing are that it tends to be less expensive - both in terms of material and labour - than analogue, while changes to a digital proof can be made more quickly, also resulting in less expense, as films do not have to be regenerated.

Digital proofing systems are now being developed to incorporate Hexachrome six-colour system and HiFi colour.

Soft proofs

Soft proofing is a system of using a carefully colour calibrated monitor as the proofing medium, without producing an analogue or digital hard copy proof.

Soft proofing has found difficulty in establishing a place in the array of proofing systems now available, due mainly to the difficulty of equating transmitted colours on the colour monitor with those of a printed result.

The soft proofing colour monitors, however, lend themselves to a remote colour proofing facility, so giving a reasonable presentation of how the printed result will appear.

Soft proofing can, of course, be used as part of an overall proofing sequence, where the parameters of the proof are approved on the screen, with a hard proof only taken as final confirmation. ColorSync software, part of the Mac operating system, is an industry-standard colour management technology that aims to deliver consistent and reliable rendering on the monitor, the proof and the printed sheet. High quality monitors and controlled ambient lighting conditions for viewing are also important in improving the perception of the resultant images.

Many of the large manufacturers of prepress equipment have developed remote colour proofing links or interfaces with their own and other suppliers' equipment - linking up, for example, a workstation to a colour scanner to give pre-scan and post-scan viewing, and then to a digital proofing system.

An interesting development related to soft proofing is in the area of video/computer links where, for example, one Mac user can link with another user, through Apple Quick Time Conferencing *(QTC)*; transferring work from one system to the other, or communicating through video conferencing on the small on-screen window. Although the screen resolution of most monitors is relatively low, the system does present the possibility of what has been termed *whiteboarding*, where the recipient can mark-up/annotate the proof, so ensuring very swift turnaround of at least positional and content issues related to the proof.

Remote proofing is gaining momentum in the industry, where printers and/or repro houses are linking up with major clients by ISDN. Colour jobs are downloaded and viewed on digital proofing systems at each site, which have been calibrated to ensure uniformity and consistency between the two parties. Barco and Radius have developed a series of high quality calibrated monitors suitable for good rendition remote control soft proofing in such circumstances.

Conventional colour proofing systems

It should be noted that although much prepress currently centres around a DTP/digitally driven front-end, the workflow and working practices frequently revert to film output and conventional platemaking processes. This results in a situation where conventional analogue/film-based proofing systems are still much in demand, especially at the high quality end of colour proofing - ie - *target* and *contract proofs - see page 132.*

There are two main types of analogue-based proofs which are still extremely popular - photomechanical, often referred to as *dry proofs,* and *wet proofs* which are generated from printing plates.

Photomechanical proofs

Photomechanical proofs are produced from four-colour process separated films and do not require the use of printing plates in their production. There is now a wide range of photomechanical colour proofs starting from the initial, low-entry level desktop machines to the large format A1 machines: two different processes are used, one based on toner being applied to the base sheet and one on coloured foils.

Toner-based

The original Cromalin system, still widely used, employs colour toners and is based on photopolymerisation. Photopolymers are substances which, when excited by light energy, are transferred from a monomer into a polymer state. Their chemical and physical properties usually change as a result. In the Cromalin system the monomer is a tacky substance. Exposure to an ultra-violet light source converts it into a polymer, which is no longer tacky. If this material is exposed under a colour separation film, the unexposed sections remain tacky and, therefore, accept the coloured toner during the toning process.

The proof is composed of a base, paper or board sheet, the laminates to which the toner adheres to in the image areas, and a protective top layer. The laminates are bonded onto the base material, exposed to UV light, and exposed in sequence to give the full colour result with a final protective top clear laminate sheet.

Coloured foil-based

This entails a system where coloured foils, one for each of the four process colours, are transferred onto a base sheet by heat and pressure in a laminator. A common processing sequence is where the colour foils are exposed in turn through the colour-separated film in a contact frame with a UV light source: each colour foil, after it has been exposed, is peeled away from the base paper, leaving a colour image of the film separation, building up for all four colours.

Examples of this type of analogue proof are Agfa 'PressMatch Dry and 'Agfaproof', DuPont 'EuroSprint', Fuji 'ColorArt', Konica 'Konsensus' and 3M 'Matchprint'.

Photomechanical proofs are increasingly becoming available as dry processing systems without any need for a water supply or chemical processing unit.

Wet proofs

The traditional method of producing colour proofs is by the use of printing inks and printing plates on a specialist flatbed proofing press or even a production press. Wet proofs produced on flatbed proofing presses are often favoured by printers because the proofs have similar physical printing properties to the final printed result.

Flatbed proofing presses, as the name implies, are flatbed in construction and are available in single-, two- and four-colour configurations, in either approximately B2 or B1 printing size. Machine speeds are very slow as most machines are hand-fed one sheet at a time. The machine consists of the flat printing bed on which the printing plates are clamped - it is fitted with a cooling unit which keeps an even temperature over the entire surface - a paper/board feed with loaded grippers for holding the sheets in position, a blanket cylinder, an inking unit and a dampening unit.

The most recent flatbed proofing presses are fitted with automatic wash systems and have computerised inking facilities which electronically measure colour bars to assess the amount of ink to release. Flatbed wet proofs have the advantage of being printed on the correct substrate; also it is possible to produce progressive proofs which are invaluable to the printer - *see following page*.

Special colours, such as the PANTONE matching system, are easy to incorporate on a wet proof, and it is also possible to produce backed-up proofs. Wet proofs are particularly popular where ten, 20 or 50 sets of proofs are required, since the cost per copy becomes much more favourable compared with dry, or digital proofs.

Presentation of proofs

Apart from the production of different types of proof for varying purposes, the make-up and presentation of proofs also can vary considerably as follows:

- **Single proof** - proof produced on its own: these would normally be produced by digital methods such as dye sublimation or inkjet, alternatively as a photo-mechanical proof.

- **Backed-up proofs** - proofs which are printed on both sides, and normally on the job stock: these would normally be produced on flatbed proofing presses, or on digital colour printer, such as a Xeikon machine - *see Chapter 10, 'Computer-to-print and beyond'*.

- **Imposed page/multiple-image proofs** - proofs to show the laydown of pages/multiple-images in the correct position as printed: if produced on a flatbed proofing press and approved without correction or amendment, they can then be regarded also as press plates without the need for remaking plates for the machine. Alternatively, a large digital printer/proofer will be used.

- **Scatter proofs** - proofs which do not have the printed matter imposed in a particular position on the proof sheets. This type of proof is often used in magazines, brochures and catalogues, where the publication is a mixture of mono-chrome and four-colour work, and where all the coloured pictures are randomly arranged or *scattered* over the full sheet area for proofing.

It is a very cost-effective way of proofing a large number of colour images/pages, with the customer approving the pictures in the overall flat sheet, or individually as cut-out and pasted-up page by page on a dummy of the magazine. Again the proofs would be produced on a flatbed proofing press or a digital proofing system.

- **Progressive proofs** - these are, as the name suggests, a progressive combination of printed proofs in a particular colour sequence. A typical progressive proof of four-colour process sequence is as follows: first cyan on its own followed by yellow on its own, then cyan and yellow combined; magenta on its own, then cyan, yellow and magenta combined; finally black on its own then cyan, yellow, magenta and black combined to show the final printed result. This type of proof is usually produced on the job stock on flatbed proofing presses, or occasionally on production presses, and is highly regarded by printers as a quality control and check on ink weights, trapping, registration, colour guide and so on, as separate and combined process colours. Due to the high cost of producing progressive proofs and the decline in the use of specialist proofing presses they are only used on a limited basis. It is interesting to note, as previously stated, that digital proofing systems have now been developed, such as Kodak 'Approval' and Polaroid 'Dryjet', which can be produced on different job stocks: also that an overlay film system can be used to produce a *visual-type progressive*.

- **Production proofs** - these are the *ultimate proof,* as they are produced on the production press on which the job is going to be printed: all other types of proofs at best can only be an approximation of the variables encountered in the printing of a job. One solution to the high cost and time spent on producing separate production proofs is to arrange for the print customer to *pass on press*, having previously approved a range of proofs reflecting position, registration and general colour quality. The job in question is made-ready and approved against the previous proofs and/or originals by the printer and line managers, with the customer then approving and agreeing for the production run to start. This arrangement is much more practical when the section or job in question can be completed in one press pass - for example, on a four-unit sheet- or web-fed press.

Proofing, it must be remembered, is a means to an end, not an end in itself.

It is unhelpful and bad practice to produce a so-called 'perfect proof', which is pin sharp with a range and density of colours which cannot be produced by the relevant printing process. The proof should reflect what is possible and achievable, bearing in mind the limitations of four-colour process, with or without special colours. The colour proof is an *intermediate stage,* between the prepress arrangement of the elements of a job, and the finished printed result.

To ensure quality control is maintained and to bring more objective standards to printing - which has essentially been a subjective process - it is necessary to establish guidelines, specifications and controls to monitor and assess standards at every stage of the printing reproduction process: working with 'standard' ink densities, screen angles, dot gain, etc, on the press, assists in the calibration of proofing systems and monitors. In recent years there has been a move to clarify the terminology and understanding of the purpose of different types of proofs: four major areas have been identified, and these are as follows:

- **Visual proof** (also referred to as colour visual) - such as DTP thermal, laser or inkjet proof, usually produced by a graphic designer or client, to indicate the overall concept and design required in the finished product.

- **Typographic** (also referred to as positional or content) proof - such as an ozalid, dylux, laser proof or bromide, which is produced to enable the client to check the typesetting, position of graphics and imposition of pages at the initial stages of a job or just before the platemaking stage.

- **Target proof** - such as Cromalin - analogue or digital, Matchprint and Agfa-proof, or wet proofs, which are produced to represent as closely as possible the expected printed result, conveying press characteristics such as dot gain and colour accuracy.

- **Contract proof** - such as 'pass on press' pull or approved target proof, which is 'signed off' by the customer for the machine printer to match and use as the master pass sheet.

A 'target' or 'contract' proof should reflect what is possible when printed on a production printing press, with feedback having taken place from the beginning between the customer, repro area, proofer and printer, to get the best out of the originals and the printing press.

Print specifications and standardisation

In the past it has been considered reasonable that a set of plates would give a different result when printed on different presses, but would otherwise, under identical conditions on the same substrate, produce the desired predictable result. With the growth of multi-coloured printing and the developments and advances in printing presses and the processes, there has been an increasing drive to make the finished product more predictable by the establishment of agreed parameters of print specifications. There are many variables which affect the printed result, including *graphic repro, plates, paper/board, ink, different printing processes* and the *human element* - all of which impact on the final printed job: in the case of offset litho, fount solution, type and shore hardness of the blanket are other considerations.

A possible standard reproduction print specification for a magazine to be printed by heat-set web-offset is as follows:

1 *Film required* - positive film to be 0.004" wrong-reading emulsion-side up. All hard dot film with no strip-ins or patch-ups.

2 *Screen ruling/frequency* - 47 lines per cm.

3 *Screen angles* - black 15°, magenta 45°, cyan 75°, yellow 90°.

4 *Film identification* - all films to be marked for colour.

5 *Halftone range* - on coated stock- highlight 5%, shadow 90% maximum.

6 *Proofing sequence* - cyan, magenta, yellow, black.

7 *Ink density* - yellow 0.90, magenta 1.3, cyan 1.3, black 1.8. Tolerance +/- 0.10. The above readings measured on an appropriate densitometer.

8 *Printing control strips* - all proofs and progressives must carry colour control targets, positioned across the line of inking. These must be included on all proofs. Only original strips supplied by the manufacturer to be used.

9 *Dot gain* - this must be allowed for during the reproduction and proofing stages. The recommended readings are as follows: Gretag CSM2 40% tone to record 18%, 80% tone to record 12%. Tolerance +/- 2% - *see Figure 8.1.*

10 *Undercolour removal* - 260-300% lower and upper limits.

It should be noted that the above represents only one particular type of reproduction print specification and that different specifications need to be drawn up to address the many variables applicable to each circumstance, or group of circumstances.

A comprehensive list and explanation of print specifications is included in the International Federation of Periodical Press *(FIPP)* publications *'Specifications for European Offset Printing of Periodicals'* and *'Guidelines for the Reproduction of Halftone Separations and Pre-proofs for Gravure Magazines in Europe'.*

Colour control bars or strips

Colour bars or colour strips allow accurate and meaningful quality control comparisons to be made between colour proofs and the printed sheet. They permit individual colours to be densitometrically measured; in the actual printing process, the process colours are superimposed and, therefore, cannot be measured separately. Colour strips or bars are available from many different sources including Gretag, GATF, Hartmann, FOGRA and Brunner.

GATF allows a simple method of detecting changes such as dot gain, dot loss (sharpening), lateral and circumferential slur, and doubling by visual inspection without the use of the densitometer.

FOGRA permits visual and instrumental control of colour strips whereas Gretag, Hartmann and Brunner require the use of a densitometer to establish measured values.

Measuring the colour control strips of a proof and the printed result with a densitometer introduces the element of *objectivity* which is essential to print standardisation. Density and dot gain are two of the most important areas which must be controlled and taken account of when predicting the final printed result.

Colour control bars increasingly feature on comprehensive electronic imposition software - *see page 119*. Also, on DK&A 'INposition v2.0' for example, a further feature is automatic press calibration with screening densitometer linked into the GATF colour control bars.

Figure 8.1 shows the DuPont Eurostandard Cromalin test forme which provides colour matching elements for both analogue and digital proofing workflow. It can also be used to compare analogue and digital proofs made from films and electronic data. A test forme is available in an analogue version as colour separated film, or as an electronic data file, for use on imagesetters and colour recorder systems.

After exposure and platemaking, the test forme, in conjunction with the appropriate plate exposure test target, can be printed to give visual and measurable information on overall performance - notably dot gain, ink film thickness (density) and colour values.

This practice of calibration, using a standard range of printed images, is often referred to as *fingerprinting printing presses*, where the recorded values referred to above, are compared to previous records and standards. Deviations outside the established optimum setting standards are noted, with steps being taken to ensure the print quality is maintained at the required level.

It can also be used to compare analogue and digital proofs made from films and electronic data. Analogue and digital control strips are also available to ensure a good match between the proof and printed result.

Digital Cromalin control strip. The main difference from the analogue strip is that it includes three alignment squares or patches to monitor black (**k**), cyan (**c**), magenta (**m**) and yellow (**y**) fit/register. Other patches such as the grey balance, solid and dot percentage, can be used for visual assessment when compared with the printed sheet or measured to give comparative readings.

Analogue Cromalin control strip. This has been designed so that the analogue and digital strips can be laid side by side for general comparison if required, such as where work has been initially digitally proofed, followed by a film-based proof and/ or the printed result. Visual checks are again used, especially exposure, where only the correct exposure results in the reproduction of the DuPont logo - *see Figure 8.2*.

Control strips are now available in digital proofing systems - eg - Scitex 'Iris/ Realist' inkjet proofers have a System Brunner control strip built in; Imation/3M 'Rainbow' a Gretag control strip.

Figure 8.1: DuPont Eurostandard Cromalin test forme suitable for both analogue and digital use

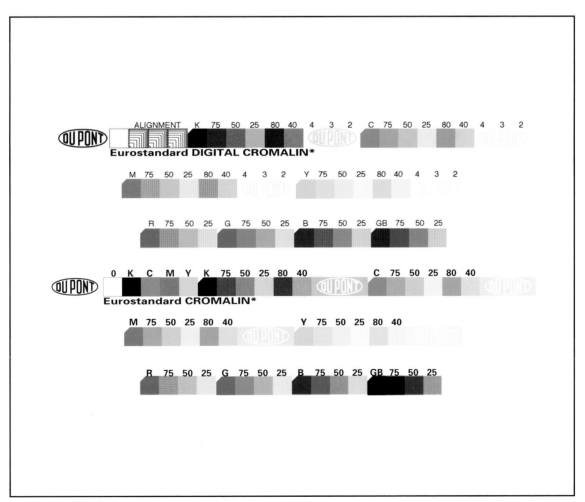

Figure 8.2: DuPont analogue and digital control strip

Dot gain

Dot gain (dot loss is also possible but less common) takes place at almost every stage in the printing/reproduction process. From the time each dot is first created from a contact screen or digitally, it is liable to change in size in contacting or platemaking. The aim at all stages is to keep the change to a minimum and on the whole this is done, though with more success in the film stages than in the platemaking and printing stages, with conventional reproduction techniques.

However, once plates are made and inked, dot gain is much more difficult to control for then the dot size will vary with the type of paper or board surface, the ink, the press design and condition, the press room conditions, press settings and the machine manager's skills plus, in the case of offset litho, the blanket and damping solution - although it must be emphasised that dot gain occurs in all printing processes.

Dot gain can be considered from two aspects - the *physical* and the *optical*.

• **Physical dot gain** covers any uncontrolled change that takes place between the creation of the first dot and the platemaking, as well as the uncontrollable changes on press when the fluid ink is subjected to pressure in the press 'nip'.

• **Optical dot gain** is caused by the scatter of reflected light which occur when viewing the printed image. A gloss, or very white paper reflects more light back to the eye around each dot, and this has the effect of making the dot appear smaller than it really is: conversely, a matt or dull paper will make the dot seem larger. The paper or board used also affects the physical dot gain as a poorer quality/uncoated material will not allow as sharp a dot as a high quality one. It therefore follows that the proofing material should match the production substrate if further elements of dot gain are to be avoided.

A further point to note is that dot gain is affected by screen frequency in that dot gain increases in relation to the overall perimeter area of dots, rather than linear measurement - ie - the finer the screen frequency, the greater the number of dots present, and therefore the higher the overall peripheral area of the dots, resulting in higher overall dot gain.

Total dot gain, a combination of physical and optical gain, can be as high as 30% in the midtone (50%) dot areas, so it is obvious that, without a considerable degree of standardisation, no consistency can be achieved.

Every press has its own dot gain characteristics: whilst other print variables such as ink trapping and solid density can be controlled on the press, dot gain is more difficult to control. With the dot gain controlled as far as possible for a particular press, the printer should seek the remedy for any unexpected dot gain variances at the repro stage, rather than by further attempting to change the characteristics of the press.

To assist this process, it is possible to set up templates in the prepress system for each of the designated printing characteristics. However, if flexibility is required to switch printing from one press to another, then press characteristics would need to be similar for the desired result to be achieved, or another set of plates would be required. When proofing on a proofing press, the exposure during platemaking should be controlled to produce proofing plates with a dot that will print the same size when proofing as the result on the production press: additionally, proofing inks can be formulated to give a dot gain comparable to that given by the final production inks.

Whether printing plates are produced through an entirely digital- or analogue-based system, dot gain must be built in to whatever system is being used. To be truly effective, proofing systems need to allow for and/or simulate the dot gain experienced by printing presses.

Conventional, film-based systems, seek the remedy to dot gain by generating film which allows for the identified dot gain of a press - eg - if the dot gain for a press is assessed at 10%, then the film would be produced with just over a 90% dot, so resulting in an overall 100% printed dot

Digital proofing systems have to overcome the problem in a different way as no film is used, also a different randomised screening method is normally used, resulting in a continuous tone effect. The digital proofing system needs to have the ability to simulate dot gain through software adjustment, and setting facilities, resident on the machine.

Figure 8.3 illustrates how even a small change in dot size changes the overall printed result compared to the desired result - note conventional halftone dots have been used in this example. The centre illustration represents the *reference standard,* - ie - agreed closest reproduction to the values of the original. All other illustrations are reproduced with varying amendments to the magenta dot. The illustration in the top left hand corner is reproduced with a 2% dot loss; top right hand corner with a 2% dot gain; bottom left hand corner with a 4% dot loss and bottom right hand corner with a 4% dot gain.

The wider band of +/- 4% often represents the tolerance band for standardised offset printing, whereas the +/- 2% tolerance is being adopted by more and more printing companies and print buyers in a drive towards higher quality and more controlled printing standards. Dot gain tolerances are given as +/- 2% in the print specification example for a heat-set web offset magazine on *page 133.*

137

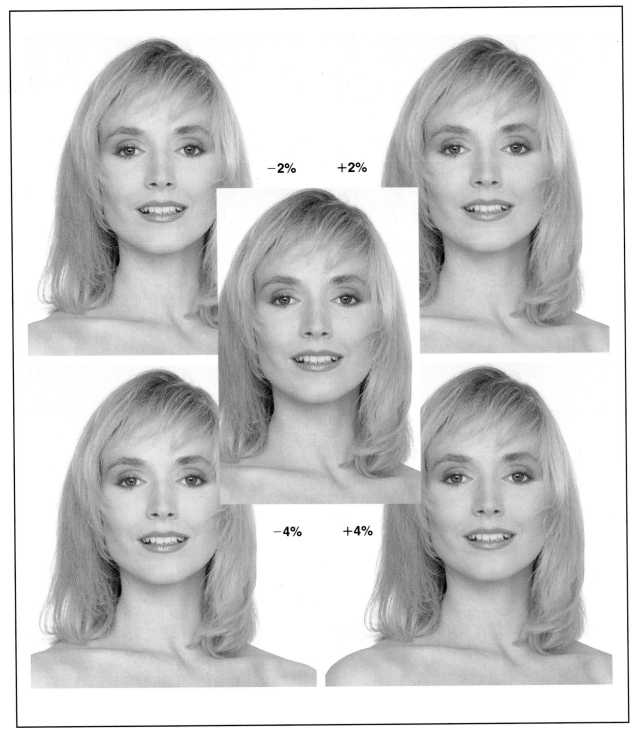

−2%   +2%

−4%   +4%

Figure 8.3: Effect of dot loss and dot gain on the printed result

Reproduced by courtesy of Bespoke Publications Ltd and DuPont (UK) Ltd from Chapter five, Colour Proofing, *of the series* 'Colour Concepts'

Colour profiles and calibration

A colour profile is the recording of the particular characteristics related to a colour device. The accepted standard for drawing up colour profiles is the International Colour Consortium *(ICC)*. ICC structured colour profiles are written by manufacturers of colour output devices to describe the characteristics of their equipment: these colour profiles represent the ideal standard scenario, but changes over time and circumstance do occur, so additional calibration and adjustment needs to be undertaken to cover the wide range of circumstances that can occur.

Often desktop proofing systems are bundled with colour profiles and colour management system. It should be noted that colour management systems cannot change the capabilities of the selected output device, so the standard of the colour reproduced is dependent on the quality, accuracy and consistency of the colour management system and output device combined - *see colour management systems* on *page 67*.

The important issue is to be able to validate a proof's ability to match the printed result consistently and to the standard expected with colour profiles and calibration facilities helping to achieve this.

nine

OUTPUT MEDIA AND PREPARATION OF PRINTING SURFACES

Output media, with the development of digital systems, can now take many forms, including film and plate imagesetting; laser and other technology printers; computer-to-plate systems; colour proofing systems and digital printing systems. The same digital information can also be 'repurposed' for other multi-media applications to provide outputs to CD-ROM, the Internet or web sites, video and slides for presentations.

This chapter will focus on imagesetters and laser printers, along with computer-to-plate systems, plus related areas.

Chapter 8, 'Proofing, print specifications and standardisation' covered colour proofing systems, including the main range of digital printing technologies used in the industry: *Chapter 10, 'Computer-to-print and beyond'* covers an outline of digital printing systems.

The brief history of mechanised output media can be traced back to hot-metal machines, which were introduced in the late 19th century, in the form of the Linotype and Monotype machine to replace the slow and laborious hand setting of individual metal characters from a specially arranged type case.

The Linotype machine, and its 'sister' machine, the Intertype, produced solid lines or slugs of typematter, whereas the Monotype system produced single pieces/characters of relief type, similar to the hand-set typematter used since movable type was first introduced in the mid 1500s.

All the output media in terms of typesetting up until the latter part of the 20th century were developed to address the needs of the dominant printing process - ie - letterpress, with the other printing processes having to adapt to the situation that all major output media systems were targeted at relief image letterpress printing: their main option was to take hard printed copies of the relief type and use these for reproduction.

It was not until the 1950s and 1960s that photographic means of generating typematter began to develop in a commercial way, with the fast development of offset lithography being the main driving force.

Phototypesetters

Phototypesetting was the first specially devised method of cold composition to follow hot-metal setting. Hot-metal setting was ideally suited to flatbed letterpress, but not to offset lithography which required a flat photographic-type finish on paper or clear film.

The answer was the development of phototypesetting where, instead of the system pumping molten metal into a recessed or engraved matrix and allowing it to solidify into metal type, the melting pot mechanism was replaced by an *exposure unit* and the letter matrices by negative masters. As light was shone through a matrix an 'opposite' positive image was exposed onto the photographic bromide paper or film. Negative masters were available in many forms, depending on the system, either in strip, concentric disc or drum form; and finally in digital form.

Negative master   after exposure through negative master

Figure 9.1: Example of the phototypesetting principle, illustrating the word PRINT created in a negative master form and the resultant positive form, as would be generated by the phototypesetter system, on bromide paper or film as required

Imagesetters

Through the development of digital generation and storage, imagesetters have been developed which, free from the restrictions of photographic masters, can create images not only of type, but also of a wide range of graphics including line, tints and photographs, by reproducing in a predetermined dot or other shaped pattern.

The development of imagesetters, and laser printers, has allowed full DTP and WYSIWYG - ie - full make-up on screen, to flourish, as all elements on the computer screen can be reproduced in the desired finished form. Previously, with phototypesetters, 'windows' or gaps needed to be left into which the screened pictures or other graphics would be stripped.

Imagesetters are driven from application programs which can output their information in a page description language called PostScript, which is a *device-independent* programming language. This means that the Postscript file can be output on any device, regardless of its resolution. As a programming language, PostScript can support any level of graphic complexity: it is a *page-dependent* description language - ie - the entire file needs to be interpreted prior to imaging a single page.

The process of imagesetting essentially consists of two parts - a Raster Image Processor *(RIP)* and a *high resolution printer or output unit* normally using laser exposure. Despite their versatility, the earliest examples of digital typesetters and imagesetters were limited in that, when connected to a front-end system to produce and output whole pages, most could not perform all the commands that were required of them.

RIPs

A RIP operates by transforming the front-end instructions from the host DTP/EPC system, which are stored in PostScript language, into a 'digestible' bitmap form of managed data the output device can understand and utilise.

A RIP has to perform three functions:

1 Interpret the page description language from the application program, such as QuarkXPress or PageMaker.
2 Create a list of all the objects on a page, known as a 'display list'.
3 Create a page bitmap for the output device, which tells it where to place the 'dots' that form the page image - to draw the objects on a page.

There are two types of RIP - *hardware*, which exists as a separate piece of physical hardware or box, coming between the computer-driven front-end unit and the output unit - ie - the imagesetter; alternatively there is *software*, which resides in the computer front-end.

Traditionally, hardware RIPs have been used, but there has been a major swing to software RIPs in recent years as computers and processing power have increased and improved so dramatically during the mid to late 1990s. The software option tends to be the cheaper one, with upgrading a simple job of increasing the processing power of the host computer, or in fact changing the computer, whereas the hardware upgrade path can mean a start-again cycle.

Imagesetters have traditionally been faster than RIPs, resulting in the imagesetter at times having to wait for the RIP to catch up, with the required data being sent in chunks so leading to 'banding' (visible bands of lines across tint and solid areas).

Several solutions exist to minimise or avoid banding:

● the use of a RIP which is faster than the imagesetter
● page-buffering, which retains the rasterised data 'on hold', until it can be sent to the imagesetter in one complete unit
● multiplexing, in the form of using several RIPs in parallel, so achieving a very fast and powerful RIP operation
● a 'doubling' capacity feature, where the RIP can simultaneously convert and queue files, while writing a file to an output device.

Each RIP has a limit on the overall size of each single graphic it can handle at any one time - with just below A3, for example, being the maximum some RIPs can handle. Adobe, the originator and developer of PostScript, has issued licenses for RIP designs which continue to improve to take account of developments such as PostScript levels 2 and 3.

Most forms of powerful output device are controlled by a RIP from, for example, colour copiers transformed into colour printers, to imagesetters and CTP systems. RIPs are designed to run AppleMac, PC or UNIX platforms, some as dedicated/proprietary units, and others as relatively general purpose RIPs driving a wide range of output devices. The MGI 'Jetstream' RIP, for example, has the facility to support colour copiers, electrostatic and inkjet printers, as well as imagesetters on the AppleMac, PC or UNIX platform.

Major prepress companies such as Linotype-Hell (now Heidelberg Prepress) and Agfa have developed RIPs to drive their specific range of imagesetters with built-in upgrade path. Linotype-Hell developed the 'Delta' RIP (which is in the form of a modular software RIP developed from their previous hardware RIP experience) to drive some of their imagesetters: it consists of three parts, DeltaSoftware, DeltaWorkstation and DeltaTower. The Delta Software drives the A3+ Quasar, B2 Herkules and DrySetter imagesetters; the DeltaWorkstation is based on a PC running Windows NT; and the Delta Tower looks after the screening requirements.

Agfa has developed the 'Cobra' software RIP, a powerful, upgradable product run on a UNIX platform SPARC workstation which is capable of driving imagesetters and other input and output devices simultaneously. Electronics for Imaging *(EFI)* are well known in the industry for their Fiery RIPs converting colour copiers into colour printers: the range has now been extended to cover large format digital printing.

Apart from the relatively proprietary/dedicated RIPs developed by major prepress companies, 'open' systems have been developed by companies such as Harlequin which has, for instance, produced its own PostScript interpreters, rather than licensing them from Adobe, producing powerful, feature-rich RIPs which are very popular in high-end workflows driving imagesetters, platesetters, digital proofing systems and digital presses.

Imagesetters

Imagesetters generate and expose dots onto photosensitive material - such as film, bromide paper and in some cases polyester and film plate material. The material is mainly supplied in light-tight removable cassettes in roll form to different widths depending on job requirements and the capabilities of the machine; photosensitive material is also supplied in sheet form in some applications. Often two sizes of film can be held in the imagesetter for ease of switching work.

There are two main types of imagesetter - capstan and drum:

- **Capstan imagesetters** use a flatbed system, utilising a drive mechanism which moves the photosensitive material, such as film, up to and past the imaging head in the form of a platen. Due to the mechanical nature of the capstan system, which relies on the correct amount of tension being present at all times, it has generally been regarded as an inferior product to the drum option and one which is often not considered appropriate for fine and accurate colour registration work. It must be acknowledged, however, that the latest capstan imagesetters are far more accurate, and create work to far higher tolerances than their predecessors. Many are capable of producing four-colour separations for printing - with resolutions to 200+ line screen.

- **Drum imagesetters** come in two main types - *internal* and *external* drum. With the drum-type imagesetters, the material to be exposed is held or attached internally or externally around a drum or cylinder. With internal machines, the light source/imaging head moves along the inside of the rotating drum, imaging as it traverses; conversely, with the external machine, the drum not only spins but also traverses while the imaging head remains stationary. One advantage of the external drum machine is that the laser light path to the film is very short compared to the internal drum, helping to achieve very accurate imaging.

Imagesetters are continuously improving in terms of quality of result, such as screen frequency and precise positioning, but also in speed by use of multiple laser beams for imaging.

The wide range of exposure technologies on modern imagesetters includes argon-ion, infra-red, laser diode, HeNe, YAG, and visible red lasers. Holographic technology is now being applied to some imagesetters, resulting in double the imaging speed of other systems, along with improved screen quality and reduced banding problems.

Laser light is highly intensive, but cannot be easily switched on and off, while retaining high speeds and stability. To overcome this problem, the laser light is passed through a crystal-based prism which deflects the light differentially, simulating switching on and off.

A further necessary component is a spinning mirror which delivers the imaging dots onto exactly the required positions: alternatively a deflecting mirror mechanism without a prism system can be used to introduce the 'on - off' imaging cycle to create the micron image dots.

As covered in *Chapter 5, 'Handling images/graphics'*, the higher the resolution used, the greater the range of tones that can be reproduced in halftone form - eg - to reproduce a 150lpi screen frequency with up to 256 grey levels requires an imagesetter which can generate an output resolution of at least 2400dpi. For text, line and relatively coarse halftone work, 1200 dpi is generally considered adequate.

Modern imagesetters come with a range of output resolutions, which allow each job to have the resolution best suited to its own specific requirements and characteristics, alongside the most efficient use of 'RIPing' and imaging/outputting times. The resolution range offered by imagesetters now covers from around 900dpi to over 16 000dpi in some cases. In recent years there has been a considerable trend towards printers installing imagesetters to match the size of their biggest press - eg - B3, B2, B1 or above. The drive towards electronic imposition has accelerated this move to output one-piece composite punched pin register film, ready for platemaking. Imagesetters are, in fact, available in a wide range of format/film output sizes through A4+, A3+, A2+, A1+ to 2 B0 and above.

B2 imagesetters can output a four-page A4, imposed flat in under five minutes; with B0 imagesetters capable of generating a 16-page A4, imposed flat in under 15 minutes at 2540dpi. It should be noted that the more complex and fine the data to be output, for example, a halftone image as against typematter, or 300lpi rather than 150lpi, the slower will be speed of the output device.

B3 imagesetters give the small-size sheet printer a very cost-effective, flexible system, producing film output for high-end process colour work and polyester plates for general commercial work. Some devices offer film and polyester processing on the one machine, and developments are being worked on to include CTP with metal plates, which will result in a truly multipurpose output device.

On-line processors

To help streamline workflows, many printing companies are installing on-line film processors which automatically take the exposed film from the imagesetters, through a processing unit delivering dry film ready for platemaking, or further operations such as retouching or planning as required. Some imagesetter and on-line processor combinations produce plate-ready film and polyester plates ready for press.

With environmental and economic pressures forcing printers to work more cleanly and efficiently, systems have been developed in which the imagesetter and on-line processor work in an 'intelligent'/linked relationship. In these systems, the imagesetter instructs the processor what type of images have to be reproduced - eg - light or heavy, type or tone, etc, with the processor releasing just the right amount of developer and fixer to the units concerned, along with closely monitored temperature control, establishing the optimum working environment.

A further development in this area is the specialist application, dry film imagesetter, which is process free, in terms of processing, after the plate has been exposed. These machines have been developed to meet the growing demand for environmentally friendly working practices, reducing and eliminating the need for chemicals, and faster and cleaner working practices, while retaining a high quality result.

Laser printers

Monochrome laser printers are relatively ubiquitous in business, office, and many home environments, in that the vast majority of computers have at least a monochrome laser printer as an output device. Desktop laser printers have improved considerably in terms of speed and quality since they were first introduced: originally the printers started at A4 size and 300dpi, with the machines used predominantly for proofing work, consisting of text and relatively coarse tints.

The machines come in a wide range of models running on the PC platform - eg - PCL and HP models, plus PostScript printers which run on AppleMacs, but are also PC compatible, while having inbuilt networking capabilities.

Laser printing machines are now available, producing much higher added value products, with resolutions of up to 1800 and 2400dpi in A3+ format size, so positioning them as plain paper imagesetters or platesetters, rather than simply proofers.

Laser printers usually consist of an inbuilt RIP and a print engine, although sometimes a separate RIP is used on a Mac or PC.

The RIP executes the PostScript commands, taking the digital data, interpreting it and translating or processing it into a series of raster images, which are then output on the appropriate output device - ie - the 'print engine'.

The *print engine* operates by directing extremely fine beams of laser light, via a revolving hexagonal mirror, onto a light photosensitive drum. The laser beam pulses 'on and off' in response to the instructions received from the RIP, creating charged toner particles on the drum in the image areas only. The particles of toner are then heated and fused onto the chosen carrier or substrate from the loaded drum as they come into contact, producing the printed result.

During printing, the application and software program builds up a description of every object on the page, which is translated by the printer driver software, into PostScript commands. With the PostScript description language being device independent, it is the output device - ie - the printer, that defines the output resolution.

If a printer does not have a resident PostScript interpreter, it has to rely on the host computer to create the pattern of dots, so considerably slowing down the printing process.

Desktop laser printers are capable of speeds of up to 16 pages per minute with larger, more powerful, stand-alone machines, generating speeds of over 100 pages per minute. Actual printing speeds, however, will depend on the complexity of the page to be printed - eg - a highly illustrated page will take longer than a simple text page, as will an A3 image compared to an A4 one, due to pages having to be created and imaged before the print engine can deliver pages through the laser printer.

Dot scanners

Specialist flatbed CCD scanners have been developed to create digital data from line artwork, continuous tone or colour separated (pre-screened) negative and positive film, transparencies and reflection colour prints.

The machines come in scanning format sizes from A3+ up to B1+, taking existing imposed film flats, or pasted-up artwork, and digitising them in planned form.

The scanner has the facility to reproduce each single dot or line of a pre-screened original. This *'dot-for-dot'* procedure will operate where the size and screen ruling in the originals match the required result at a 1:1 ratio.

In circumstances where the screened material needs changing and manipulating, a descreening process is undertaken, along with retouching and manipulation as required.

The dot scanner consists of two main parts - the front-end/job preparation station and the scanner:

- The **job preparation station** consists mainly of a high performance PC, interfaced to the scanner (and often networked to a company's general digital workflow), along with software packages covering data compression, picture replacement and manipulation, automatic registration and digital descreening, etc.

- The **scanner** has a flatbed copyholder construction, available in varying sizes to suit requirements. Input scanning resolution is from at least 1270dpi up to 2540dpi, with output/interpolated resolution at 5080lpi. In terms of speed, it takes approximately 90 seconds to scan an A4 image at maximum resolution.

Copy dot scanners in this category are the Purup-Eskofot 'EskoScan', Scitex 'Monoscan' and Tecsa 'TS 3000 series': in addition, some scanner manufacturers also offer a 'copydot' add-on option to their existing conventional scanner.

Mixed media

One of the problems to be overcome by many printers is having to work with mixed media, in the form of digital and analogue (film and bromide) media.

Many printers operate in an environment, such as in newspapers and magazines, where they regularly work with publishers, advertising and design agencies, etc, who supply at least some film or camera-ready copy for jobs, along with digital data in its many forms of storage media and transfer.

To operate efficiently, printing companies have to find a common working environment, and that increasingly involves a digital workflow.

Apart from the external influences of printers being supplied in non-digital data form, there is often an immense amount of useful archived material in film form, at least some of which would prove invaluable, if available in digital form.

One answer to this problem lies in the use of a scanner or scanning systems, which will digitise the analogue media, so creating a common digital working environment with electronic make-up and imposition, outputting in composite plate ready film flats or complete-to-plate - *see dot scanners* on the previous page.

Mixed media output systems

A further option which addresses the mixed media scenario and, in fact recognises and embraces the status quo, is the use of products which allow exposure of digital source data, and conventional planned film on the same plate, masking off selected areas of the plate to suit the circumstances required.

Manufacturers such as Misomex and DuPont/Cymbolic Sciences have developed such mixed media output devices in the form of the 'Laserstepper' (Misomex) and rebadged 'Platejet' (DuPont/Cymbolic Sciences).

They also create the possibility of providing either film or metal plate output - thereby assisting in the process of meeting conventional imagesetting needs for film, as well as being able to image 'direct to plate'.

Preparing printing surfaces

Different printing processes require different printing surfaces, usually in the form of a printing plate, cylinder or stencil.

Each type of image carrier, or printing surface, has its own particular properties by which the essential characteristics of each printing process are met.

Lithographic printing plates are produced in a *planographic form* with ink-accepting image areas and water-accepting non-image areas.

Plates for letterpress or flexography are produced with *relief image areas*; gravure cylinders or plates are produced with the *intaglio image areas in recess*; and the screen process relies on *stencil processed meshes*, where areas are left unblocked to form the image areas.

Lithographic platemaking

For modern commercial printing, the lithographic surface may be of metal, paper or plastic; conventional platemaking makes significant use of the photographic process in one form or other, except for certain paper and plastic plates, on which the image may be directly typed, drawn, or produced using a direct-to-plate system. Alternatively thermal imaging is used on some CTP systems - *see pages 156* and *157*.

For the conventional lithographic process to operate, the plate must have two properties; it must be both *hydrophilic* (water-attracting) and *oleophilic* (oil-attracting). These two properties do not exist naturally on lithographic plate material and have to be created by the appropriate processing. During the printing operation, a water-based solution is first applied to the plate, followed by the ink. The water solution flows onto and is retained by the non-image areas, with the image areas repelling the water; when the ink is applied, it is retained in the image areas, while the non-image areas repel the ink.

The first metal lithographic plates were of zinc, a metal which was found to have a good affinity for oil and ink, but required surface treatment to improve its relatively poor affinity for water. Today the material most widely used for lithographic plates, including all single metal plates, is aluminium. The processes of graining, anodising and presensitising, help to give aluminium the properties required for offset lithographic metal plates:

- **Graining** roughens the surface of the plate, providing a better anchorage for the ink and water, as well as reducing the surface tension and improving the 'wettability' of the plate.

- **Anodising** is an electro-chemical process which converts the surface of the aluminium metal which has been treated into aluminium oxide; this creates a tough, damp-accepting surface area, resistant to abrasion as well as helping to protect the plate from oxidisation.

Plates are *pre-coated or presensitised*, with a thin layer of a photosensitive emulsion, to generate the image areas required.

The application of photography, or *photolithography* as it was first called, brought about a revolution in lithographic platemaking techniques. This revolution and improvement in the chemistry and materials used, have been instrumental in making lithography the most commercially successful method of printing today.

In conventional platemaking, film is the main means of arranging the printed elements in a form which can be printed down onto a light-sensitive plate surface. It may be in the form of complete pages or one large composite piece of film; and if colour work, as separations of the various colours. The film may be in negative form, with the printing areas transparent; or positive, with the printing areas opaque and the non-printing areas transparent.

In the UK, positive film is used extensively for four-colour process work, with negative film more popular for monochrome or spot colour work; there is no set rule however, except that the printing plate must relate to the system used, both negative- and positive-working plates being available.

The assembled foils of negative or positive films in position are arranged wrong-reading emulsion-side up so that, when platemaking, the films and plate surface will form an emulsion-to-emulsion right-reading surface.

Both film and assembly foil must remain stable when subjected to likely changes in temperature, or humidity, as any shrinking or stretching would affect registration of the colours.

Litho plates, practically without exception, are sold pre-coated ready for processing as positive- or negative-working.

Printing-down and plate processing

Conventional exposure of the printing image onto a litho plate is made in a printing-down frame - *see Figure 9.2*. The prepared montage foil is positioned carefully on the plate, preferably using a punch register system to ensure accuracy.

After the glass top has been cleaned, the plate with the foil on top is placed in the printing-down frame. The glass top is then closed, after which the vacuum pump is operated to extract all the air from the frame causing the planning foil, or flat, to make the closest possible contact with the plate during exposure.

The printing-down frame can be in the form of a flip-top, or it can be freestanding, where the frame is exposed on the horizontal plane, or swivelled for exposure into the vertical position. The light may be xenon, metal halide or sometimes mercury vapour. Freestanding frames are common if the plate is particularly large and, in such a case, the light will also be freestanding, positioned at the correct distance from the vacuum frame (facing the plate) and illuminated for the required period. After exposure the plate is removed from the printing-down frame and processed in the manner appropriate to the chemistry of the plate.

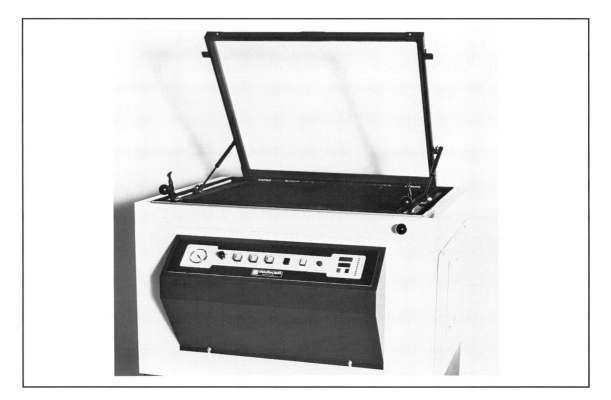

Figure 9.2: Example of a printing-down frame/platemaker

The effect of exposure through a negative film is to harden, or render insoluble, the coating beneath the transparent image area. In the processing, the soft or soluble non-image area is developed or washed away by a chemical solution or, increasingly, water, depending on the process. The hardened coating in the image area then provides a site for attracting and retaining ink.

In positive-working systems, light passing through the non-image areas of the film softens, or renders soluble, the plate coating, rather than hardening it. The non-image area is again developed away in the processor, leaving the image area hard and available to receive ink. When processing is complete, polymer or finisher is applied to the plate by hand or, increasingly, automatically, to desensitise the non-image areas and preserve them. As long as the desensitising layer of gum/finisher remains on the surface of the plate, the non-image areas will be protected.

The dried finisher coating also protects the non-image areas when the plate is stored - this is due to the buffered dry coating possessing large molecular structures which are difficult to remove and wash out when absorbed into the pores of anodised aluminium.

Processing of plates is increasingly being carried out on automatic plate processors which develop, process, gum/finish and dry the plate. The processing machines are often configured on an in-line basis, where the operation is continuous, from the stage where the operator feeds in the exposed plate to the finished processed plate ready for machine. Automatic plate processors are now mainly able to process both negative and positive plates, using the same processing chemistry, whereas, previously, separate processors and/or chemicals were used for each type.

The lithographic plate selected depends on the class of work to be printed, the length of run, and the requirements of the particular press to be used. For work in more than one colour a plate must be made for each printing colour from separately assembled foils.

Horsell Graphic Industries has developed the *Gemini platemaking system*, which allows the combining of negative and positive film onto a single positive-working plate. The negative film is first exposed to the positive-working plate; then it is passed through the *Gemini unit*, where controlled heat converts the negative image to positive. The positive film is then exposed to the same plate in the normal way. Finally, it is developed as a positive-working plate.

Plate-baking

Baking presensitised positive-working plates in a specially constructed oven for five to ten minutes at approximately 200° to 250°C will normally increase the plate life by up to threefold; baking of negative-working presensitised plates will result in only a relatively small increase in plate life. Image deletion is not practicable, or possible, once a plate has been baked.

Offset litho printing companies, which specialise in long-run work or printed work with a high probability of repeat orders, requiring plates to be used again at regular intervals, favour baking positive-working presensitised plates because of their greater press life and resistance to chemical attack and oxidisation.

Step-and-repeat machines

Printed work can be *multiple-set* in which two or more identical images are printed on the same plate. In order to achieve this, the image is exposed in various positions over the plate, which can be done by manually repositioning the foil between exposures. Traditionally, printers with general requirements for multiple-image printing such as in carton/packaging, label, ticket and voucher printing, have extensively used step-and-repeat machines. In this case the film is placed in a holder, moved over the face of the plate and exposed when in the correct position. The holder is accurately located by manual or computer-controlled operation. Multiple-image plates produced on step-and-repeat machines are more accurate and dependable than hand-planned multiple images, which can often lead to some film images being laid down slightly out of register.

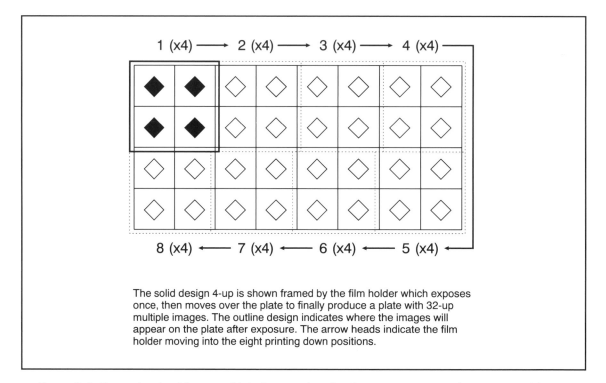

The solid design 4-up is shown framed by the film holder which exposes once, then moves over the plate to finally produce a plate with 32-up multiple images. The outline design indicates where the images will appear on the plate after exposure. The arrow heads indicate the film holder moving into the eight printing down positions.

Figure 9.3: Example of a 32-up multiple-image plate laydown on a step-and-repeat machine

Apart from the improved accuracy and time saving gained from the use of a step-and-repeat machine, there is also a considerable film saving.

Figure 9.3 illustrates the operation of a step-and-repeat machine to produce a 32-up multiple-image plate. The exposing head or holder has a four-up image mounted on it, necessitating an eight-stage step-and-repeat operation to complete the plate. This is repeated, changing the four-up film master as appropriate, until the required number of colour plates are completed - ie - four plates for a four-colour process set. It should be noted, however, that the requirement for creating multiple-image laydowns is increasingly being carried out via a software application - ie - created and verified on an electronic/computer-based system - *see page 119.*

Projection platemaking systems

This method of processing and producing plates is ideally suited to bookwork, and high-pagination directory-type work, with the need to produce a large number of plates in a short period of time. The method also has the ability to store printing images, and to recall and remake plates with relative ease.

Rachwal, an example of this system, consists of three main components - the camera station, the control unit and the projection platemaking unit. Camera-ready copy is photographed by the camera station onto 70mm film at speeds of up to 220 shots per hour. One length of film is long enough to take 1000 A5 pages, or 500 A4 pages. After automatic developing and drying in a processor it is ready for projection. The platemaking unit is controlled by the control unit, with operation data such as plate size, page sequence and exposure time programmed and stored on disk. The pages are projected to final size onto the correct position on the plate and exposed. A further option on this system involves a link into a phototypesetting/imagesetting system which exposes fully made-up pages directly onto the 70mm roll film without the need for the intermediate stage of producing camera-ready copy.

Direct-to-plate systems

Several different direct-to-plate systems are available, with all having in common the ability to produce a printing plate without the intermediate use of negative or positive film. There are three main types of direct-to-plate systems, suitable to offset litho platemaking:

1 Direct from artwork-to-plate using a camera system or other form of analogue exposure.

2 Direct from imagesetter, laser printer-to-plate, or specialist platesetter/platemaster.

3 Direct from computer-to-plate *(CTP).*

Artwork-to-plate using a camera system, or other form of analogue exposure

In this type of system, offset litho plates are produced on specialist cameras with a reversing mirror to obtain a right-reading plate. The plate material can be metal, using the electrostatic process, with liquid or powder toner to produce a plate suitable for newspapers and bookwork, for example: alternatively, the plate material can be silver-coated paper-based and polyester/Silvermaster-type material, suitable mainly for the small- to medium-sheet size market in quick-print and general commercial printing, plus relatively short-run large format size printing, predominantly single and spot-colour, for book and magazine printers.

Examples of machines in this area include Silver Master 'CP', A B Dick Itek Graphic 'Camera-Platemakers' and Agfa 'Supermaster SP560'.

The cheapest type of plate in this category is, in fact, the paper plate or master, where the specially-coated paper sheet receives the image areas by being passed through a photocopier, or camera-based system - this type of plate would only be suitable for small offset short-run single-colour work in text only, or text with coarse tints.

Imagesetter, laser printer-to-plate, or specialist platesetter/platemaster

These systems are a form of computer-to-plate, relying on digital data to create an offset litho plate in paper, plastic or polyester material - generating a higher quality image quality than in *(1)* outlined on *page 153*, as no intermediate stages are encountered. In addition, the platemaking process is very fast, with the facility to retain data on digital storage media for future accessing and platemaking.

Polyester plate material, although inexpensive and suited to the type of work outlined above, suffers from stretch so making it unsuitable for very close register work, also fine screen work is unsuitable as the maximum screen frequency possible is around 120 to 133lpi. It should be noted, however, that with the pace of change and development currently under way, such as imagesetters exposing direct onto presensitised metal plates, the distinction between this group and high-end CTP systems will become blurred.

Some imagesetters and laser printers can be used to produce paper and polyester as well as film-based plates, with some multi-purpose imagesetters now capable of outputting presensitised metal plates.

SRA3 small-offset-size plates are the main product of this specialist/desktop platemaker/platesetter systems category, although SRA2 plate size is also available. Systems which have been developed to meet this requirement consist of, for example, an imagesetter, scanner, RIP, graphics arts camera and in-line processor, all built into the one unit.

Depending on the configuration, the system is able to scan in and reproduce analogue media such as camera-ready copy and pre-screened or continuous tone photographs; plus on a digital basis, input electronic files through the resident RIP, with interfaces to Mac and PC platforms, finally outputting on the imagesetter/platesetter at over 2500dpi on Mega paper or polyester plates.

Examples of such systems are the A B Dick Itek Graphix 'DPM 2000', AMI/ Eskofot 'DPX-420' and Kimoto 'Platesetter 1000'.

Computer-to-plate systems

Interest in high quality metal computer-to-plate *(CTP)* systems steadily grew through the 1990s as digital workflows matured and improved, with different parts of the electronic jigsaw coming together, such as digital flightcheck systems and digital proofing, to provide an integrated digital solution.

As an output device/media, CTP shares a lot in common with imagesetters to the extent that both require a powerful RIP and exposure system to operate. As stated elsewhere in this chapter, imagesetters have been designed to mainly use flexible photosensitive material such as bromide paper and film, although some machines will produce polyester plates. Because of the relative similarity between imagesetters and CTP platesetters, it is likely that more hybrid machines will become available, capable of outputting film or plates as required.

The first range of CTP machines launched used laser exposure units and light-sensitive plates, which cannot be operated under simple daylight plate-loading conditions, so they have to rely on auto plate holding and releasing in darkroom cassettes.

Temperature is another major area that needs to be tightly controlled and monitored to ensure the light sensitive plates hold the definition required across the fine line/highlight, mid-tone and solid tone range.

The initial metal CTP systems were large/very large format machines aimed at specialist printers such as large format book, catalogue and magazine printers with the higher volume market of B1 and B2 being developed later. The very large format machines cover up to over 32-page A4 imaged plates imaging a full size plate, for example, at 1200dpi in under seven minutes, 2400dpi in under 10 minutes and 3200 at under 16 minutes: at the other end of the scale B3+ and B2 metal CTP systems are now available.

CTP systems will normally have the following features:

- overall construction ensuring light-tight operation and clean air environment inside the machine
- tightly controlled and monitored temperature range
- up to two processors on-line
- range of output resolutions from around 1200dpi to over 3000dpi
- plate handling and plate cassettes on-line covering a range of plate sizes
- bin indicator lights showing quantity of plates still unexposed
- automatic slip sheet removal between plates allowing direct loading from original packaging
- automatic queuing, loading, exposing and processing
- external daylight operation environment.

The main types of CTP metal plate systems which have developed are as follows:

Silver halide metal, where the plate is pre-coated with a layer of silver halide coating: after exposure the background/non image areas are developed out, leaving exposed silver halide image areas. Examples of plates in this category are DuPont 'Silverlith SDB' and Agfa 'Lithostar'.

Hybrid, which uses a combination of silver halide and photopolymer/diazo, is available in two types. In the first type, the metal base plate has a first layer of diazo coating, followed by a middle layer of adhesive, then silver halide top layer. After exposure the silver halide is developed out leaving a mask: the plate is then re-exposed to UV light. Finally diazo and adhesive coating layers are developed out in the non-image areas. The second type is a form of hybrid IR *(infra-red)*, where instead of the surface silver halide coating, there is an overall IR mask layer on the surface of the plate. Examples of plates in this category are Polychrome 'CTX' and Fuji 'FNH'.

Photopolymer, which consists of a metal base, middle layer of photopolymer coating and a clear top coating layer. After exposure the photopolymer is developed out leaving the image areas. Examples of plates in this category are Agfa/Enco 'N-90', 3M 'Viking' and Western Litho/Mitsubushi 'Diamond Plate'.

Thermal consists of a plate with a presensitised photopolymer coating layer which is exposed to an IR heat-based laser source.

The major difference with the thermal plate and the light sensitive plates is that the thermal imaged plate is created with heat, not light. The processing of the plate depends on reaching the threshold temperature, if this is not reached no image will be formed, not even a partial image - *see Figure 9.4.* The result is that the plate cannot be over- or under-exposed. Examples of plates in this category are Kodak 'Direct Image', Horsell Anitec 'Electra' and Sakurai 'Platemaster'.

Silver halide diffusion transfer plates, hybrid and photopolymer plates are able to be exposed by a wide range of laser and UV light sources such as Argon Ion and F D Yag, but the plates, as previously mentioned, cannot be handled in daylight conditions and relatively complex plate processing is required.

Thermal CTP plates have been developed aimed at offering advantages over light sensitive CTP plates, including the following:

- plates cannot be overexposed
- run lengths when baked, can be over one million impressions, two million has been achieved
- allows standard plateroom safelight conditions
- long latent image stability
- holds very high resolutions and sharp images, therefore well suited to stochastic screening
- generally works with conventional plate processors
- the dot from the platesetter is the exact dot produced on the plate.

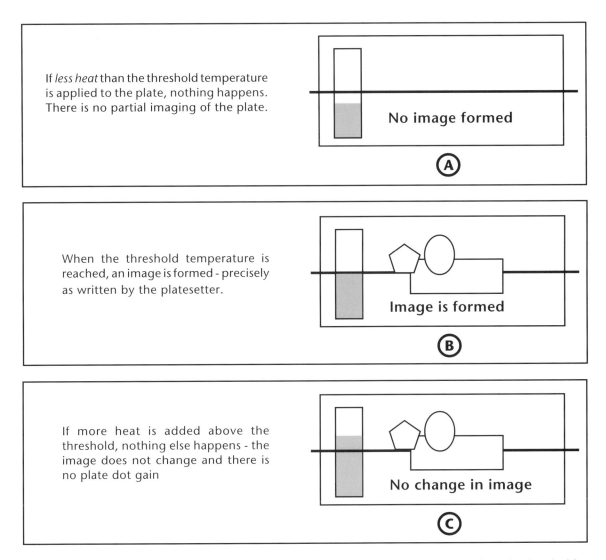

If *less heat* than the threshold temperature is applied to the plate, nothing happens. There is no partial imaging of the plate.

No image formed

Ⓐ

When the threshold temperature is reached, an image is formed - precisely as written by the platesetter.

Image is formed

Ⓑ

If more heat is added above the threshold, nothing else happens - the image does not change and there is no plate dot gain

No change in image

Ⓒ

Figure 9.4: Figures illustrating the stages of thermal platemaking. (A), being below the threshold temperature does not form an image; (B), on reaching the threshold forms an image, and (C), exposing beyond the threshold temperature stills forms the image exactly as (B), but has no other effect - eg - no dot gain or image growth.

Letterpress blocks and plates

Relief letterpress plates, usually referred to as blocks in flatbed printing, consist of areas of raised printing surface, accepting ink and transferring it to the substrate such as paper or board, with the non-printing areas, being lower, receiving no ink.

Letterpress plates were traditionally made in two types: *originals* made from etched zinc or copper; or duplicates - ie - copies of an original, made again from metal, or moulded from rubber or plastics. Except in very exceptional circumstances all the traditional forms of letterpress plate have been replaced by photopolymer.

Photopolymer plates

Photopolymer plates are made of a photosensitive plastic, which hardens under the action of ultra-violet light, of which two separate systems exist.

In one system the material consists of a solid photopolymer material bonded to a metal backing sheet, which assists in securing it to the press, either in a rigid flatbed form, or a flexible material, which can be easily curved round a cylinder for rotary printing.

The photopolymer material for making the plate is purchased ready for processing and is held in contact with a right-reading negative, emulsion-side down, while being exposed to ultra-violet light in a contact frame which protects the operator from the UV rays. The length of exposure varies according to the sensitivity of the material and nature of the subject. The ultra-violet light hardens the photopolymer in the printing areas, which are transparent on the negative, the opaque areas of the negative holding back the light.

After exposure the plate is subjected to a high-pressure spray of solution which, increasingly is just plain water, or some form of weak solvent solution. The liquid solution washes away the unhardened photopolymer, leaving the hardened printing area raised in relief. After drying, the final stage is to expose the whole plate to light to post-harden it, after which it is ready for use. The photopolymer material is also often given an initial overall pre-exposure, through the back of the material, to help form a firm base and side edges/channels of the relief areas.

In the second system, the plate material is available as a photosensitive liquid resin, where the liquid is poured on top of the negative which is in a contact frame and protected by a fine plastic film, so forming a laminate. As it is poured in, the liquid is levelled by a doctor blade, which also releases air bubbles to form a clear plate.

A film or board base is then rolled onto the surface, or back of the liquid, and the resulting assembly exposed from the back and front. After exposure, the plate is removed, washed as with the first system and, after post-hardening, is ready for use.

Photopolymer plate systems are usually installed by letterpress and flexographic printers to produce plates in-house, in much the same way as the lithographic printer produces litho plates.

Of the two systems described, the first has found favour with the general commercial printer, while the second has been used mainly by newspaper printers for newspapers and by flexographic printers for packaging and paperback books - with the solid photopolymer being the most popular product overall.

Flexographic printing plates

There are two main types of flexographic printing plate - *rubber* and *photopolymer* - both of which are produced conventionally and digitally. Each follow a different series of processes, resulting in the production of a relief printing surface.

Rubber

Rubber has been used to produce relief flexo plates, normally referred to as *stereos*, since its earliest development as a printing process. The properties of high tear strength, high resistance to abrasion and ozone resistance make it an ideal flexo plate material.

A rubber stereo or plate can be produced as *engraved/cut* or *moulded:*

Engraved/hand-cut rubber stereos are produced by tracing or copying the required image onto a sheet of rubber, and then cutting away the non-image areas of rubber to leave the image areas in relief. The hand-cut rubber stereo is mainly restricted to the lower quality of paper bags and cheaper ranges of printed packaging.

Moulded rubber plates are produced using a recess mould of a suitable material, such as thermosetting plastic, which sets with heat permanently, onto which rubber material is placed, and through heat and moulding pressure a relief image rubber plate is produced to the correct depth.

Photopolymer plates - *see previous note under letterpress*

This is the most popular type of material for flexographic printing as a range of different plates and/or properties can be produced, depending on requirements. Photopolymer has a stable base, which makes it suitable for reproducing print stretch/disproportioning allowances required in rotary relief printing , along with register and print repeat lengths which are calculated from standard formulae. Photopolymer plates are also suitable on which to produce step-and-repeat images, along with the use of punch pin register systems.

Computer-to-plate relief photopolymer systems

CTP relief photopolymer systems are now coming on stream as front-end digital systems are becoming established in flexo and letterpress printers, linked to specifically developed output systems, or hybrid/dual purpose systems which can, for example, output flexo and offset litho plates.

The available CTP flexo/letterpress options are as follows:

Laser-engraved plate or roller

This method allows flexography to produce very fine definition, high quality printing plates - also known as *engraved cylinders* or *rollers.* The system utilises a computer-controlled CO_2 laser which selectively removes the non-image rubber areas from a rubber covered roller or sleeve.

After engraving there is no need for further processing other than mounting, if appropriate. The computer-controlled laser engraving head can produce relief printing surfaces with built-in automatic disproportioning stretch, (essential for retaining a high print quality result without distortion), step-and-repeat images and seamless jointing, etc. Image data instruction or control of the laser operates through either a scanning unit responding to colour-separated negative or positive film, linked to an electronic workstation. A built-in option allows the electronic engraving machine to produce its own images or patterns for use in, for example, embossing dies and repeat patterns. Laser-engraved relief platemaking is still relatively rare although great use is made of laser-engraved anilox rollers used in flexographic presses.

Platesetters

This is the latest development in flexo platemaking and letterpress, following developments of offset litho platesetters, and imagesetters adapted to output a wide range of media, including plates.

An example of a dual imagesetter/platesetter is the basysPrint 'UV-Setter 710', which can expose photopolymer flexo and letterpress plates as well as offset litho plates. As its title suggests, it uses UV light on a twin-head exposure unit: it works through a powerful front-end system with RIP, generating digital proofs from the system, before final plate outputting. The maximum plate size is 820 x 1120mm allowing the production of several images up on one plate, planned as multiple-images of the same job or plates covering several jobs. Through the use of the UV heads only a single exposure is required to produce a plate.

Another example of a CTP flexo system is the Misomex 'FlexoSetter 4872' which takes a maximum plate size of 1219 x 1829mm: it can also expose conventional photosensitive film. The system, as with other laser exposure systems, requires a double exposure - firstly in the FlexoSetter to ablate/remove the blank coating from the polymer layer to create a negative mask, followed by a second exposure in a UV contact frame which hardens the photopolymer in the image areas, before washout development removes the mask and unexposed polymer areas.

Flexo/letterpress platesetters are presently capable of producing plates at an output resolution of 150lpi.

CTP flexo photopolymer plates differ from conventional plates, which are exposed via a negative in a printing-down frame. The CTP photopolymer plate used with digitally generated laser exposure requires a black coating or mask over the photopolymer material. During exposure, the black coating is removed to create the image areas, with the non-image areas left intact - ie - with mask/black coating material.

Partnerships and alliances between prepress suppliers bringing together their front-end digital expertise, in software and associated equipment, along with flexo and letterpress plate material, are to be seen in the development of Barco 'Cyrel Digital Imager' *(CDI)* and BASF/Saueressig flexo platesetters, which are most likely to be used by printers/flexo plate suppliers, especially for packaging.

Gravure cylinder preparation

The modern gravure process has developed from early hand engraving and etching of flat metal copper plates, to a highly sophisticated printing process. Copper cylinders have, to all intents and purposes, replaced gravure printing plates as the image carrier.

The conventional gravure process, or *photogravure* as it is often called, consists of recessed minute cavities or cells, of uniform area and shape, but of varying depth, to give tonal variations with the non-printing or background area surrounding each cell remaining at surface level. Alterations to conventional gravure have been developed such as *variable area cylinder,* which is an inverted halftone formation in which the image areas vary in area, but are of uniform depth, and *gravure conversion,* where the recessed cells vary both in area and depth.

There are two distinct methods of producing gravure cylinders - *etching* and *engraving:*

Etching

This is the traditional method of creating gravure cylinders, now almost totally superseded by the engraving of cylinders. The conventional way of preparing an etched printing image in gravure is the *carbon tissue* method. By this means, first the screen and then a continuous tone (contone) positive are printed down by exposure onto a carbon tissue.

This consists of a layer of pigmented gelatine, attached to a sheet of paper or polyester, and rendered sensitive to light in such a way that the gelatine hardens according to the intensity of light passing through the screen and the positive during their separate exposures. The carbon tissue is subsequently attached to the smooth metal printing cylinder, the backing paper/polyester is removed, and the cylinder is developed in warm water, which washes away the soft gelatine unaffected by light during exposure.

The varying thickness of light-hardened gelatine remaining on the copper cylinder in relief enables the etching process to be controlled. Where the gelatine is thick, the resulting etch is shallow, but where the gelatine is thin, the etch is deeper.

There is, of course, no etching where the cross lines of the screen have been. In colour work separate cylinders are etched for each colour from colour-separated positives.

With gravure conversion, a film screen positive is made from a combination of exposures using a contact screen and the contone positives. This is exposed to the carbon tissue (without pre-screening) in addition to the continuous tone positive. The cylinder, when etched, consists of a series of cells varying in both surface area and depth. The result is a conventional-shaped cell in the shadow areas with a gradual variation to a small cell in the highlights.

Electronic engraving

As with other printing processes, gravure cylinders are now reproduced by both analogue and digital means - ie - through film-generated and digitally-generated engraving.

Figure 9.5: Electronic engraving machine - the Helio Klischograph K202 Simultaneous, with 12 scanning and engraving heads

Film generated (analogue) engraving

This method breaks down into three stages:

The *first stage* is the production of composite continuous tone positive film, right-reading emulsion side down. If film separations are produced or supplied in conventional screened form, they have to be 'descreened', which can be done through the scanning head of the engraving unit.

The *second stage* takes the form of the positive film being register-punched and exposed in a printing-down contact frame, to a correspondingly register-punched white film-based opaline material, which is coated with a direct reversal emulsion processed in a similar way to any photographic material. The opaline material reacts during its exposure and development similar to a positive-working offset litho presensitised plate, leaving a black continuous tone image on a white plastic background.

The *third stage*, following the exposure and processing of the opaline material, is for the opaline material to be mounted onto the analyse/input drum of the engraving machine - Helio Klischograph and Ohio are two popular cylinder engraving systems. The principle and operation of gravure cylinder engraving is similar in some ways to that of large drum colour scanners. Both systems consist of an analyse and an output unit: in the case of the colour scanner the image profiles on the illuminated analyse drum are 'read' or analysed, as electrical impulses, and sent to the output unit to activate a light source which exposes onto light sensitive film emulsion, so producing process colour separated film. The output unit on the gravure system activates a diamond stylus, so engraving copper plated cylinders in response to the electrical impulses received from the mounted opaline material.

The engraving units can engrave up to and in excess of 3200 cells per second, with screen rulings varying from around 133lpi up to 300lpi.

Digitally generated engraving

In this system, digital data is created on AppleMacs, PCs and workstations, and/or received by the gravure engraver via DAT tape, optical disks, syquest cartridges and remote digital links, such as ISDN. The digital data is fed into the host system acting as a server direct to the engraving output. Digital data takes about one-tenth of the time to download data to the engraving unit, compared to mounted opaline material: in addition much higher quality results are achieved. The very high cost of producing gravure cylinders has always been a limiting factor to the wider use of the process, other than for specialist areas and long-run, highly illustrated publications.

Screen stencil production

The modern screen printing process has developed from simple stencilling, with evidence and examples still existing going back over a thousand years.

Screen printing for many years was known as *silk screen printing*, because the material used to make the fine stencil mesh was silk bolting cloth. Silk was used for its very fine structure, and because it could easily be bonded to the image-carrying stencils.

Silk as a screen mesh fabric has been largely replaced by synthetic fibres such as nylon, polyesters or fine stainless steel wire, as they possess considerable advantages over silk - they have higher tear resistance and good resistance to chemicals, and are easier to clean and re-use.

Screen meshes

Modern synthetic meshes are made with varying properties to suit particular applications, with the *screen mesh count* - for example, 100 'threads' per cm - and *mesh gradings* of, say, light, medium quality and special purpose, varying accordingly. Both of these properties will determine the printed ink film thickness and the quality of detail.

Screen frames

Screen printing frames are made in a wide variety of sizes and shapes to suit the situation, mainly from metal or plastic. The frame needs to be strong and rigid to support screen mesh material, which must be attached securely and correctly tensioned across the frame.

Screen stencils

Stencils are prepared so that they block out the screen mesh in the non-image areas as required, leaving the printing areas clear.

The production of screen printing stencils falls into three main groups - *hand-cut, photomechanical* and *electronically generated*.

Hand-cut stencils

These are used for simple, straightforward work. The stencil image is created by the use of a sharp scalpel to cut out the required design shape from masking material, in the form of paper laminate, or adhesive-backed film.

Alternatively, the masking film is wetted, in order to adhere to the underside of the mesh.

The printing areas of the stencil are peeled away or developed, to leave the hand-cut stencil material firmly bonded to the mesh. The protective base backing material is then removed.

Photomechanical stencils

Photomechanical processing is by far the most widely used option for modern, commercial screen printing, even allowing for the growing interest and use of electronically generated stencils.

Light-sensitive material is exposed to an opaque positive image. It is then hardened and rendered insoluble by exposure to light with the unexposed emulsion image area dissolving away to leave completely open, clear stencil areas.

The production of photostencils can be divided into four clearly identifiable methods; briefly, these are as follows:

Photo-indirect where the processing is carried out before the stencil is transferred to the mesh. This method gives high definition, as there is close contact between the stencil undersurface and the printing substrate.

Photo-direct where the processing is carried out directly onto the screen, which has previously been coated with a light-sensitive emulsion. In this method, the stencil is formed as an integral part of the screen mesh. Quality definition is not as good as photo-indirect, but it normally gives a longer-run, more robust stencil.

Photo-direct/indirect is, as the name suggests, a combination of direct and indirect where the processed stencil is prepared by an unsensitised emulsion being bonded to the underside of the screen mesh. A sensitised emulsion is then applied to the screen mesh surface. After drying, it is then exposed and processed. The result is a stencil with the combined properties of high quality definition, durability and the capacity for long runs.

Photo-capillary direct is the most recent development in stencil making. A presensitised emulsion film base is adhered to the mesh with water or laminated to the mesh with sensitised emulsion. After drying, the base support material is peeled off, and the screen is exposed to a positive in a vacuum printing-down frame using a high actinic light source. The unexposed areas are developed and washed out with water. This has become a popular method of stencil making, with similar properties to direct-indirect, but with simpler, faster processing.

A further addition to the examples of screen meshes covered previously - all of which are flatbed, is the rotary screen stencil.

Rotary screen stencils typically come in two types: a sensitised microstructure photopolymer material called 'screeny' which has been developed by Gallus and supplied in rolls; these are cut into lengths as required with the use of a register system. Alternatively 'himesh' rotary metal screens, developed by Stork. The correct size and area of the selected screen mesh material, either in the flat state or wrapped round the printing cylinder, is exposed in a printing-down frame to a single- or multiple-image positive film (right-reading emulsion-side-up), covering the printing cylinder.

After exposure the screen mesh material or cylinder is washed out with water jets to leave the printed areas clear and unblocked, with the completed screen mesh material mounted on the printing cylinder frame as required.

Flatbed screen stencils are used in conventional screen printing on a wide range of substrates in sheet form; rotary screen stencils are used mainly for self-adhesive roll-fed printing, also specialist web printing such as wallcoverings and printed textiles.

Electronically generated stencils

There are two types of electronically generated screen stencils which are outlined as follows:

Electronically-cut stencils

This is a form of computerised stencil cutting operated from a workstation front-end computer aided design *(CAD)*-type arrangement where the manually- or computer-generated artwork is traced or scanned, with the controlling drafting head of the output device directing a cutting blade, or stylus, to create very intricate and accurate stencils on masking material, which is then mounted on the prepared screen mesh.

Computer-to-screen inkjet system

This is another example of a CAD or workstation-driven screen stencil making system. It works with a standard flat screen mesh coated with a photosensitive emulsion. The digital form of the image to be reproduced is used to activate the inkjet system, which deposits opaque ink to block out non-image areas on the photostencil.

The screen is then exposed and developed in the standard way as that undertaken with analogue-generated photostencils. Examples of this type of system are the Luscher 'JetScreen' and Svecia 'StencilMaster'.

ten

COMPUTER-TO-PRINT AND BEYOND

The traditional printing approach, based over centuries, has generally been one of a *production-centred approach* concentrating on economies of scale, producing the exact same printed product, time after time, at increasing production speeds.

Digital means of reproduction, through computer-to-print and beyond, presents the opportunity to turn this approach on its head, putting the customer and/or user of the information/data at the centre of the process, and concentrates on producing a product and service with built-in flexibility which can consist of a printed product with 100% variable data - ie - each subsequent copy being completely different to the previous one: alternatively it is increasingly likely that there is an element of common/fixed data and customised/variable data mix. In addition, the data can be made available in a wide range of multi-media products and services including the Internet, Intranet, WWW, CD-ROM, video and video conferencing, etc.

Factors which are accelerating the move to computer-driven media systems, including print, are as follows:

- text and graphic data now substantially created and manipulated in digital form, so making the transition to computer-to-print and other products a logical and increasingly established workflow pattern
- the move towards shorter print runs
- drive towards JIT *(just-in-time)* working practices, alongside tight stock management and project/facilities management demanded by customers and offered by printers as a means of generating high added value products and services
- growth of alternative non-print media competing with print
- faster turnaround requirements, including growth of print on-demand capability
- easier entry level for users into digital print, than conventional printing
- the whole printing process, not just prepress, but also printing and print finishing, becoming increasingly digitally controlled and monitored
- increasing ease of combining prepress, printing and finishing into an on-line or in-line integrated process, from base sheets or webs of paper or other substrate, to finished product.

Digitally based print-based systems have to a great extent, created new market opportunities and niches, rather than just be a straight replacement for conventional printing processes such as offset lithography.

Some direct substitution by digital printing systems has taken place, especially in short-run work and areas of personalisation: this is set to gain momentum and affect all areas of printing more and more in the future, as digital workflows and the experiences of printers and print buyers mature in a multi-media arena.

A major influence towards computer-to-print is the accelerating tele-communications of data transfer through modem, ISDN and networks - *see pages 41* and *42,* alongside faster data transfer rates speeding up the process and providing the opportunity for print-on-demand response.

Preflight checking of files is one of the major processes required in the digital workflow preparation of data for printing. It has become an essential process due to the greater need to check for any problems, faults and inconsistencies which may occur in the digital workflow. This is due to the fact that in a digital environment processes are generally automated and 'hidden', so making 'visual checking' practically impossible and impractical. Severe time and cost penalties will be incurred if clean and efficient workflows are not established and maintained. The main areas of preflighting include checking page construction, graphics file formats, trapping, founts, text matter and output device requirements, software related problems, along with calibration issues to ensure standards are established, monitored and verified against identified criteria. Some RIPs - eg - Harlequin, now have preflight checking and trapping features to ensure that 'faulty' files are not transferred to the imaging 'engine'.

Workflows are the designated routes, or processes, that a job has to pass through in its journey from, say, initial creation of text and graphic files, through manipulation such as page make-up, to checking such as proofing, and finally to its predetermined designation, such as computer-to-film, computer-to-plate or computer-to-print. A further important issue is in establishing close working relationships with customers, designers and other users in the digital workflow and print order processes, to ensure as smooth a transfer of data as possible, on a job-by-job and overall basis.

Mapping, analysing and defining workflows *internally* - ie - within a host system such as within a printing or repro company, and *externally,* covering a wide range of customers with varied requirements and systems in place, is increasingly important in establishing an efficient and cost effective throughput of work.

An increasing area of interest and development is in *'distribute and print',* where data is sent to designated remote sites for 'local' printing and distribution offering a relatively low cost option and high speed turnaround at least for short-run work. This has been particularly targeted by the Xerox company, with its worldwide document networked print-on-demand strategy.

Different points, or ports of entry, to the printing process and extended multi-media environment, have become available through the digitalisation of communications, which 'theoretically' simplifies the transfer of data from one party to another, or many others. Due, however, to different working practices, procedures, protocols and computer platforms, the resultant workflow patterns are often far from being seamless in most cases: this has now been largely addressed by the development of PDF *(Portable Document Format)* files and PostScript.

At the time this book was written - ie - late 1990s, printing was going though a transitional period from the old craft, mechanical-based, mainly analogue driven, conventional printing processes, to one of considerable modernisation of all printing processes, typified by an increasingly digital front end/prepress which, apart from generating the data in a form suitable for printing - ie - up to computer-to-plate or computer-to-print, could be used to set up digitally controlled presses and print finishing equipment.

Examples of this include setting up the ink profiles on a press, from the electronically imposed bit map data of a job: alternatively, setting up a folding machine, including type of folds required, adjustment of sheet size and calliper for each job, again from master job details data created on a front-end software program and/or linked into a host MIS *(Management Information System).*

A further development coined *'future print'*, along with *'distribute and print'* arrangements, places the focus very much on responding to customers needs, where printers concentrate on producing services rather than products, and the direction is focused on repurposing data for many different formats and uses. For a more indepth coverage of this changing face of print the reader is directed to the BPIF publication *'Managing Technology - strategies for profitable growth in the printing industry'*, 1997.

Printing for so long the major means of communication now has many other competing media options. Digital printing is mainly established in niche markets, rather than volume printing, which remains the domain of the conventional printing processes. It is particularly suitable for personalisation of documents, reproduction of out-of-print publications, even down to one copy; short run batch printing which allows inexpensive set-up and reprint costs, customised or regionalised brochures-type printed products, allowing specific targeting to an identified market, rather than a composite, general all-embracing brochure.

Many examples of printed work previously produced on a high volume basis by conventional printing processes, such as computer manuals, have changed to a print-on-demand basis, or are produced only on non-print media such as CD-ROM - alternatively in the form of 'electronic books', in which case the 'format' of the text has to change from 'portrait' to 'landscape' to be displayed on a monitor or terminal: the text being resident on the computer's hard disk where the individual software user can print out a hard copy of the manual, or selected parts of the manual as required on, for example, a laser printer, for their own personal use.

Data preparation for print

Printers are increasingly receiving electronic data rather than mechanical data, as confirmed by *Figure 10.1*, prepared by the British Printing Industries Federation, which reproduces data generated through responses from their members.

Input data	1995	1997
Traditional mechanical	37.5%	22.6%
Raw data	14.8%	16.5%
PostScript	10.4%	11.6%
DTP minor change	14.0%	20.7%
DTP major change	23.3%	28.6%

Figure 10.1: Changes from 1995 to 1997 in the breakdown of data received by printers from customers

All types of digitally generated input data supplied to printers from 1995 to 1997 show an increase in volume, confirming a major shift to digital media - this trend is set to continue and accelerate. Electronic files are also increasingly supplied in media other than standard diskettes, as confirmed by *Figure 10.2*.

Electronic file medium	1995	1997
Standard diskette	63.2%	44.2%
Removable hard drive	14.1%	20.9%
Telecommunications	8.5%	15.0%
Erasable optical drive	7.7%	15.4%
Tape	6.5%	6.5%

Figure 10.2: Changes from 1995 to 1997 in the electronic file medium received by printers from customers

The data in *Figure 10.2* has again been prepared by the British Printing Industries Federation through responses from its members. *It should be noted that with re-writable CDs now so inexpensive, they are bound to impact on the above figures, along with other storage/communication systems as they are introduced.*

The reduction in the use of standard diskettes is due mainly to the growth of the file sizes required, which are prepared and sent to printing companies: a standard diskette of the high density, double sided type can only hold 1.44 Mb of data when formatted, whereas removable hard drives, tape and erasable optical drives can hold substantially more, several Gb in fact, and are therefore more suitable for colour and feature-rich files. Telecommunication through ISDN and modem is set to grow at an accelerating rate, due to improved speed of data transfer and high rate of new users taking up this medium.

Electronic/digital printing

Electronic/digital printing - ie - *computer-to-print*, covers a wide range of processes with two distinctive types - *fixed image data* and *variable image data* printing.

The above classification of digital printing considers only processes where no separate, removable plate or other surface preparation such as cylinder or stencil is prepared for the printing process to operate, and the printed result is generated from a direct imaging process onto the chosen substrate.

Computer-to-plate *(CTP)*, on the other hand, although based on a complete prepress digital workflow, creates an intermediate analogue stage - ie - plate, cylinder or stencil, which interrupts and stops the digital workflow present in computer-to-print. CTP is usually a process where the plate is made *off the press*, to be followed by the separate process of mounting plates on the press ready for job setup: an alternative is where CTP involves preparing plates *on the press*, each plate being imaged directly on the press - *see Heidelberg Quickmaster DI 46-4 on pages 181* and *182.*

Digital printing has created the reality of on-demand printing, due to the absence of extensive make-ready/set-up associated with conventional printing processes.

It is certainly suited to short-run work with a cost-based break-even figure compared to, for example, sheet-fed offset litho of around 1000 copies or more, although the situation is changing all the time with the probability of digital printing encroaching more and more into areas which are currently the domain of conventional processes. A further example of encroachment of digital printing on previously conventional print territory is in the increasing use of large- or wide-format digital colour printing systems instead of screen printing for short-run poster work. Fast turnaround is recognised as one of the major assets of computer-to-print systems.

Although all the main conventional printing processes, such as offset lithography, flexography, letterpress, gravure and screen, are relatively undisputed in terms of volume and value produced each year, digital printing in its many forms is now also established as a major player in printing and print-related products.

The images to be printed are generated and manipulated in a digital form on an AppleMac, PC or other host computer system: they are then downloaded onto the host printing unit via a RIP and digital link, which can either be part of an on-line networked system, or the data transferred off-line by a storage media such as a disk or tape. The print unit/engine is then set up for the required number of copies and if a finishing unit is included and/or required, the job is collated and bound and can be completed on- or in-line.

As previously stated, whereas conventional printing processes are mostly suited to producing the same printed image time after time in volume, electronic printing has the advantage and facility to produce a different image each time from variable data, and so can produce an original copy each time the printing roller/drum rotates if required. This is due to each of the conventional printing processes requiring a relatively expensive plate, cylinder or stencil for each separate image, whereas electronic printing can literally produce a new image *(at the flick of a switch)*, each time a new page or file is downloaded digitally.

There are a wide range of printing processes or technologies which fall under the generic term of electronic or digital printing: in addition, they can also be categorised in so many different ways that a definitive list would be a difficult, if not an impossible task. This chapter will only attempt to provide an overview of the main digital printing technologies and processes. *Figure 10.3* illustrates two separate categories of electronic/digital printing and digital imaging printing.

Electronic/ digital printing				Digital imaging printing
Digital copier/ printing systems	*Variable information/ data printing systems*	*Computer-to-print systems*	*Wide-format printing systems*	*Computer-to-press systems*
- *black-and-white and colour*	- *black-and-white*	- *four-colour process*	- *black-and-white and colour*	- *four-colour process*
- eg - Xerox DocuTech 135, DocuPrint 6135, DocuColor 40, Kodak Image Source 92p and 1565, MicroPress *using electrophotography, xerography or laser*	- eg - Nipson Varypress and N70, Océ Pagestream 350, IBM InfoPrint 4000, Domino JetArray *using electrophotography, laser and for mainly personalisation inkjet*	- eg - Indigo, Chromapress, Xeikon DCP, IBM InfoColor 70, Xerox DocuColor 70 *using electrophotography* - *liquid or dry toner*	- eg - CalComp CrystalJET, ColorSpan Europe DisplayMaker, Hewlett Packard Designjet, Raster Graphics Piezo Print 5000, *using various forms of inkjet: electrostatic and laser*	- eg - Heidelberg Quickmaster DI 46-4, development of Heidelberg 74 digital press, KBA-Planeta and Scitex 74 Karat, Omni-Adast Dominant 705C DI, Goss Adopt *using mainly lithography in some form or other*

Figure 10.3: Examples of electronic/digital printing capable and suitable for variable image data; plus digital imaging printing suited more to short-run fixed image data

Electronic/digital printing systems

Electronic printing systems are now available which can produce black only, spot colour or full process colour, either for short-run work or specialist applications.

Digital copier/printer systems

The new generation of copiers, both black-and-white and colour, is the development which threatens certain conventional printing market sectors presently held predominantly by small-offset. Copiers now use technology which offersmuch higher resolution than previously, with scanning-in resulting in excellent quality, even with photographs. The more advanced system copiers are changed into a printer through, for example, an EFI Fiery colour server linked to digital data from an AppleMac or PC: alternatively RIPs are now being built-in or embedded into the machines. Some photocopiers, whether linked to a system or not, can produce spot colour work by simply using coloured toner powder.

Examples of digital copier/printers are as follows:

Xerox DocuTech Production Publisher 135 is a highly specified stand-alone or networked black-and-white copier/printer system, which can scan/digitise images in at 24 x A4 pages per minute, print out at 135 x A4 600 dpi pages per minute and binds on-line, depending on configuration and requirements.

Xerox DocuPrint 6135 with the same Xerographic engine as the Docutech, can support print-on-demand applications; functioning also as a stand-alone device and accepting electronic media on floppy disk, CD-ROM or DAT tape, with an on-screen document viewing facility using Adobe Acrobat, a PDF (*portable document format*) file.

Figure 10.4: Xerox DocuPrint 6135

Xerox DocuTech 6180 is a further black-and-white product aimed at networked print-on-demand where print files can be transported electronically through a number of means such as removable media, LAN *(Local Area Networks)* or WAN *(Wide Area Networks)* connections, plus high-speed modems or the Internet. The machine again supports both on-line and off-line finishing including tape binding, perfect binding, hard cover and signature booklet. Maximum speed is 180 x A4 pages per minute at enhanced 600dpi resolution.

Kodak ImageSource 92p printing system uses Kodak Lionheart client server software which is compatible with most industry-standard operating platforms, such as Windows, DOS, AppleMac or Sun Open Windows. It inputs from hard copy, disk, digital archive or directly off the network. It processes in excess of 100 pages per minute and prints at 92 x A4 pages per minute, at 600dpi, and has an optional folder and saddle stitcher.

Kodak 1565 copier/printer is another networked system, operated through an interpreter such as EFI Fiery: speed is seven full process colour and 28 black-and-white prints per minute at 400dpi.

MicroPress is a digital printing system developed to process and distribute work on up to four networked sheet-fed print engines producing A4 page output. The system is controlled by the Press Director which automatically schedules jobs, distributing the workload across the available print stations. The Press Director resident on a Windows-based NT PC works through different software packages as required, to make-up documents from different sources, along with an automatic OPI image server and local image database followed by drag-and-drop print requests to the PostScript RIP. The RIPped data is then passed through an electronic collator unit onto the networked print stations. The print stations are based on laser electrophotographic non-impact printing technology at 12 pages per minute in full process colour. The system is suited to variable data content with no limit to the number of variable data pages in a job, targeting the machine at short run on-demand markets.

Xerox DocuColor 40 is a sheet-fed digital colour production system, producing 40 full colour A4 pages per minute, far faster than any current copier/printer system: it prints at 400dpi x 8-bit resolution and comes with an EFI Fiery RIP or Scitex front-end.

Variable information/data black-and-white printing systems

Most digital printing systems can be adapted to reproduce at least partial variable data, through the use of software which creates flexible field areas in the document, so that personalised or variable data can be dropped in to the selected areas, varying from a single reference number to complete 100% changes, with each printed copy.

This section highlights systems used mainly in document management, print-on-demand systems, mainly for overprinting or personalising statements, flyers, tickets, vouchers and forms; or alternatively producing entire products from plain paper in sheet or reel form.

The range of on-line and off-line finishing equipment is wide and varied. Major suppliers in the area of paper handling and finishing are Lasermax/Stralfors, Dalren and Hunkeler covering sheet and roll/web-fed systems.

Manufacturers and suppliers of variable data printing equipment include Nipson, Océ, Digital Print, Xerox and IBM - some examples are included below to illustrate the range offered:

The Nipson Varypress M 700 can run at speeds of up to 105 metres per minute: output can be over 700, A4 portrait, two-up pages per minute either as a stand-alone configuration, or in-line with other compatible equipment.

The Nipson N 70 continuous stationery page printer can run at a rated speed of 70 pages per minute with up to 100% variable data on every page without any degradation in speed; apart from variable text it can print overlays, forms and logos.

Figure 10.5: Nipson Varypress M 700 variable data printing system

Océ Pagestream 350 is a continuous printer producing 300 or 240dpi at up to 350 x A4 pages per minute two-up and *Océ Pagestream 440* at up to 440 x A4 pages per minute two-up

IBM InfoPrint 4000 is a roll-fed black-and-white duplex printing system capable of printing at 436 x A4 pages per minute. The system uses IBM InfoPrint Manager, the first digital printing system to use Adobe PostScript Extreme, which is claimed to be the first simultaneous RIP-while-printing PostScript technology. The InfoPrint Manager multiprocessor RIPping relies on Adobe PDF as its internal file format: this along with IBM AFP *(Advanced Function Presentation)* architecture ensures each page is properly formatted and prints at over 26 000 x A4 pages per hour containing variable data. The machine prints at resolutions of 480 or 600 dpi and can be linked up to in-line or off-line finishing lines.

Domino Jet Array Editor 2 is an inkjet printing system aimed at the addressing/ personalisation type of work. It consists of a small print head that can be mounted on any orientation and is capable of printing onto a range of substrates including paper, polythene and coated stocks. The system is flexible and mobile, so that it can be moved around between different types of production equipment such as presses, folders, stitchers, inserters and polythene wrapping lines. It is capable of keeping up with medium range press speeds, as well as operating faster than most finishing equipment. The Editor 2 PC-based controller enables the user to create a comprehensive personalisation marketing tool with specific messages as well as full address changes.

High-speed inkjets are now being used on web offset presses at up to and beyond 50 000 personalised copies with several field changes including name, address and other variable data. The more nozzles and printheads on an inkjet unit, the greater the overall area that can be covered.

Variable information/data systems vary from limited personalisation to print-on-demand, or what is often known as *'bespoke document production'*.

Figure 10.6: IBM InfoPrint 4000 roll-fed black-and-white duplex printing system

This rapidly developing area has been driven by improving means of data storage, manipulation and handling linked to faster and more productive printers.

Although printing inks have been developed which withstand the tremendous heat generated by laser printers, printing companies often still have to exert caution when overprinting previously printed stock.

The Nipson Varypress uses cold fusing magnetography allowing a much wider range of substrate such as pre-glued mailers, plastic and cellophane type products to be manufactured which would melt with conventional hot ink jet fusion or laser.

Computer-to-print systems

Examples which fall into this category are the Indigo E-Print 1000, which is sheet-fed, plus Indigo Omnius, Agfa Chromapress, Xeikon DCP/32D, IBM InfoColor 70 and Xerox DocuColor 70, each of which are roll-fed, multi-colour printing systems. All the computer-to-print systems referred to, with the exception of the Indigo, use the Xeikon engine, although the front-end and RIPs may be different:

The Indigo E-Print 1000 accesses digital data to create the printed result from an imaging and blanket cylinder using a special liquid-based toner ink called 'ElectroInk'; the maximum printed area is A3 (297 x 420mm) running at up to 2000 four-colour A4-size images per hour (two-up). The machine has the capability of printing up to six colours perfected, collated and bound into a saddle stitched booklet if required.

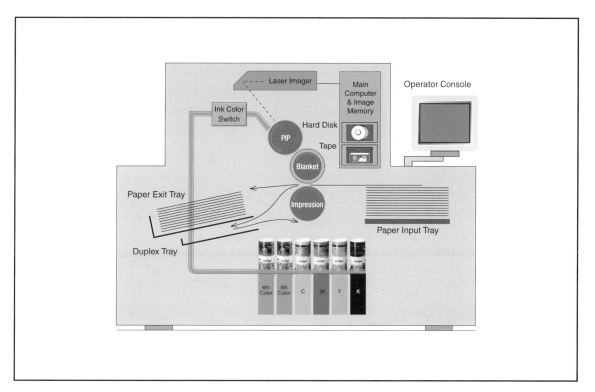

Figure 10.7: Schematic drawing of Indigo E-Print 1000 digital offset press

The E-Print 1000 was the first-ever digital offset press. As in conventional offset litho printing, ink is transferred from plate to blanket and then from blanket to paper; however, unlike conventional offset litho no residual ink is left on the blanket.

Since 100% of the 'ElectroInk' image is transferred to the substrate, the blanket can receive a different image with each revolution. In addition, on-the-fly ink colour switching technology enables each revolution to print not only a new image, but each image a different colour. The Indigo press uses only one set of cylinders for all colours, as against one set of cylinders for each colour with conventional offset litho.

Digital data input is supported via PostScript and Scitex proprietary 'Handshake' into a powerful workstation front-end for processing. Files can be input to the Indigo E-RIP from off-line Exabyte cartridge tape or via a LAN Ethernet network. Job and printing parameters are handled electronically by the electronic publishing software, or they are defined interactively by the E-RIPs graphical user interface which automatically processes the files to be printed, ensuring E-Print compatibility. The print-ready data is then transferred to the E-Print 1000, where the operator simply selects the relevant file and presses a button to commence printing. The rest of the printing process is automatic, requiring no additional operator intervention.

Figure 10.8 shows a picture of the Indigo E-Print 1000 TurboStream press which, through a very powerful front-end, speeds up workflow enhancements achieving faster job setup, allowing jobs to be grouped and printed together, so that the press runs continuously on successive jobs without the need to stop and restart the press each time a new job is introduced.

Indigo has also developed the *Omnius*, a roll-fed version based on the E-Print 1000, aimed at the packaging industry.

The Agfa Chromapress uses a printing engine based on electrophotography, producing work at a resolution of 600dpi with variable dot density, resulting in apparent image quality comparable to 2400dpi at 1751pi. The maximum roll width is 320mm with a printing speed of 35 x A4 duplex pages per minute/2100 x A4 duplex pages per hour. The component parts of the system include a powerful workstation, along with related software tools; a server which controls queue management, press databases, colour management, automatic imposition and proofing mode; facility for controlling print commands, OPI replacement, status reporting, archiving and remote diagnosis; powerful RIP; an output manager that works with the RIP to maximise the system's productivity, plus an engine controller which controls paper conditioning web movement, fusing unit and communicates with the RIP and output manager; printing engine and on-line or off-line finishing facilities.

IBM InfoColor 70 is a full process colour digital roll-fed press developed specifically for fast print-on-demand applications. It is built on an open systems architecture producing 70 colour pages per minute/35 double sided pages per minute: the machines consists of eight print stations (CMYK x two) through which the paper web or board up to 200 g/m^2 passes with a finishing gloss unit if required.

The IBM InfoColor 70 uses an electrophotographic printer utilising dry toner technology achieving 600 dpi with variable light levels per dot. It is PostScript-compatible generating the equivalent of 170lpi screen. The machine comes with variable data system software which simplifies the personalisation of documents, plus plug-ins for PageMaker and QuarkXPress. MergeDoc, a production tool, is also supplied that preflights the variable data, reporting missing images and data errors, and prepares the files for the powerful IBM RS/6000 front-end, InfoColor 70 Raster Image Processor and Xeikon engine output.

The Xeikon DCP/32D covers a range of digital colour presses using the Xeikon printing engine with basic output capabilities in line with the IBM InfoColor 70. There are, however, five separate configurations through the use of different front-end systems, which result in either the digital data being processed quicker, and/or variable data capabilities being available.

Xerox DocuColor 70 is a further Xeikon engine-based digital colour press, with a Scitex SX 3000 or EFI Fiery RIP front-end. Its basic output capabilities are very similar to that of the IBM InfoColor 70.

Developments have now led to the introduction of B2 size computer-to-print systems, such as the *Xeikon DCP/50D* and *Chromapress 50i*. The new Xeikon machine is a wider version of the Xeikon SRA3 electrophotographic machine, initially introduced as the DCP-1, then DCP/32D *(double-sided)* and DCP/32S *(single-sided)*. Paper width is 500mm with a print width of 474mm, with speed up to around 3000 duplex A4 pages per hour, running stock covering 60g/m^2 to 250g/m^2.

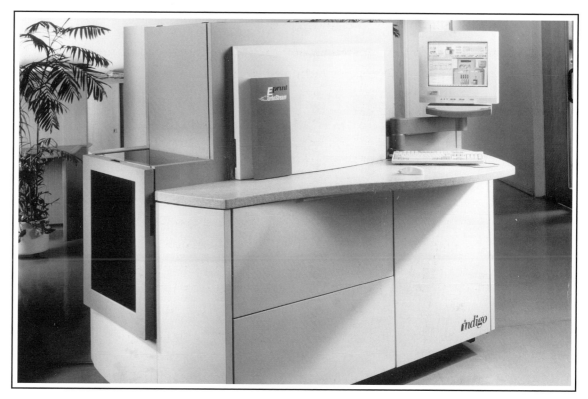

Figure 10.8: Indigo E-Print 1000 TurboStream digital offset press

Wide-format digital colour printing systems

An area which has seen significant growth in computer-to-print is in wide-format digital colour printing which is replacing conventional screen printing in short-run poster and banner printing, but is also creating significant new markets: development has now resulted in printer widths of 1000mm plus, specialist software and inks resistant to fading. Systems are typified by all computer-to-print options - the creation of digital data which is then interpreted/RIPped to a digital printing engine.

In the area of large-format digital printing systems the vast majority are roll-fed inkjet units with four printing heads, CMYK, generating the image in traversing lines across the width of the print unit. Speed of machines vary greatly from over $30m^2$ per hour in draft mode to $8m^2$ in high quality, photo-realistic mode. Some machines are now available where the printed substrate can include - apart from paper - cloth, canvas, backlit film, rigid board or vinyl, etc.

Apart from the most popular process of inkjet, thermal transfer and laser colour printing systems are used. Electrostatics is mainly used for mono and spot colour large-format digital printers.

A selection of wide-format digital colour printing systems is as outlined below:

Color Span Europe DisplayMaker - two models are available in this series, the 400 with a maximum width of 1070mm and the 5000 at 1320mm. The machines are continuous inkjet systems with what is claimed as an apparent 1200dpi resolution. Maximum speed is rated at $5.3m^2$ per hour.

Hewlett-Packard Designjet machines are available in a series including the 755cm, CP2000 and CP2500, all with a maximum width of 900mm. The machines are water-based inkjet systems, capable of 300 to 600dpi resolution. Maximum speed is rated at $3m^2$ per hour.

RasterGraphics Piezo Print 5000 - as its name suggests - is a piezo inkjet-based system with a maximum width of 1360mm. Maximum resolution is 307dpi, with maximum rated speed of $35m^2$ per hour.

CalComp CrystalJET is a 1370mm-width colour inkjet printer which can print at the fast speed of 13m² per hour at 360dpi. It can operate with any type of ink including pigments and dyes, water, solvent or glycol based. The machine has been developed with a selectable dot size feature allowing it to generate halftone dots up to a resolution of 720dpi.

Figure 10.9: CalComp CrystalJET wide-format digital colour printing system

Digital imaging printing systems

Computer-to-press systems

Computer-to-press digital colour printing systems, which offer the high print quality of the conventional printing processes along with networked digital data inherent in the system, have been slow to develop.

Heidelberg has produced two machines in this category, firstly the GTO-DI, an A3 sheet-fed machine which has been withdrawn to be replaced by the Quickmaster DI 46-4.

The Heidelberg Quickmaster DI 46-4 is a four-colour computer-to-press machine which prints by waterless sheet-fed offset litho from direct-imaged polyester plate material: maximum sheet size is 460 x 340mm with a maximum printing speed of 10 000 sheets per hour. The Quickmaster DI is aimed at short-run colour work positioned between colour toner print systems and traditional offset litho printing, retaining high quality offset litho printing combined with short set-up times and directly linked to digital prepress.

In the production of the direct imaged plates - ie - without any intermediate film stage, PostScript data from the digital front-end system is converted in the RIP processor of the Quickmaster DI into screen data which, in turn is converted into control signals for 64 infra-red laser diodes (16 x 4 colours).

The laser beams created by the laser diodes are then bundled into precise rays of controlled light which are focused onto a multi-layer polyester-based plate, ablating material to leave small depressions in the image areas.

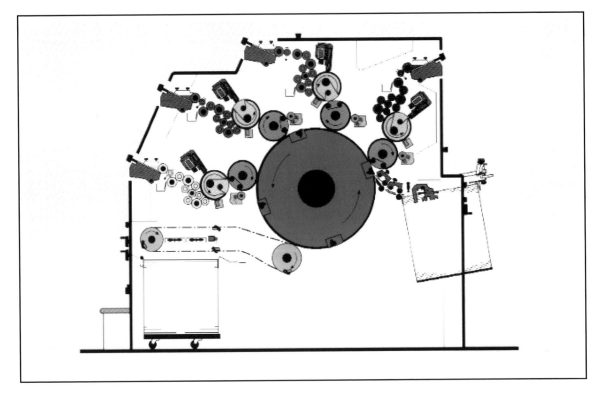

Figure 10.10: Schematic drawing of Heidelberg Quickmaster DI 46-4 digital press

It is these depressions which accept and form the inked image areas, leaving the untouched silicon layer to form the waterless non-image areas. Two different resolutions are available - 1270dpi or 2540dpi creating up to 150lpi screen resolution.

Due to the digital control process of the press, a new job with four plates can be set-up/made-ready in six minutes. The machine operates a plate spooling system which automatically renews the printing plates in all four units on press.

Each job is prepared through the RIP and held in a page buffer unit on the press: the operator then selects and controls the print sequence of jobs. Automatic imaging of all four printing plates along with the cleaning/processing of the plates takes under 10 minutes in total. Ink profiles on the four printing units are preset from the digital data file and register is 'automatic' with the plates being exposed direct on press: the operator can of course override settings manually if this is required.

The press is unusual in that it is of satellite construction with a quadruple-size central impression cylinder, allowing four-colour printing in one gripper closure, enhancing high standards of registration. The press operates a network interface on Ethernet running Windows NT, using PostScript with Harlequin RIP/interpreter.

Future developments in high quality digital printing presses

One of the major restrictions to relatively high standard digital colour printing up until the time the publishing of this book was the maximum overall print size which could be generated. The maximum sheet size of the copier/printers and digital printing systems was around A3, with the Heidelberg Quickmaster DI 46-4 press at B3+ (460 x 340mm) and the maximum width on the roll-fed digital colour presses around 320mm.

Due to the restriction of the basically oversize A3 maximum size, other than the wide format printers, which are relatively slow and suited to specialist/niche markets, several manufacturers had stated they intended to make a B2 digital press, either on their own, or through an alliance/partnership arrangement.

B2 computer-to-print systems covering the Xeikon and Chromapress machines will be among the first to be launched.

Developments in the area of computer-to-press systems were also coming thick and fast towards the end of the millennium.

Heidelberg announced in 1998, the launch of a B2 digital press modelled on their conventional sheet-fed SM 74 offset litho press, to go alongside their B3+ Quickmaster DI 46-4 press. The new digital press will have an imaging area of 500 x 700mm and be available in four-, five- and six-colours, plus in-line varnishing.

Further digital press developments are as outlined below.

Omni-Adast Dominant 705C DI which has a maximum sheet size of 486 x 660mm, with image resolutions of 1016, 1270, 2032 and 2450dpi and maximum screen ruling of 200lpi. The press has a maximum press speed of 10 000 sheets per hour with configurations of two, four or five print units with converting units to allow perfected printing. Press plates have been developed by Presstek, forming a waterless-aluminium silicon coated base plate imaged on an on-press version of the Sakurai platesetter.

The press is aimed at general commercial print markets, rather than specialist, niche short-run work, currently providing the bulk of the work for the A3+ digital presses, with job changeovers targeted at no more than seven minutes per job.

Goss ADOPT (Advanced Digital Offset Printing Technologies Concept Press). The machine works by imaging a copper-based solution onto a nickel oxide coated cylinder digitally, then erasing it after the required print run, avoiding the need for printing plates. The process uses single fluid lithography which works on the basis of ink and water mixed into an emulsion. A preset shear force on the last roller of the ink train ensures that image areas are inked and the non-image areas accept water, both of which are tightly monitored and controlled during the print run. The machine uses conventional heatset or coldset inks.

Due to both the printing and blanket cylinders being gapless - ie - complete unbroken cylinders, the machine also works on changeable variable cylinders - eg - 22", 26" wide, etc: being a shaftless press this makes for economical working.

KBA-Planeta and Scitex 74 Karat is a full B2 format press, 520x740mm, operating by waterless offset lithography at up to 10 000 sheets per hour. It has a revolutionary 'Gravuflow' keyless, self-calibrating inking system with all four inking units located one above the other at one end of the press.

The machine uses fully-automatic thermal processed plates, capable of 200lpi via a cassette system, around a single triple-size central impression cylinder requiring no sheet transfer: each sheet runs through the press twice in one gripper control while the four colours are applied. There is a fully-automatic make-ready cycle of under 15 minutes; are all press functions, controlled from the console via an operator-friendly graphical user interface.

Digital prepress data, including raster image processing, colour management, proofing and imposition are transferred to the press via various open digital front-end systems including Scitex PS/M or Brisque.

Figure 10.11: KBA-Planeta 74 Karat digital press

Many digital printing systems are constantly being developed or existing ones being amended or upgraded, so inevitably this publication can only include a representative selection of equipment, which is changing over time.

Most of this chapter also appears in the 'Introduction to printing and finishing', the companion publication to this one. This is a deliberate decision as electronic/digital printing overlaps both the areas of pre-press and printing but increasingly is being recognised as having more in common and closer links with digital prepress than actual printing.

Adobe Acrobat and PDF (Portable Document Format) files

One of the major problems inherent in the development of DTP-driven systems has been the difficulty of transferring digital data and documents without incurring major incompatibility problems through the use of different platforms, software programs and applications. This has now become possible through the use of PDF files which take the form of a page-orientated object database.

The philosophy behind PDF is to create a digital master which is independent of format, so allowing it to be used across the wide media spectrum which is available from once-only created digital data.

It provides the means to considerably improve and automate digital workflows, through creating an open system, overcoming rather than be locked into proprietary systems, and being ideally suited to distributing proofs electronically, trapping and providing OPI support.

Anyone with a Web browser and Adobe Acrobat software can instantly access PDF files, and because Acrobat is independent of platforms, applications, and distribution media, it is the ideal basis for long-term information distribution, archiving, and retrieval strategy.

PDF files using Acrobat can be created from any application and form such as hard copy or digital form: with software such as PageMaker, QuarkXPress or Microsoft Word and Excel it is simply achieved by selecting 'Create Adobe PDF' from the file menu, creating a PDF file which appears visually as the original document, along with fonts, graphics, images, and page layout, retaining it in a wide range of formats. For high-end use, it is necessary to print Postscript to disk and run the PostScript file through Distiller.

As can be seen from *Figure 10.11*, paper documents can be scanned and OCR'd into PDF image files, and/or imported and viewed in a wide variety of image types which can make the electronic documents created feature-rich by indexation and search features.

The user and creator of the PDF file is then in the position to send that file anywhere without concern as to its accessibility by, or transferability to, other parties through disk, ISDN, modem, CD-ROM, email, Intranet and or Internet. PDF once created takes on the properties of a true transportable means of digital file exchange.

Acrobat software is particularly suited to electronic web publishing as it integrates the viewing of PDF files directly into the major web browsers: further features are the facilities to scale, search, zoom in on, and print at full resolution, along with compression features that make PDF files extremely small in comparison to, say, one created in PostScript - eg - down from a 40Mb file to one of 4Mb, making access and transfer of data considerably faster. There are reduced storage needs in respect of large colour files.

Adobe Distiller is used to create the PDF file from the PostScript output and from this to create a considerably flattened and simplified object list compared to most other systems, allowing much easier and quicker RIPing/processing of data to final selected output media. This PDF workflow is the most significant change in prepress since the introduction of PostScript in the mid 1980s.

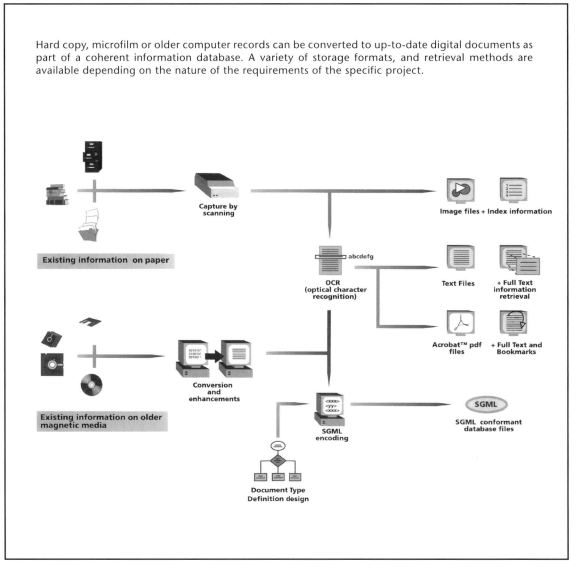

Hard copy, microfilm or older computer records can be converted to up-to-date digital documents as part of a coherent information database. A variety of storage formats, and retrieval methods are available depending on the nature of the requirements of the specific project.

Figure 10.12: Flow diagram illustrating a range of conversion services available to create digital data - reproduced by kind permission of Pindar plc.

The Internet

The Internet, often referred to as the 'Net', is a combined series of networks which allows a device or user connected to one network to communicate with another device or user resident on the combined network system.

It has been in development for over 30 years, having its roots in the USA where government departments developed a program to create computer hardware and software that could send messages between computers over telephone lines. It was then advanced further by US universities setting out to achieve the goal of facilitating communication between scientists and academics.

During the early 1980s, TCP/IP protocols which define the Internet, *see page 46*, were developed that allowed different types of computer to work and link together on the same network, regardless of what operating system was used. This process eventually produced what now is known as the Internet, which has been taken up as a major means of communications by individuals and especially by businesses which view the Internet as a massive commercial opportunity, such as newspapers and magazines, which allow subscribers to access on-line electronic, often interactive, copies of their publications.

The main uses of the Internet for a printing company is for transferring data files and to support email communications: in addition, companies are increasingly using the Internet to advertise their products and services through specially designed, interactive web pages and as a digital communication link with other organisations including suppliers as well as customers.

Computers are linked to the Internet by a modem which converts computer codes, through *modulation*/*dem*odulation through the conversion of purely digital signals from a computer to the normal audio analogue signals required for transmission over the telephone lines, then back again to digital signals into the receiving computer, setting up a client server arrangement - *see page 41*, with users and providers supplying, exchanging and accessing information across the Internet. Increasing use is being made of ISDN *(Integrated Services Digital Network)*, which offers a digital transfer of data throughput - *see pages 41* and *42*.

To operate on, and access the Internet the following components are required - a computer, modem, telephone line, supporting software, and an ISP *(Internet Service Provider)* account such as Demon or Pipex: this allows the user to connect with the ISPs services which includes an email address, along with access to servers for World Wide Web, email and other digital services. Browsers, such as Mosaic or Netscape, allow users to view, interact with, and retrieve files through the use of a user-friendly interface to Internet resources.

Intranets are a form of internet which work on the basis of one single service/host provider and one access point, with multiple computers connected to it - ie - it has dedicated restricted access.

A typical installation would be a networked intercompany system, as against the Internet which has multiple providers of the system. Through the application of an Intranet, companies are able to create private networks, linking individuals, departments and remote sites. The benefits to a large organisation are considerable, such as providing a much more secure system than the Internet, which is faster than the fax, as well as being more cost-effective than the post.

World-Wide Web

The WWW *(World-Wide Web)* was originally created by CERN, the European Council for Nuclear Research, and has now developed into the most-used service on the Internet. This can be confirmed by the number of WWW web site addresses appearing in increasing amounts on a large range of communications, eliciting response or access to information supplied by a user. All WWW addresses start with 'http:', a URL *(Universal Resource Locator)*, which identifies the protocol needed to log onto the web site.

The World Wide Web means of communication is constructed using *hypertext*, which allows separate documents to be linked, so that the user can easily move about between them, overcoming the limitations of conventionally printed publications. An example of this flexibility is where, for example, a document prepared in hypertext contains a particular word or reference, then this can be made a *link* to an on-line dictionary: the user only needs to click on the selected word or link to access and read the related explanation or definition, then click to return to the required place again in the document.

A piece of text which is underlined or highlighted is an anchor or hyperlink; graphics can also be links, which are often accessed by clicking on buttons or thumbnails of pictures. If the user has jumped somewhere, they can go back by clicking the 'back' or 'return' button. Due to the vast amount of data that can be accessed through the WWW, directories and search facilities are available to assist the user: an example of a WWW search facility is WebCrawler.

The WWW uses HTML *(Hypertext Markup Language)*, a simple programming language which allows World Wide Web documents to contain graphics, sound, video and links to e-mail and other services. HTML is a subscript of SGML, using it to define document structure suitable for use on the WWW.

SGML *(Standard Generalised Markup Language)* is an open, nonproprietary language for describing information, structuring it on the lines of a database, allowing documents to be published in multiple media, as well as to be converted to different formats. Documents prepared are constructed by content rather than form, with SGML providing a language for describing a class of document through the DTD *(Document Type Definition)*. HTML has developed into a DTD which describes the class of documents that appear on the World Wide Web.

Electronic mail (email)

Email is a further digital means of communication used for sending and receiving text messages over a telephone link. The following are required to operate email: email account with an Internet Service Provider, access to the ISP's email server computer and email client software; plus computer and modem.

To send an email the exact address of the recipient will be required: the message can be prepared by the sender with the receiver's address off-line, so to speak, while not linked up to the Internet. Once connected to the Internet the message(s) can be sent via the ISPs mail server which takes the form of an electronic sorting office for the email, passing messages on as directed. On an incoming basis email is delivered straight to users whose computers are operating on-line: if a user is off-line at any stage, they can pick up their emails when they connect again to their ISP's mail server.

Emails can often be enhanced by attaching electronic post-it notes to emphasise a point or change. There is a range of software available to allow the user to enhance the media of emails.

CIP3

CIP3 stands for International Co-operation for Integration of *prepress, press* and *postpress* and has been drawn up by a group of major companies serving these three main areas of print.

From this co-operation PPF *(Print Production Format)* was developed by IGD *(Fraunhofer-Institut für Graphische Datenverarbeitung)* in agreement with all the member companies with the aim of computer-integrated manufacturing of print products.

The PostScript language has been adopted as the encoding method, along with the PPF interface being vendor-independent, forming the digital link of all production processes in prepress, press and postpress. The overall objective of CIP3 is to reduce costs in terms of time and materials throughout all areas of the printing process.

The data contained in a CIP3 PPF file includes the following:

- administrative/job set-up data
- preview images for each colour separation to facilitate presetting of the ink zones on the printing press
- transfer functions
- colour and density measuring information
- register mark
- cut data
- folding procedures
- private/specific data which can be used to store application or vendor-specific data - eg - machine settings for repeat jobs.

The benefits from using CIP3 PPF include:

- once-only data acquisition
- shorter production cycles
- better quality control
- avoidance of film chemistry
- reduced water wastage
- less substrate wastage.

Member companies of CIP3 include Adobe, Agfa, Baldwin, Barco Graphics, Creo, R R Donnelley & Sons Company, Electromat, Inkflow, KBA, Kolbus, Komori, Linotype-Hell, MAN Roland, Mitsubishi, Muller Martini, Polar, Scitex, Screen, Ultimate Technologies, Wohlenberg and Xerox.

It is now possible to preset jobs from prepress through to print finishing and completion with CIP3 standards built into a growing amount of member companies, equipment and processes.

As all printing equipment becomes more and more digitally controlled, CIP3 will assume a higher priority in deciding and controlling workflows.

Links between CIP3 and MISs (*Management Information Systems*) have been slow to take off, although both have the potential to provide printers with a very effective combined system - the MIS identifying the most cost-effective job route and the CIP3 ensuring that it is followed in the most efficient manner - *see Figure 10.13.*

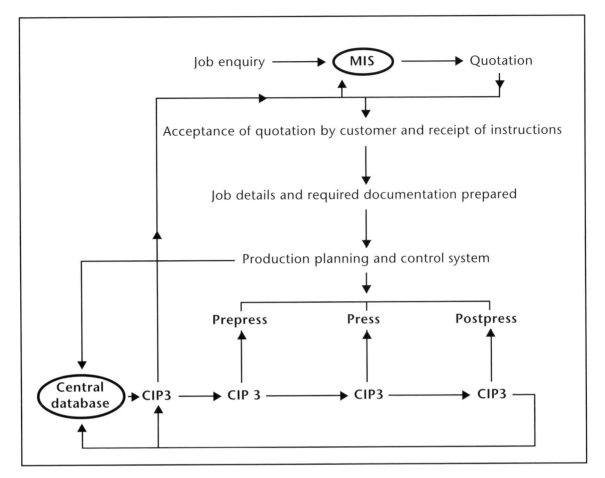

Figure 10.13: Flow diagram of a possible link-up of CIP3 and an MIS

Glossary

．．

This glossary is intended to be used as a means of reference and explanation to expand on some of the technical and operational terms used in prepress- and digital printing-related areas.

Access To recall data from a computer storage area.

Acoustic coupler A method of transmitting data over telephone lines or radio links using the microphone and ear piece to transmit and receive an audible digital sound. To transmit computer data over telephone lines, the data must be converted into electrical tone signals. See *modem* and *ISDN*.

Additive primaries Coloured lights in red, green and blue, (R, G, B), which when combined with each other in equal proportions, produce white. Other colours may be produced by mixing different proportions of each light source. Video monitors use this principle to produce colour television images. Input scanner detectors sense red, green and blue components of the scanned image before electronic conversion to printing colours of cyan, magenta, yellow and black.

Airbrush An instrument having a small reservoir to contain liquid ink and so arranged that a controlled current of air is blown over the ink surface which is broken down into an atomised spray and ejected through a nozzle. Used by artists when working traditionally - ie - without the aid of a computer system with art/design facilities, to obtain graduated effects on drawings, photographs and lithographic printing surfaces.

Alignment Horizontal positioning of type to ensure that the base of each character is perfectly in line with the next.

Artwork Text, graphic and illustrations arranged individually or in any combination for subsequent printing. Artwork may conventionally be drawn in black-and-white on suitable artpaper or board; or may be computer-originated, in which case it may be supplied as digitised data on a floppy disk or other means of electronic data. Artwork may also be in the form of a full-colour drawing or picture which requires specialist reprographic colour separation. This enables the separation to be printed in the four basic printing process colours (cyan, magenta, yellow and black).

Ascender Top part of the lower-case letter stretching above the x-height of the character, as in d, h and k.

ASCII *American Standard Code for Information Interchange*. This is a standard coding system used within the computer industry to convert keyboard input into digital information. It covers all of the printable characters in normal use and control characters such as carriage return and line feed. The full table contains 127 elements. Variations and extensions of the basic code are to be found in special applications.

ASPIC *Authors' Symbolic Prepress Interfacing Codes*. Standard mark-up or code system which indicates a change of typesetting format. See *SGML*.

Author's corrections Corrections made by the author on proofs, that alter the original copy. The cost of making such alterations is charged for, in contrast to printer's errors or house corrections.

Backslant Where a typeface can be made to slant backwards, in the opposite way to italic.

Bandwidth The rate at which data is sent over a network.

BASIC *Beginners All-purpose Symbolic Instruction Code*. The earliest, most popular language used on microcomputers.

Bit *Binary information transfer* or *binary digit*. The basic unit of information in computer imagesetting; it represents a pulse, electrical charge or its absence. Each bit stands for one binary digit, 0 or 1. Bits are usually grouped together in blocks of eight to make *bytes*. Most computer operations work on byte-sized pieces of information.

193

Bitmap	An image arranged according to bit location in columns. Resolution of a PostScript file processed through a RIP will have a bitmap image with the characteristics and resolution of the particular output device - eg - laser printer at 300dpi up to 1800dpi, imagesetters at 1270dpi up to 5080dpi.
Black box	Colloquial term for a device or program which converts information from one form to another.
Bold	A typeface that is heavier than normal weight, available in most type families.
Bromide	A photographic paper used in graphic reproduction, phototypesetting and imagesetting on which a photographic image is created. See *PMT*.
Browser	A program which retrieves and displays information from on-line services.
Byte	The standard measure of computer information and memory, consisting of eight bits. See *bit*.
Calibration bar	This takes the form of a strip of tones and solids used to check printing quality throughout the process as a negative, positive, proof or printed copy. See *colour control bar*.
Camera-ready artwork	Finished artwork that is ready, without further preparation, to be photographed.
CD ROM	*Computer disk read-only memory,* on which computer program information is stored.
Chip	The basic building block for computers, made from silicon.
Choke	A specific adjustment or distortion whereby the perimeter, in total or in part, of an element is slightly pulled in (*choked*) towards the centre of the element. Choking of an element is normally used in conjunction with the spreading (see *spread*) of a neighbouring element to ensure that colour registration standards are achieved. Choking of an element may be performed in a number of ways, manually, photomechanically or digitally, with various computer programs.
Client	Any computer or workstation that uses the resources of another computer. See *server*.
CMYK	Initial letters indicating the printing 'subtractive' primary colours - *cyan, magenta, yellow* and *black*.
Coarse screen	A halftone screen up to 35 lines per cm used in preparing illustrations for newsprint and similar rough surfaced papers.
Colour control bar	A coloured strip on the margin of the sheet which enables the platemaker and printer to check by eye or instrument the printing characteristics of each ink layer. See *calibration bar*.
Colour proofing	This term describes a wide range of techniques which have been developed to reproduce full colour images from the film or digital data available, prior to the actual print run; thus allowing the client, colour separation house and printer to view the 'proofed' result, prior to the actual print run.
Colour separation	In photomechanical reproduction, the process of separating the various colours of a picture usually by colour filters or electronic scanning so that separate printing plates can be produced.
Compression	The compacting of data so reducing the size of image files. See *decompression*.
CTP	*Computer-to-plate.* The generation of a printing plate direct from digital data. See *platesetter*.
Computer-to-press	Printing direct from a computer system without any intermediate stage.
Contact screen	Used to produce a halftone from continuous tone film or artwork using cameras or scanners.
Continuous tone	Term often shortened to *contone*, it describes images which contain an apparently infinite range of shades and colours smoothly blended to provide a faithful reproduction of natural images.
Contract proof	A coloured, hard copy representation of the printed image, made from films or digital data, which will be used to make the final printing plates. The word 'contract' comes from the fact that, when signed by the client, a contract is formed, which states that the final printed job should be a close match to the contract proof.

Control target	Quality aid available in digital or analogue (film) form containing specific elements designed to highlight any variation in reproduction or printing quality.
CPS	*Characters per second.* This refers usually to the output speed of imagesetting systems.
CPU	*Central Processing Unit.* In large computers, this may consist of a circuit that contains a number of chips, but for microcomputers the CPU is almost invariably a single chip, the microprocessor.
CRT	*Cathode Ray Tube.* An electronic vacuum tube with a screen on which information (text or pictures) may be stored or displayed. They are used as displays in video display terminals, and to expose letter images onto film or paper in phototypesetters/imagesetters.
Cursor	A moveable guide point on a VDU screen which allows the operator to identify a position on the display.
Customisation	The personalisation of printed matter through the use of a digital printing system.
Daisy wheel	A printing head used on typewriters and computer printers where individual characters are on the ends of 'petals'.
Database	A collection of data items which are used frequently by programs. A database of any size would be kept on a disk, several disks or CD ROM, etc.
DCS	*Desktop colour separation.* An image format which consists of four separate CMYK separations files at full resolution, plus an EPS file for placement purposes only. Also referred to as *EPS 5*.
Decompression	The expansion of compressed data normally back to its original size. See *compression*.
Densitometer	A device for measuring film or a printed product, either by reflected or transmitted light. Densitometers vary in their sophistication and the number of features provided, such as colour, black-and-white, read-out memory, computer printout, etc.
Descender	Part of the lower-case letter below the x-height of the character as in g, q and p.
Diffusion transfer	See PMT *(photomechanical transfer)*.
Digital	Describes the use of digital pulses, signals or values to represent data in computer graphics, telecommunications systems and word processing.
Digital fount (font)	An electronically-stored type font with characters stored as a series of digital signals.
Digital page composition	DPC, also known as EPCS *(electronic page composition system)* or CEPS *(colour electronic page system)*. A system designed to take a range of page elements (text, linework and images) and integrate them into a user-specified format. Image and text input to the system arrive on magnetic tape, by direct system interconnection or directly from an input scanning system.
Digital printing	Range of printing processes that take digital data from a front-end computer system and output direct to a digital printing system.
Digital workflow	An all-digital workflow would be represented by all data being created and captured digitally, from the very beginning of the printing process to outputting on a digital printing press or other form of digital output - eg - CD ROM or Internet.
Display matter	Type displayed such as title pages, headings, jobbing work, as distinct from solid composition or body matter.
Dot gain	Refers to the fact that the percentage size of a halftone dot on film (printable dot) changes size as it is transferred from film to printed paper/substrate. This is dependent/interrelated to the type of film image (negative or positive), the method of printing and the substrate used. If working traditionally - ie - with film, the press dot gain must be anticipated at the film stage and the dot size reduced to counteract the percentage gain. This is not a linear change as it varies depending on the original film dot size.
Dot matrix	Imaging method in typewriters and computers. Each letter is made up of dots using a matrix of 5 x 7 or greater.
Download	The transfer of digital data from one computer system to another.
Driver	A program or routine that allows a computer to communicate with, and control, a peripheral device such as a printer or scanner.

DTP	*Desktop publishing.* The generic term given to the introduction of personal computers (PCs) to typesetting, page composition and image handling. The combination of all these gives electronic control within a single system of what was traditionally a specialist and segmented series of operations.
Dummy	A sample of a proposed job made up with the actual materials and cut to the correct size to show bulk, style of binding, etc. Also a complete layout of a job showing position of type matter and illustrations, margins, etc.
Duotone	A two-colour halftone produced from two halftone images of the same original. Different visual effects can be obtained by using different screen angles, contrast ranges, special screens, etc.
Duplex halftones	Two-colour halftone plates made from a monochrome original, the second plate being used as a tint.
Dye sublimation	This is a form of printing used mainly in the graphic arts for proofing where coloured dyes on plastic film carriers are heated to the extent that they vaporise and fuse onto the substrate as required.
EDI	*Electronic Data Interchange.* A term which describes any commercial data transfer.
Electrophotography	The printing process used by many electronic printing systems where a laser or LED *(light emitting diode)* and photoconductive drum are used to create charged image particles of toner that are transferred and fused to the substrate forming the printed result.
Electrostatic printing	A term used to describe where the printing plate, drum or belt is charged overall with electricity and light is reflected from the non-image areas of the original being copied, destroying the charges in these areas. Toner powder is then applied, which adheres only in the still-charged image area, fusing itself to the substrate by heat. See also *laser printing.*
Encoder	A mechanism for converting data in one format to data in another - eg - RGB to CMYK.
Encryption	The encoding of data to make it more secure.
EPS	A file format, *Encapsulated PostScript,* used to transfer PostScript image information from one program to another. An EPS file has two parts - a 72dpi PICT file used to display the file on a monitor and the PostScript code that describes the page.
Ethernet	A networking system enabling the high-speed transfer of data between computer systems and peripherals over a co-axial link.
Extranet	The use of Intranet technologies to set up link up groups of users together, such as companies with their suppliers.
Facsimile (fax)	The transmission of copy, artwork or separations electronically from one location to another; also to produce a duplicate (facsimile) of the original data.
File	Generic term for a specifically created group of data in the form of a document or application, which is referred to by its unique name and stored as such.
Filmsetting	See *phototypesetting.*
First-generation film	An original plate-ready film, which has been exposed either through a camera or, more typically, through a laser imagesetter, and photographically processed.
Fit	Proportion of space between two or more letters which can be modified - eg - tight fit by adjusting the set-width.
Fixed space	Space between words or characters not variable for justification purposes.
Floppy disk	A removable magnetic storage medium with most common used size being 3.5".
Flush left or right	Type lining up vertically, either to left or right.
FM screening	*Frequency modulated* screening. See *stochastic screening.*
Font	American for fount. Both are pronounced 'font'. See *fount.*
Formats	Repetition of typographical or other commands. Formatting is used to program a computer by a single command to simplify repeated changes to text matter after it has been set and printed out - eg - the updating of a price list.

Fount	A set of type characters of the same design (and with hot metal, also the same size) - eg - upper and lower case, numerals, punctuation marks, accents and ligatures.
Four-colour process	Colour printing by means of the three subtractive primary colours (yellow, magenta, cyan) and black superimposed; the colours of the original having been separated by a photographic or electronic process.
FPO	*For Position Only.* The use of a low-resolution image in a document, so as to illustrate the position and format of the final high-resolution image.
Front-end system	The part of a computer or imagesetting system responsible for the control of input, correction, manipulation and storage; as opposed to the 'back-end' which forms the output device.
Function codes	Codes which control setting system's functions, as opposed to input codes which produce characters.
Generic mark-up	A method of mark-up which describes the structure and other attributes of a document or print job in a rigorous and system-independent manner, so that it can be processed for a number of different applications. See *SGML.*
Graphics tablet	Used in computing and page make-up for layout or system control. A 'mouse', pen or puck on a drawing board controls movement on the video screen, traces in outlines or permits selection of commands from a 'menu'.
Gravure printing	A process in which the printing areas are below the non-printing surface. The recesses are filled with ink and the surplus is cleaned off the non-printing area with a doctor blade before the paper contacts the whole surface and lifts the ink from the recesses.
Grey balance	The condition in colour reproduction where the dot size values of the subjective primaries are balanced to give a visual neutral grey - eg - cyan - 60%, magenta - 48% and yellow - 46%.
Greyscale	The depiction of grey tones between black and white. A greyscale monitor is able to display grey pixels as well as black and white, but not colour pixels.
Grid	A regularly spaced set of lines in two dimensions to form a series of positional references. In electronic systems they may be used to position accurately text and image information for on-screen page layout.
Gutter	The binding margin of a book.
H & J	Hyphenation and justification.
Half-sheet work	See *work-and-turn*, also *work-and-tumble.*
Halftone image	Represents an image which has had the tones translated into solids and various dot sizes to represent to the eye, a continuous tone result. The visual effect is of different tonal levels depending on the ratio of printed dot area to page/substrate background.
Halftone screen	Glass plate or film, cross-ruled with opaque lines and having transparent squares; used to split up the image into halftone dots. See *contact screen.*
Hard copy	Typed or printed copy produced simultaneously with a tape or recording which allows operators to read and correct before photosetting or imagesetting.
Hard disk	A fixed magnetic storage medium in which the data holding element cannot be removed. Hard disks have very large storage capacity of several Gb, enabling data to be rapidly accessed and manipulated.
Hardware	The electronic components of a computer, as opposed to the programming *(software).*
Headline	In composition, it takes the form of a line of type at the top of a page separated from the text by white space. A running headline is the title of a book repeated at the top of every page of text, or at the top of left-hand *(verso)* pages, with the chapter headings of the contents of the two pages on the right-hand *(recto)* pages.
Highlight	The whitest part of a halftone when printed.
House corrections	Corrections in proofs, other than those made by the author.
HTML	*Hypertext Markup Language.* The language used to create text for the World Wide Web; including codes to define layout, founts, embedded graphics and hypertext links. See *hypertext.*

Hue	The colour defining component of a point in an image. *Hue* combined with *saturation* fully defines a colour.
Hypertext	A means of writing and displaying text which structures the text to be linked in several ways, so enabling related documents to be set up.
Icons	Symbols used to make explanations shorter, relating to the manipulation of specific menus on screen. The AppleMac system and PC Windows are examples of the use of icons.
Image	The ink-carrying areas of a printing plate.
Image master	Photographic original for founts of typefaces used in photosetting.
Imagesetter	An output typesetting system which has the ability to combine all the elements of a page - text, tints, graphics, etc - directly onto paper/bromide, film or polyester plate material.
Impose	To plan film or pages prior to platemaking.
Imposition schemes	Plans for the arrangement of the pages of a book so that they will follow in the correct sequence when folded.
Indented	A shortened line of type set over to the right of the normal margin.
Inferior characters and figures	Letters or numbers which are smaller than the text size and are positioned on or below the baseline, also known as *subscript*.
Inkjet	A non-impact printing process in which droplets of ink are projected onto paper or other material, in a computer-determined pattern.
Inner	An imposition containing the pages which fall on the inside of a printed sheet in sheetwork - the reverse of the *outer forme*.
Input	Data for processing by a computer prior to outputting.
Input device	Any device that can apply an input to the computer. This includes the keyboard, disk drive, tape unit, voice recognition and any other peripherals that supply input signals.
Interactive	Term which relates to the situation when the operator working on a VDU or system can see what is happening and acts immediately to alter anything as required.
Interface	A general term used to describe the method by which two independent systems may communicate with each other. The term interface is usually used in reference to electronic system interconnection, but may also refer to the way in which users relate to the equipment they operate.
Internet	A world wide network of computers.
Intranet	An internal network within a single company/organisation using Internet technology.
Ion deposition	Non-impact printing process in which ions are projected from a replaceable print cartridge onto a rotating drum to form a latent dot matrix image.
ISDN	*Integrated Services Digital Network*. A telephone network service which carries data, voice transmissions by digital means, not analogue.
Justification	The even and equal spacing of words and blocks to a predetermined measure: 'to justify a line' is to space out a line of type to the required measure.
Kerning	The process of altering the space in between type characters to achieve a more aesthetically pleasing arrangement of the letters of a word.
Key	The outline of a drawing which is transferred or used as a guide in the production of printing plates so that the various colours will register with each other; also relates to the design which acts as the guide for position and registration of the other colours. Further examples of the term include the character key on a typesetting keyboard and to set via a keyboard.
Landscape	Oblong loose or folded printed sheet, or book, having its long sides at head and foot.
Laser	*Light Amplification by Stimulated Emission of Radiation*. A fine beam of light, sometimes with considerable energy, used in imagesetting, colour scanning, copy scanning, platemaking, engraving, plus cutting and creasing forme-making.

Laser engraving	The process of engraving an image onto a printing plate, or as a further example a printing cylinder coated with rubber, using an intense laser beam. It is used for continuous patterns where a conventional printing plate join would be revealed in the printed image.
Laser imagesetter/ recorder/plotter	Descriptions identifying the film/plate material output devices of various manufacturers. Film exposed at high resolution using laser light source direct from digital information stored on hard disk.
Laser printing	A form of electrostatic printing in which the image is not created by reflection from an original (electrostatic copying) but by switching a laser on and off according to digital information from a computer.
Lead	Term covering strips of metal less than type-high, used as general spacing material (thickness: 1pt, 1.5pt [thin], 2pt [middle], 3pt [thick]); also to lead, in all composition, to add space between lines of type. The term comes from hot-metal letterpress printing, in modern setting systems it is more often referred to as *interlinear spacing*.
Leader	A type character having two, three or four dots in line, used to guide the eye across a space or other relevant matter, as in tables.
LED	*Light emitting diode.* A semi-conductor that produces a light when a voltage is applied. In small sizes used in photocomposition/imagesetting and colour scanning.
Letterpress printing	A process in which the printing surface of metal, plastic, photopolymer or rubber is raised above the non-printing surface. The ink rollers and the substrate touch only the relief printing surface.
Letterset	Offset letterpress printing, using a wrap-round relief plate on a litho press; also called *dry offset*.
Letterspacing	To increase the standard space between characters to fill a line or enhance the visual look of the words. See *kerning*.
Ligature	Two or more letters joined together, and forming one type character as fi, fl, ff, ffi, ffl.
Light pen	Light-sensitive stylus used with certain VDUs for design or editing.
Line art	Artwork without any gradations of tone. In digital terms the term covers images containing only black-and-white pixels; also known as *bilevel*.
Line block	A relief block produced from a line drawing and without the use of a halftone screen.
Line caster	Hot-metal typesetting machine that produces lines or slugs of type.
Line drawing	A typical drawing which would be produced with pen and brush when using a full charge of ink, thus making lines of comparable photographic value.
Line feed	The distance, usually in points, between base lines or successive text lines in phototypesetting/imagesetting.
Line printer	High-speed, tape or computer-activated machine producing typewriter-like printouts.
Lithographic printing	A process in which the printing and non-printing surfaces are on the same plane and the substrate makes contact with the whole surface. The printing part of the surface is treated to receive and transmit ink to the paper, usually via a blanket (see *offset printing*), the non-printing surface is treated to attract water and thus rejects ink from the ink roller, which touches the whole surface.
Logo	An image or symbol constructed from shapes, designs and letters, designed to represent an organisation, trademark, etc.
Lower case	Term covering small letters of the alphabet as distinct from capitals; also the divided wooden tray used for hot-metal founders typesetting.
Matrix, also matrice	A *two-dimensional array of CCD elements,* as used on some CCD scanners. Traditionally in typefounding and typesetting it covered a copper or brass mould from which a typeface or slug of metal was cast.
Menu	The choice of operations displayed on a VDU.
Merge	A method of combining matter on two or more tapes or disks into one, using a computer to incorporate amendments or new copy into existing copy and to produce a clean tape or disk for typesetting.

Mesh (screen printing)	The weave dimension and angle of the fabric of material used for preparing silk screen stencils.
Microcomputer	A small computer, usually made to sit on a desktop.
Microfiche	A sheet of film, typically 150 x 150mm, holding in reduced size, many pages of larger documents.
Microprocessor	The 'chip' that forms the central processing unit of a computer.
Mixing	Having more than one typeface, style or size in a line of text.
Modem	*Modulator Demodulator.* A modem is a device which accepts a digital signal from a computer and adapts it for transmission over an analogue channel - ie - a telephone line.
Modification	With digital imagesetters/photosetters and display setters, characters can be condensed, expanded or italicised by digital or optical means.
Moiré pattern	In colour printing, using traditional halftone screening, the term describes an irregular and unwanted screen clash patterning, either over the whole image in certain combinations or in specific areas. To avoid moiré the screen angles of the colour separations need to be changed.
Montage	Term used in the graphic industry for a number of operations: *photomontage* - combination and often blending of images; *montage of pages* - page make-up; *montage of film* - mounting several colour separation films of one printing colour in register for subsequent transfer to the printing plate.
Mouse	Electronic device, used on a graphics tablet, for drawing or 'pointing' to certain areas of the screen on a computer.
OCR	*Optical Character Recognition.* Typewritten or printed matter capable of being read opto-electronically using a scanner, for subsequent imagesetting/phototypesetting.
Off-line	Not connected - eg - a computer printer may be disabled by switching it off-line. Another use is where information entered into a computer is processed at a later time, without the operator being present. Many EPC and graphic systems manipulate the actual data after the job to be done has been set up by an operator. The off-line component of the job often takes much longer than the initial set-up. This may be referred to as post processing and forms a major limiting factor to the efficiency of such systems.
On-line	The opposite of off-line - ie - the transfer of data from one device to another is done via a direct link. On-line connections require that the linked devices understand their data formats and structures and are able to keep track with the speed of data transfer.
Operating systems	Software that directs and controls the basic functions of a computer, such as storing files, linking with peripheral devices, etc. Mac OS 8.1 (AppleMac) and Windows 98 (PC) are examples of operating systems.
OPI	*Open Prepress Interface.* A process which enables low-resolution images to be replaced automatically with high-resolution ones at output stage.
Original	The term applied to copy which is to be reproduced.
Original plate	A letterpress block or relief printing plate produced by a block maker, or by a photomechanical etching process, as distinct from electrotyping or stereotyping.
Orthochromatic	A photographic film insensitive to red light; used for monochrome reproduction or on scanners using non-red lasers.
Outer	An imposition containing the first and last pages of a printed sheet in sheetwork; as distinct from *inner* forme.
Paged	A book is said to be paged when the pages are numbered consecutively; as distinct from folioed.
Palette	A range of colours, accessed on electronic systems from a colour data base and displayed on the screen, used for a specific job. The palette which may consist of colours classified according to PANTONE or other colour systems, may be updated and changed in seconds.
Panchromatic	A photographic film or plate sensitive to all visible colours of the spectrum.

PANTONE	PANTONE® is a registered trademark of Pantone, Inc. for colour standards, colour data, colour reproduction and colour reproduction materials, and other colour-related products and services, meeting its specifications, control and quality requirements.
Paste-up	Any matter pasted up as copy for photographic reproduction.
PDF	*Portable Document Format.* A format which allows a document to be saved, opened and viewed, without the need for the original application used to create the file: best example of a PDF is Adobe Acrobat.
PDL	*Page Description Language,* such as PostScript, identifies the parameters of a page as a set of co-ordinates and with the use of a compatible raster image processor translates the data into a suitable form for outputting. See *Postscript*.
Photolithography	The process of reproducing an image on metal by photography for lithographic printing.
Phototypesetting	The setting of type matter on film, or photographic paper, through the use of a negative master; also known as photosetting.
Pi characters	Characters omitted from a normal type fount or master, for example, accents, mathematical signs but included on a separate fount.
Pixel	From *Pic(x)ture element*, the smallest part of a picture on a computer screen.
Plate	Any relief, planographic, or intaglio surface; also an illustration of a book printed separately from the text and usually on different paper.
Platesetter	A development on from the imagesetter where the output from a platesetter is a printing plate produced from digital data without the need for the intermediate stage of film. See *computer-to-plate*.
Plate cylinder	The cylindrical surface on a rotary printing press, which carries the printing surface.
PMT	*Photomechanical transfer*. A method where an image is photographed and screened onto a paper negative which by chemical transfer produces a bromide print - referred to as a *PMT* (Kodak) and *copyproof* (Agfa). This may be reproduced dot-for-dot in platemaking, or pasted-up with unscreened text for further reproduction. The term also refers to *Photomultiplier Tube* - the light sensing device used on drum scanners.
Point system	The use of a typographic standard 12-pt pica of 4.217mm to which all other measurements are referred.
PostScript	A PDL *(Page Description Language)* developed by Adobe, which describes the contents and layout of a page. PostScript also serves as a programming language whereby the PostScript code is executed by a PostScript RIP in the output device in order to produce a printout or film containing the page. See *PDL*.
Preflighting	The process of checking and monitoring digital data to ensure the smooth running of a digital workflow through its complete cycle with the objective of eliminating problems at source. Preflighting software has been developed to undertake this role including examining such features as page geometry, graphics file formats, blends, trapping, fonts, text and output control settings, etc.
Pre-sensitised plate	A printing plate precoated for direct exposure, made in positive or negative form.
Printer	The unit that prints out information from a computer, and can take the form of a daisy wheel, dot matrix, laser, ink jet or thermographic device.
Printing cylinder	See *plate cylinder*.
Process colours	The printer's subtractive primary colours: cyan, magenta, yellow and black.
Program	The instructions *(software)* that enable a computer to carry out the tasks desired.
Progressive proofs	A set of proofs showing each plate of a set printed in its appropriate colour and in registered combination to act as a guide for the printer.
Proof	A version of a document or colour illustration produced specifically for the purpose of review prior to reproduction.
Protocol	An agreed set of rules/standards which allow computers to communicate with each other.
Quad left, right	Term used to describe commands to make lines flush left, right or centred.

Qwerty	Standard typewriter keyboard layout used in the printing industry; the term also applies to the arrangement of keys on the upper left-hand of the board.
Ragged right	Term used to describe command to use a fixed word space, not allowing type to line vertically on the right; also known as *unjustified*.
RAM	*Random Access Memory,* also referred to as *main memory,* is used by a computer to store and access programs plus other data; it is erased when the computer is switched off.
Raster	The method used in most imagesetters and VDUs to 'draw' the image, each image being made of a series of parallel, or rastered, lines which are switched on and off as they cross the image area. The alternative method is to use *vectors*.
Register	The printing of two or more plates in juxtaposition so that they complete an image or montage of images if printed on the same side of the sheet/web or back up accurately if printed on opposite sides of the sheet/web.
Register marks	Marks placed in the same relative position on sets of printing plates so that when the marks are superimposed in printing the work falls into correct position assuming the plates have been made correctly.
Retouching	The manipulation treatment of a digital image, photographic negative or positive, so as to modify tonal values or to compensate for imperfections.
Reverse leading	A setting function allowing the film/paper to be moved in the opposite direction to normal, thus achieving typographical effects, such as in multicolumn work or maths setting.
Reversing	Altering the original from left to right in the reproduction and vice versa.
RGB	The acronym covering red, green, blue (the additive primary colours) as opposed to Y, M, C and (K), (the subtractive primary colours).
Right reading	Paper/film, positive/negative from a imagesetter which can be read in the usual way - ie - left to right.
RIP	*Raster Image Processor.* Graphic workstations usually produce files in a very compact form based on vector definitions. However, these are not directly suitable for output as all plotters and scanning systems need raster data to operate. RIP technology provides the link between *vector* and *raster* systems. PostScript is an example of a vector data generator.
ROM	*Read-Only Memory.* A type of memory chip where the contents cannot be altered by writing data, nor by switching off power. ROM is used for storing operating systems so that the system is available as soon as the machine is switched on.
Rosette	The pattern created when all four-colour halftone conventional screens are placed at the traditional angles. The rosette pattern is clearly visible under a magnifying glass.
Scanner	Electronic colour scanners produce, from colour transparencies or colour copy, colour corrected screened separations for the four printing ink colours; specialist scanner systems, linked to engraving heads are also available, for generating gravure cylinders.
Screen printing	Often called *silk screen printing* from the material formerly used for the screen mesh. A stencil process with the printing and non-printing areas on one surface. The printing (image) area is open and produced by various forms of stencil. The substrate is placed under the screen and ink is passed across the top of the screen and forced through the open (printing) areas on to the substrate below.
Screen ruling	The number of halftone dots per linear inch or centimetre.
Scrolling	This is a technique used on a VDU to recall information from the display memory: as each line is recalled, all existing lines move on the screen up or down by one line to make room for the next line.
Search engine	Software that searches out sites on the Internet.
Separation	Term used in the reprographic industry to describe the films which represent the yellow, magenta, cyan and black content of an image: by printing these four separations one on top of the other, most of the mixed colours of the image can be regenerated in the printing process.

Server	A computer that provides a service or supplies resources to other computers. See *client*.
Service provider	An organisation which provides connections to the Internet.
Set	The width of a type character.
SGML	*Standard Generic (or Generalised) Mark-up Language*. A versatile code used to mark-up and identify the various elements of a document for outputting in photosetting or other form. See *ASPIC*.
Sheet work	A certain number of pages are imposed in two formes, one printed on one side and the other on the reverse side (backing-up) - *inner* and *outer* - each backed-up sheet producing one perfect copy; also sometimes known as *work-and-back*.
Side notes	Short lines of matter set in the margins.
Slug	A complete line of type, as produced by a linecaster's machine.
Software	The programs that enable the computer to perform its tasks.
Solid	Type set without leads (as in hot metal setting) or additional feed between the lines - eg - 10 on 10pt or 11 on 11pt.
Spaces	Metal blanks less than type-height used for spaces between words or letters such as hair, thin, middle, thick, as used in hot metal setting; term also used for the same purpose in imagesetting.
Spot colour	Any area of colour that is not printed using a CMYK process set; coloured areas reproduced using self-coloured inks, such as PANTONE inks.
Spread	The process generally carried out enlarging the width of line work. The inverse function, *choke*, is used to reduce the width of line work by using the same process but from the positive image. This is done to ensure that there is no gap between the linework and the surround area. The line work now larger, spreads over from its original area to give an overlay, simplifying the printing process by reducing the need for absolute accuracy of the press; also helping to compensate for shrinkage and stretch in the substrate to be printed. See *choke*.
Standing matter	Printing material such as planned film or plates used on a previous job which are retained pending possible reprint.
Stochastic screening	Also known as FM *(Frequency Modulated)* screening. With conventional halftone screening, the variable dot size formed, creates the optical illusion of various tonal values; however, the dot centre pitch distance is constant. In the case of FM screening systems, the dots are randomly distributed to create this tonal change illusion. The greater the number of dots located within a specific area, the darker the resultant tone. The dots produced in this way are usually smaller than conventional halftone dots, resulting in improved definition, although greater care and attention to detail is required at the platemaking stage. See *FM screening*.
Superior characters	Letters or numbers which are smaller than text size and are positioned above the top of the body.
TCP/IP	*Transmission Control Protocol/Internet Protocol*. The procedure set up to regulate transmission on the Internet.
Thermal printing	Non-impact printing process in which heat is transferred from a digitally-controlled print head to a substrate causing a change in colour.
Thick space	A type space having the width of one-third of its own body.
Thin space	A type space having the width of one-fifth of its own body.
TIFF	*Tagged Image File Format*, a file format for exchanging bitmapped images (usually scans) between applications.
Tint laying	Term used to cover preparing the many patterns of mechanical shading.
Tints	Mechanical shading in line areas, normally available in 5% steps from 5% to 95%.
Titling (founts)	Any fount of capitals, generally full-faced and used for headlines or titles.
Type-height	A traditional flatbed letterpress printing plate is said to be type-high (23.317mm) when it is mounted to the correct height for machine printing.

UCR	*Under-colour removal.* In the four-colour printing process, removal of part of the cyan, magenta and yellow, while adding extra black: its use leads to the overall reduction of the total quantity of ink used.
Unit system	Term based on the division of the em of the body size, each character of a fount having its own unit value. These systems, which vary according to manufacturer, are essential for justification and tabulation of lines. See *set*.
Unjustified	Text setting where lines of type align vertically on one side, while being ragged on the other: wordspacing is kept to a constant value.
Upper case	Term for capital letters (caps), also the type case which held the capital letters.
URL	*Uniform Resource Locator.* The address of a web page.
Variable space	The space inserted between words to spread and justify the line to the required measure.
VDU/VDT	*Visual display unit/visual display terminal.* A display unit which consists of a cathode ray tube on which characters may be displayed, representing data read from the memory of a computer. The unit also incorporates a keyboard on-line to the computer to manipulate data within it.
Vignette	This term usually refers to a single dot pattern that may start at 50% dot and gradually decrease to say 5% in a smooth graduation.
Visual	The design concept drawn, either manually or electronically, in colour to provide an impression of the final image.
White-out	Term covering to space out composed matter to fill the allotted space, or to improve the typographical effect; also to paint out matter not required for reproduction on artwork.
Word processing	The input, editing, organisation and storage of words/data using computer-based equipment.
Work-and-back	See *sheetwork*.
Work-and-tumble	When matter is printed in its entirety on both sides of a sheet by using a different gripper edge on the back-up, than on the first printed side.
Work-and-turn	When matter is printed in its entirety on both sides of a sheet by using the same gripper edge.
WORM	*Write Once Read Many times.* This describes a digital storage medium (usually optical) to which you may send information - eg - an image. This image is then stored permanently on the disk which cannot be erased or altered, but can be read many times. It is a method of storage which is extremely useful for archive purposes.
WWW	*World Wide Web.* A hypermedia system consisting of millions of websites forming the publishing heart of the Internet.
WYSIWYG	*What You See Is What You Get.* An acronym used to describe a visual display showing a representative replica of the resultant output in paper or film form.
Xerography	Proprietary name for a form of electrostatic printing - as used in the Xerox Docutech Production Publisher.
x-height	The height of lower case letters having neither ascenders nor descenders, as x, m and u.

Bibliography

The books and other literature listed below are intended as useful reference material for enlarging on, or are complementary to, subjects covered in this publication. Additional current information will also be found in the wide range of trade press publications, plus printed and multi-media products from prepress suppliers, software and associated companies/organisations.

Adobe Type 1 Fonts Communication Handbook
(Adobe Systems Inc., 1993)

Agfa's 'Meet the family' educational publication series consisting of:

An Introduction to Digital Color Prepress

A Guide to Color Separation

Working with Prepress and Printing Suppliers

An Introduction to digital prepress for Flexography and Packaging

An Introduction to Digital Scanning

An Introduction to Digital Photo Imaging

A Guide to Digital Photography

An Introduction to Digital Color Printing

PostScript Process Color Guide

A Guide to Digital Imaging
(AM International, 1997)

Amato, L., *PostScript in Prepress, a guided tour*
(Scitex Europe, 1993)

Barnard, M., Berrill, C., Peacock, J., *Pocket Print Production Guide*
(Blueprint, 1995)

Broback, S. and Williams, R., *Beyond the Little Mac Book*
(Peachpit Press, USA, 1997)

CREF - *Computer Ready Electronic Files*
(Scitex UK user group, 1994)

CTP - *A Film Free Future?*
(Purup•Eskofot Ltd., 1998)

DATIC - *Digital Advertisement Transfer Guidelines and Recommendations*
(Digital Advertisement Transfer Industry Committee, 1995)

Digital file transfer checklist
(BPIF, 1998)

Graphic design on the desktop computer
(Adobe Systems Inc./Tektronix)

Guide to legal typeface use
(FontWorks, 1993)

Electronic printing
(Graphic Arts Intelligence Network [for Intergraf], 1994)

Home, S., *Introduction to typography*
(Pira, 1998)

Label Buyers' Guide to Prepress Terms and Definitions
(BPIF, 1991)

Managing technology - strategies for profitable growth in the printing industry
(BPIF, 1997)

Mortimer, T., *Colour reproduction in a digital age*
(Pira, 2nd edition 1998)

Paris, P., *Trouble Shooting for Printers*
(BPIF, 2nd edition, 1993)

PDF Printing and Publishing
(Agfa/Micro Publishing Press, USA, 1997)

Profit through Prepress
(Pira, 1997)

Standard folding impositions
(BPIF, 1992)

Tritton, K., *Colour control in lithography*
(Pira, 1993)

Yeo, P., *The DTP Manual*
(Pira, 1994)

Index